"Drawing upon a range of Jewish and Christian sources, Veling finds in Levinas the universal thinker who is nevertheless rooted in Jewish particularity. At once a personal reflection and a scholarly account, both learned and accessible, this book makes an important contribution to understanding why Levinas matters."

—Michael Gillis
The Melton Centre for Jewish Education
The Hebrew University of Jerusalem, Jerusalem, Israel

"Levinas is a complex and elusive writer. Veling rightly tells his readers that he can only supply one reading. But what a reading it is! Veling offers a fresh and penetrating take on Levinas's central theme. Both those new to Levinasian ethics and more experienced readers will benefit enormously from Veling's profound and poetic interpretation."

—Neil Pembroke
School of History, Philosophy, Religion, and Classics
University of Queensland, Queensland, Australia

"In this splendid book, Jews and Christians meet as part of one family. Terry Veling explains the writings of the post-war Jewish philosopher Emmanuel Levinas with skill and with deep respect. It is a lucid introduction to contemporary theology that transcends traditional denominational boundaries. It is both illuminating and inspiring."

—John S. Levi
Asia-Pacific Centre for Inter-religious Dialogue
Australian Catholic University, Melbourne, Australia

For You Alone

For You Alone

*Emmanuel Levinas
and the Answerable Life*

Terry A. Veling

CASCADE *Books* • Eugene, Oregon

FOR YOU ALONE
Emmanuel Levinas and the Answerable Life

Copyright © 2014 Terry A. Veling. All rights reserved. Except for brief quotations in critical publications or reviews, no part of this book may be reproduced in any manner without prior written permission from the publisher. Write: Permissions, Wipf and Stock Publishers, 199 W. 8th Ave., Suite 3, Eugene, OR 97401.

Cascade Books
An Imprint of Wipf and Stock Publishers
199 W. 8th Ave., Suite 3
Eugene, OR 97401

www.wipfandstock.com

ISBN 13: 978-1-61097-717-3

Cataloguing-in-Publication data:

Veling, Terry A.

    For you alone : Emmanuel Levinas and the answerable life / Terry A. Veling.

    xxii + 186 pp. ; 23 cm. Includes bibliographical references and index.

    ISBN 13: 978-1-61097-717-3

    1. Lévinas, Emmanuel—Criticism and interpretation. 2. Philosophy and theology. 3. I. Title.

B2430.L484 V45 2014

Manufactured in the U.S.A.

Acknowledgment is gratefully given for permission to reprint as follows:

Leonard Cohen, "Coming Back to You" and "If It Be Your Will." Excerpted from *Stranger Music: Selected Poems and Songs*. Copyright © 1993 Leonard Cohen. Reprinted by permission of McClelland & Stewart.

Adrienne Rich, "Natural Resources." Copyright © 2002 by Adrienne Rich. Copyright © 1978 by W.W. Norton & Company, Inc, from *The Fact of a Doorframe: Selected Poems 1950–2001* by Adrienne Rich. Used by permission of W.W. Norton & Company, Inc.

Karen Brodine, "June 78." Reprinted from *Illegal Assembly*. Copyright © 1980, by permission of Hanging Loose Press.

To my father,

Ben A. J. Veling

(October 5, 1929–February 3, 2013)

IN PARADISUM

Thus we come back to the love "as strong as death." It is not a matter of a force that could repel the death inscribed in my being. However, it is not my nonbeing that causes anxiety, but that of the loved one or of the other, more beloved than my being. What we call ... love, is *par excellence* the fact that the death of the other affects me more than my own. The love of the other is the emotion of the other's death. It is my receiving the other—and not the anxiety of death awaiting me—that is the reference to death.

We encounter death in the face of the other.

—Emmanuel Levinas, *God, Death, and Time*

Contents

Preface: An Answerable Life   xi

Abbreviations   xxi

1   Introduction: "Jerusalem Writings"   1

Part One: For You Alone

2   Indifference: Nobody Asks after You   19

3   Under Your Gaze   31

4   For You Alone: The Miracle of Exteriority   48

5   Sociality: More than One, Every One   67

Part Two: The Talmudic Ocean

6   The Talmudic Ocean   89

7   "We Will Do and We Will Hear"   124

8   "Love Your Neighbor as Yourself"   142

9   Suffering for Nothing or Suffering for You   163

Bibliography   177

Name Index   185

Preface

An Answerable Life

Scene One: A Thinker Sits Alone in a Room

René Descartes is sitting by the fire, wearing his winter dressing gown, and says, "Today I have suitably freed my mind of all cares, secured for myself a period of leisurely tranquillity, and am withdrawing into solitude."[1] He is trying to find a firm foundation for his thinking, something that is undoubtable, something he can therefore build upon with confidence and reliability. "I realized that I had to raze everything to the ground and begin again from the original foundations . . . I will apply myself earnestly and unreservedly to this general demolition of my opinions" (59). He decides to take nothing for granted, to question every assumption, to subject everything to doubt, "so that eventually all that remains is precisely nothing but what is certain and unshaken" (64).

His meditation is arduous as he discovers that there is very little he can affirm—"the air, the earth, colors, shapes, sounds, and all external things are but the bedeviling hoaxes of my dreams" (62). He finds himself growing suddenly dizzy, as though he had "fallen into a deep whirlpool" (63). He is living in a world of shadows and unreality, not even certain that the sheet of paper in his hands is real. Maybe the whole world is but a dream, an illusion, a grand deception.

He is confident, nevertheless, that if he could strip away all that is false he will find the one thing that is certain and unshakeable. So he challenges everything, questions everything, dismantles everything—until suddenly

---

1. Descartes, *Discourse on Method* and *Meditations on First Philosophy*, 59 (subsequent references in parentheses).

Preface

he realizes: "As I converse with myself alone and look more deeply into myself . . . I realize I am a thing that thinks, that is to say, a thing that doubts, affirms, denies, understands a few things, is ignorant of many things, wills, refrains from willing, and also imagines and senses" (70). Through his long and difficult meditation he at last arrives at the certitude he sought: "Here I make my discovery: thought exists; it alone cannot be separated from me. I am; I exist—this is certain." And so from this thinker, sitting alone by the fire in his dressing gown, we receive one of the best-known maxims of philosophical thought: "Noticing that this truth—*I think, therefore I am*—was so firm and so certain . . . I judged that I could accept it without scruple as the first principle of the philosophy I was seeking" (19).

René Descartes was a courageous thinker. Against the weight of human history, with its treasured store of knowledge and traditions, he dared to place his reasoning self as the sole arbiter of truth and authority. Nothing can be assumed. Everything must be tested. Generations followed him along his path of "methodological doubt." He opened the gates to the "age of enlightenment," to the realm of autonomous, critical and rational thought. As a fellow philosopher would later say, "Have courage to use your own reason!"[2] At the source of this great transformation of the human world, we find Descartes' "thinking self," the bold and courageous Ego.

Scene Two: A Thinker Is Interrupted by a Visitor

Martin Buber is sitting in his study, presumably enjoying the delights of reading and writing, surrounded by his books—a time of "religious enthusiasm," he calls it—when he has a visit from a young, unknown man. He responds to the young man with friendly conversation, but isn't really present to him "in spirit." He listens and is not disrespectful, yet this is just another one of those usual meetings with a student, and he pays it no more or no less attention.

Later, not long after this visit, he learns that the young student is no longer alive, and it dawns on him: "He had come to me not casually, but borne by destiny, not for a chat but for a decision. He had come to me. He had come in this hour."[3] He realizes that his absorption in study and writing prevented him from giving his full attention to another human being, to the real concerns of life that were presenting themselves to him with immedia-

---

2. Kant, "What Is Enlightenment?" in *Critique of Practical Reason*, 286.
3. Buber, *Between Man and Man*, 14 (subsequent references in parentheses).

cy and urgency. He finds himself stripped down to a bare and unshakeable certitude, to this essential truth: "I possess nothing but the everyday out of which I am never taken. The mystery is no longer disclosed, it has escaped or it has made its dwelling here where everything happens as it happens. I know no fullness but each mortal hour's fullness of claim and responsibility . . . I do not know much more. If that is religion then it is just *everything*, simply all that is lived in its possibility of dialogue" (14).

Martin Buber calls this event a "conversion" and a "judgment." It is the conversion from a solitary *I*—an I enclosed in a world of thought and reflection—to a world of "claim and responsibility," whereby another speaks and requires my response. "You are called upon from above, required, chosen, empowered, sent, you with this your mortal bit of life are referred to . . . You are not swallowed up in a fullness without obligation, you are willed for the life of communion" (14).

Scene Three: A Writer in a Sculptor's Garden

I am sitting on a country road, admiring the sunlit valley, listening to the wind. A stranger comes up to me and we start talking. At first he is suspicious and I feel myself under scrutiny. He has come to inquire into this strange scene, this stranger sitting by the road. I comment on the beauty of the valley, ask him whether he lives in the house nearby, and if it is all right for me to sit a while. He smiles and I see his suspicion ease.

We begin to talk and I am suddenly involved in a personal and friendly conversation. He learns that I teach theology at a Catholic university, that I had come to the mountains to sit and write a while. He says he has lived in this valley for twenty-five years, since his retirement. He is now in his eighties. He speaks with a noticeable Czech accent, and I learn that he immigrated to Australia just after the Second World War.

Maybe it was because I was sitting there writing—I am not sure—but he says, "I am a sculptor—would you like to see my work?" At first I think of politely declining, but then I feel the wind's breath prompting me. So we walk up the road a little, talking about art and religion, his life and his work, until we approach the front gate of his property. I stop in my tracks, stunned. Before me is a huge granite stone with these words chiseled into it:

All knowledge begins with feeling.

I immediately want to rush back to where I had been sitting, take up my pen, and practice this saying.

Preface

We follow the tree-lined pathway leading to his house, and along the way there appear various statues—like ancient ghosts, with singular dignity, carved from solid rock, yet filled with fluid forms: women, dancers, dolphins, birds, children. In another part of his garden, where he set himself to work, I see three or four solid masses of raw rock. From one of these emerged a half-formed figure as if breaking free from the stone.

I stand in this sculptor's garden, full of bewilderment and marvel. I have ventured into a stranger's home—what am I doing here? He then opens the door to a large shed. He asks me to take off my sandals, as his wife liked to keep the floors clean. The shed is filled with examples of his work. In his heyday, he had received various prizes. It seems like quite an intimate moment to me. He is sharing his memories, his treasure.

As I leave, I begin to wonder what brought us together—two strangers, one trying to write, another trying to wrest shape and form from stone. Was it the wind? The strange and wandering Spirit that blows where it will? Did this stranger come to me as a teacher? How is it, I wonder, that a person who deals in rock and granite, in hard and solid forms, nevertheless inscribes at his gate: *All knowledge begins with feeling*. To carve feeling from rock, to let shape and form emerge from solid mass, to trust the chisel, to love, rather than fear, the raw beauty of ancient stone. Perhaps he really did come to teach me, perhaps the wind was right: latent in every aspect of life, even in the difficulty of rock, there is spirit and there is friendship—if only we could feel.[4]

"For You Alone"

"Beyond the desert of criticism," Paul Ricoeur writes, "we wish to be called again."[5] The experience of "being addressed" is an important experience in human life. I am thinking, for example, of an enlightened world or modernity that placed all assurances and confidences in our hands, and then a "postmodern" world that stripped these bare and put an end to both God and us, so to speak. Against both worlds, one marked by assurance, the other by a void, Ricoeur wonders whether it is possible to be called again. Perhaps this is why Levinas' writings carry such appeal and resonance. He lets us *hear* again. We are spoken to. We are asked after, called, required. There is revelation, transcendence, the voice of God, our neighbor—not

---

4. Veling, "Personal and Spiritual Life," 20–21.
5. Ricoeur, *Symbolism of Evil*, 349.

simply our selves alone but also something other, someone other. "You are there." Rather than "the desert of criticism," it is this "being addressed" that I am keen to evoke in this text.

To be "for you alone" is very different than "to be alone." The "aloneness" in this statement is not the aloneness of a solitary being but the aloneness of a dedicated being. I give myself, not to anyone or anything, but to you alone. It is the dedication of one for another. This is called a sacrament in the Catholic tradition and a covenant in the Jewish tradition. The rabbis see this dedication encapsulated in the Song of Songs, of which Rabbi Akiva says, "If nothing had been given to us of Torah but the Song of Songs it would have been a sufficient guide for human conduct." Of all the scriptures, the Song is the most sacred of all.[6] It reflects passion and desire—a "beautiful obsession"—not in any heedless way, but a way that is filled with love.

"I slept, but my heart was awake. Listen! My beloved is knocking" (Song 5:2).

Here I am, for You. This for-the-other is often perceived as a seed of folly, an obsession, a "sickness"—"I am sick with love," the Song says. Yet for Emmanuel Levinas, *Here I am* is "a marvelous accusative: here I am under your gaze, obliged to you, your servant. In the name of God" (*GCM*, 75).

The Way Ahead

The Jewish mystical tradition, Kabbalah, speaks of writing as a process of "combining the letters" and allowing the creative energy of God's love to flow. The following text is pinned above my desk:

> Take hold of ink, pen, and tablet. Realize that you are about to serve your God in joy. Begin to combine letters. A few or many, permuting them and revolving them rapidly until your mind warms up. Delight in how they move and in what you generate by revolving them. When you feel within that your mind is very, very warm from combining the letters, and that through your combinations you understand new things that you have not attained by human tradition nor discovered on your own through mental reflection, then you are ready to receive the abundant flow, and the abundance flows upon you, arousing you again and again.[7]

---

6. Heschel, *Heavenly Torah*, 196 (citing *Song of Songs Zuta* 1:1 and *Mishnah Yadayim* 3:5).

7. Matt, *Essential Kabbalah*, 103.

Preface

Finding a way to structure or organize a book is never an easy task. Dividing a work into chapters is perhaps one way to aid clarity, yet it can also create artificial divisions that are never seamless. I often defer to Paul Ricoeur's principle that "the symbol gives rise to thought."[8] To be guided by a primary symbol is a helpful way to formulate a text, "to receive the abundant flow." A key symbol in this text is the word *you*. In his translation of the Psalms, Norman Fischer suggests that *you* is the one English word that best evokes the feeling of relationship, both mysterious and intimate at the same time. The word *you* is a form of address that includes "sadness, intimacy, and power, for in the word *you* God becomes painfully close, utterly unreachable in his nearness."[9]

Along with the Introduction, this book is divided into two parts, with four chapters in each part. Part One, For You Alone, explores the dialogical, intersubjective or relational quality of Levinas' work. Our lives are always "twofold" rather than "one." Part Two, The Talmudic Ocean, explores the religious or revelational quality of Levinas' work. A relational life is dependent on encounters that are revelatory. Revelation means that life is no mere "sameness" but is tied to the revelation of "the other," to you.

I offer below a brief synopsis of the chapters that follow.

Chapter 1: Introduction—"Jerusalem Writings"

Levinas is a survivor of disaster. This chapter introduces Levinas' life and works around his primary question, "What right do I have to be in the face of the other person's suffering?" It also outlines the genesis of my own interest and engagement with his works, beginning in Jerusalem some fifteen years ago.

PART ONE: FOR YOU ALONE

Chapter 2: Indifference—Nobody Asks after You

Levinas spent five years in a German prison camp. His early work, "written for the most part in captivity," struggled with the phenomenon of "indifference." To live in a responseless world—a world devoid of responsibility—is to live in a world of indifference and disregard. It is a world without obligation and without weight—where nothing matters, nothing calls, nothing

---

8. Ricoeur, *Symbolism of Evil*, 348.
9. Fischer, *Opening to You*, xxi.

Preface

answers, nothing counts. This chapter explores Levinas' stunning conviction (especially given his wrenching background) that the world around us and the relations between us are *personal* and *bearing goodness* rather than *impersonal* and propelled by blind and *indifferent* forces.

Chapter 3: Under Your Gaze

A principal concern in Levinas' work is the face-to-face relation, the proximity of person to person, the proximity of one's neighbor. The first part of this chapter explores Levinas' notion of responsibility for the face of the other as presented in his first major work, *Totality and Infinity*. Echoing themes from Levinas' second major work, *Otherwise Than Being*, the second part of this chapter explores the metaphor of "being faced" (with the sense of weight and obligation this urges upon us) in contrast to our more familiar and usual stance of "facing being" (with the sense of anxiety and questioning this produces in us).

Chapter 4: For You Alone—The Miracle of Exteriority

This chapter reclaims the word *transcendence* over against a world "drugged by the opiates of immanence." We generally hold in great esteem words such as *mutuality, reciprocity, equality, inclusivity, oneness*. This chapter draws attention to words such as *separateness, asymmetry, difference, otherness*—not as words of negativity but as words of excess and beyond, words of "excedence" and "transcendence"—*more than* and *other than*. Levinas always privileges You before me, You above me, You in front of me. It is as if transcendence magnetizes relation, always attracting and drawing me toward you, yet also resisting and refusing my assimilation of you.

Chapter 5: Sociality: More than One, Every One

According to Levinas, the face-to-face ethical relation of being-for-the-other is written into the very fabric of life. It is the most primordial datum in human experience. Yet given Levinas' primary concern for this fundamental ethical relation, we are nevertheless left wondering about relations that extend into the larger concerns of society, that is, "forms of togetherness" that are implicated in more than the immediacies of the face-to-face relation. This chapter asks how Levinas' "face-to-face" ethics can help us with the necessary questions engendered by the conditions of *social* existence. Social existence means existence with *more than one*, which brings before

Preface

us questions concerned with *every one*—forms of togetherness that necessarily involve questions of politics, society, equality, justice, etc. In other words, how does Levinas' insistence on the singular call to responsibility—the face-to-face relation, the one-for-the-other—also address the social and political dimensions of human existence?

Part Two: The Talmudic Ocean

Chapter 6: The Talmudic Ocean

Levinas' Talmudic commentaries hold a very great place in his life and his work. He often credits his mysterious teacher, Chouchani, in his Talmudic lectures, yet in very few places does he actually spell out "the method" he learned from his teacher. This chapter distills seven "principles" or hermeneutical practices that lay at the heart of Levinas' approach to navigating the "Talmudic ocean."

Chapter 7: "We Will Do and We Will Hear"

Levinas often cites a well-known verse: "we will do and we will hear" (Exod 24:7). This verse raises a perplexing question. How can doing come before hearing? Surely we must first hear or know what we are to do before we can do it? Surely we must first "work it out" (theorize) before we can put it into practice (application)? Surely we must first understand something before we can act on it? "We will do and we will hear" is a puzzling verse because of its strange reversal—and, as Levinas says, the rabbis "keep being astonished by it." Chapter 7 explores this strange verse that places doing before hearing, practice before theory, acting before knowing, to see what merit it may hold for us.

Chapter 8: "Love Your Neighbor as Yourself"

"Who is my neighbor?" is one of those questions that defy ready-made answers. It is a question that resonates anew in the lives of human beings who are forever learning to live together in the contours of their own personal lives and in the changing social contexts of human history. However, there is another question hidden in the verse, "love your neighbor as yourself." Rather than ask, "who is my neighbor?" this question asks, what does "as yourself" mean? This chapter offers seven responses to this question, adopting a type of Talmudic style, with various voices (ancient and contemporary, rabbinic and Christian, philosophers and theologians) entering the dialogue. The responses represent commentary on a verse that, as Hillel says, "is the entire Torah" and, as Jesus says, "sums up the entire law and the prophets."

Chapter 9: Suffering for Nothing or Suffering for You

It is perhaps not surprising that Levinas, as a survivor of the Nazi regime, addresses the question of suffering. Why? What purpose? What reason? A philosopher, so-called, could hardly avoid these questions. Levinas suggests that rather than try to find a meaning or reason for suffering, we may be better to admit that suffering is "useless" and amounts to nothing. A question nevertheless arises. Is all suffering useless? Or can we speak, for example, of "redemptive suffering"? Not so much as "useful" suffering, but as non-useless suffering that evokes human compassion, healing, and solidarity? Levinas transforms "suffering for nothing" into "suffering for you."

Abbreviations

Works by Emmanuel Levinas

AT	*Alterity and Transcendence.* Translated by Michael B. Smith. New York: Columbia University Press, 1999.
BI	"Beyond Intentionality." Translated by Kathleen McLaughlin. In *Philosophy in France Today*, edited by Alan Montefiore, 100–115. Cambridge: Cambridge University Press, 1983.
BPW	*Basic Philosophical Writings.* Edited by Adriaan T. Peperzak, Simon Critchley, and Robert Bernasconi. Bloomington: Indiana University Press, 1996.
BV	*Beyond the Verse: Talmudic Readings and Lectures.* Translated by Gary D. Mole. Bloomington: Indiana University Press, 1994.
CPP	*Collected Philosophical Papers.* Translated by Alphonso Lingis. Dordrecht: Kluwer Academic, 1993.
DF	*Difficult Freedom: Essays on Judaism.* Translated by Seán Hand. Baltimore: Johns Hopkins University Press, 1990.
DwEL	"Dialogue with Emmanuel Levinas." Emmanuel Levinas and Richard Kearney. In *Face to Face with Levinas*, edited by Richard A. Cohen, 13–33. Albany: State University of New York Press, 1986.
EE	*Existence and Existents.* Translated by Alphonso Lingis. The Hague: Martinus Nijhoff, 1978.
EI	*Ethics and Infinity: Conversations with Philippe Nemo.* Translated by Richard A. Cohen. Pittsburgh: Duquesne University Press, 1985.
EN	*Entre Nous: Thinking-of-the-Other.* Translated by Michael B. Smith and Barbara Harshav. New York: Columbia University Press, 1998.
GCM	*Of God Who Comes to Mind.* Translated by Bettina Bergo. Stanford: Stanford University Press, 1998.
GDT	*God, Death, and Time.* Translated by Bettina Bergo. Stanford: Stanford University Press, 2000.

Abbreviations

IRB	*Is It Righteous to Be? Interviews with Emmanuel Levinas.* Edited by Jill Robbins. Stanford: Stanford University Press, 2001.
IwEL	"Interview with Emmanuel Levinas." Edith Wyschogrod. *Philosophy & Theology* 4 (1989) 105–18.
LR	*The Levinas Reader.* Edited by Seán Hand. Oxford: Blackwell, 1989.
NeTR	*New Talmudic Readings.* Translated by Richard A. Cohen. Pittsburgh: Duquesne University Press, 1999.
NTR	*Nine Talmudic Readings.* Translated by Annette Aronowicz. Bloomington: Indiana University Press, 1990.
OB	*Otherwise Than Being or Beyond Essence.* Translated by Alphonso Lingis. Dordrecht: Kluwer Academic, 1991.
OS	*Outside the Subject.* Translated by Michael B. Smith. Stanford: Stanford University Press, 1993.
PI	"Philosophy and the Idea of the Infinite." Translated by Alphonso Lingis. In Adriaan Peperzak, *To the Other: An Introduction to the Philosophy of Emmanuel Levinas*, 88–119. West Lafayette, IN: Purdue University Press, 1993.
PN	*Proper Names.* Translated by Michael B. Smith. Stanford: Stanford University Press, 1996.
TE	"Transcendence and Evil." Postface to Philippe Nemo, *Job and the Excess of Evil.* Translated by Michael Kigel. Pittsburgh: Duquesne University Press, 1998.
TI	*Totality and Infinity: An Essay on Exteriority.* Translated by Alphonso Lingis. Pittsburgh: Duquesne University Press, 1969.
TN	*In the Time of the Nations.* Translated by Michael B. Smith. London: Continuum, 2007.
TO	"The Trace of the Other." Translated by Alphonso Lingis. In *Deconstruction in Context*, edited by Mark C. Taylor, 345–49. Chicago: University of Chicago Press, 1986.
UH	*Unforeseen History.* Translated by Nidra Poller. Urbana: University of Illinois Press, 2004.

1

Introduction

"Jerusalem Writings"

> With the appearance of the human—and this is my entire philosophy—there is something more important than my life, and that is the life of the other.
>
> —EMMANUEL LEVINAS

A Life

Levinas was born in 1906 to Jewish parents in Lithuania.[1] His father owned a bookshop, and he was introduced to the great authors of Russian literature (such as Dostoyevsky and Tolstoy). He also learned to read the Bible in its original Hebrew and grew up in a climate of enlightened Jewish orthodoxy. In 1923 he moved to France and studied philosophy under Husserl and Heidegger, whose works he is credited for introducing to French thought. He became a French citizen and in 1932 married his childhood sweetheart, Raïssa, a talented musician. They had two children, Simone and Michael. For many years Levinas served as director of the École Normale Israélite Orientale (ENIO), a school established to train

---

1. Peperzak offers a brief biography in *To The Other*, 1–12. See also Malka, *Emmanuel Levinas: His Life and Legacy*. Levinas offers his own unique autobiographical sketch in "Signature" (*DF*, 291–95).

Jewish teachers in the Mediterranean region. The Levinas family resided in an apartment above the school, where he and Raïssa lived until 1980.

Levinas was not well known in the French philosophical scene until the publication of his first major work, *Totality and Infinity*, in 1961, at the age of fifty-five. In the 1980s he began to attract attention as a rising star in Europe. Nevertheless, he was always anxious that his thinking and his themes never be turned into slogans; he would decry any movement that might be built around his name, such as "the Levinas Fashion."[2]

Levinas lost his parents, brothers, and parents-in-law in the Nazi genocide. As a French army officer, he was spared deportation to the concentration camps and placed in a prisoner of war labor camp, where he spent five years as a woodcutter in the forest. He recounts a story from this period about a friendly dog named Bobby. When returning to the camp after a day of labor, he and his fellow prisoners would face the glares and insults of the villagers and prison guards, who saw them as nothing more than dirty *Juden*. Bobby, however, befriended them. "When we used to come back from work," Levinas says, "he welcomed us, jumping up and down . . . This dog evidently took us for human beings" (*IRB*, 41; *DF*, 151–53).

Levinas' wife and daughter escaped the Nazi death machine with the help of his lifelong friend, Maurice Blanchot, and "found refuge and protection among the nuns of St. Vincent de Paul" (*TN*, 163). Though he writes rarely of these horrific times, the memory of the Shoah has always accompanied his thinking. "It is dominated," he wrote, "by the presentiment and the memory of the Nazi horror" (*DF*, 291). He dedicated his second major work, *Otherwise Than Being or Beyond Essence*, to the memory of the victims of Nazism and to "the millions on millions of all confessions and all nations, victims of the same hatred of the other man," along with a Hebrew dedication to his lost family members, "that their souls may be kept in the bundle of life."

Aside from his philosophical works, Levinas also wrote widely on Jewish themes, including various collections of his own Talmudic commentaries. He credits his Talmudic learning to an enigmatic and mysterious teacher, Chouchani, a genius and master of Talmud who influenced Levinas in the postwar years, but of whom little is known (*IRB*, 73–79). As one commentator notes, when you open Levinas' books, "you will find phrases or paragraphs without references and without footnotes, but which, while reading them, you can feel are fundamentally Jewish thoughts."[3]

2. Malka, *Emmanuel Levinas*, 288.
3. Ibid., 139 (citing Jean Halperin).

Introduction: "Jerusalem Writings"

Among Christian thinkers, Levinas had a special relationship with the philosopher Paul Ricoeur and with Pope John Paul II. He was regularly invited to the pope's summer residence, Castel Gandolfo, on the outskirts of Rome. Paul Ricoeur, who also attended these gatherings, recalls, "The pope attended the discussions twice a day, remaining completely silent. He would invite us to share a meal. On one of these occasions, Levinas said, 'You sit at the pope's right, and I'll sit on his left . . . A Jewish philosopher and a Protestant philosopher sitting with the pope!'"[4]

The only time Levinas did not attend the pope's gatherings was in the fall of 1994. Ricoeur recalls that, at the time, "he was filled with the pain of his wife's death," and the pope took Ricoeur aside and asked him, "Would you please give my regards to Levinas and tell him of my respect and admiration."[5]

John Paul II read Levinas' work and saw him as "the model of a great Jewish thinker."[6] Similarly, Levinas had a deep appreciation for the pope's religious vision. John Paul II's conception of the human being "as an opening onto the divine" resonated with Levinas' moral vision of the face-to-face relation.[7] "From the human, we very quickly get to God," Levinas was once heard to say; "Besides, this is the incarnation."[8]

Levinas died on December 25, 1995, the eighth day of Hanukkah. Levinas' son, Michael, recalls: "It was in the morning. He didn't feel well. It was eleven o'clock. I lit the last Hanukkah candle, he took the prayer book, he kissed the book, he kissed my hand, we left for the hospital and he passed away a few hours later."[9]

Paul Ricoeur and Jacques Derrida offered eulogies to their venerated friend, to this man of "question-prayers."[10]

A Survivor's Question

Levinas is a survivor. He survived the death of millions. He survived what his friend Maurice Blanchot calls the "countless cry . . . the utter-burn where

4. Ibid., 192–93.
5. Ibid., 193.
6. Ibid., 209.
7. Ibid., 224.
8. Ibid., 227.
9. Ibid., 269. Malka offers a description of Levinas' funeral "in the winter grayness," xxix–xxxi.
10. Ricoeur, "In Memoriam Emmanuel Levinas"; Derrida, *Adieu*, 1–13.

all history took fire."[11] He survived the death of his mother, his father, his brothers, his wife's parents. He survived, and yet deeply inscribed within his thought there lies the penultimate question that plagues virtually every survivor: What right have I to survive, to live, when so many have died? "In starting from the Holocaust," Levinas says, "I think about the death of the other man; I think about the other man for whom one may already feel—I don't know why—like a guilty survivor" (*IRB*, 126).

In his philosophical writings, Levinas transforms this question of survival into the very question of *being*. The burden of survival—what right do I have *to be, to live*—becomes the very burden of being: How is being justified? (*IRB*, 97, 163).

Levinas then takes this question of being and makes it an *ethical* question at the very outset (*OS*, 48, 92). It now becomes: What right or justification do I have to be *in the face of the other person's suffering and death*? This is Levinas' primary question.

The burden of survival and the question of being could only be answered for Levinas when, as he says, "the burning of *my* suffering and the anguish of *my* death were able to be transfigured into the dread and concern for the *other man*" (*BV*, 4). For Levinas, existence *for itself* is not the ultimate meaning; rather, it is existence *for the other*. The only justification for surviving, for living, for *being*, is when the anxiety over my own life and death are transfigured into concern for the life and death of my neighbor. "The human is the possibility of being-for-the-other. That possibility is the justification for all existing" (*TN*, 112). This is Levinas' primary response to his question. This is his subject matter, what matters most to him.

In raising this concern for "my neighbor," Levinas often speaks of the "face of the other." In language resonant with the Hebrew Scriptures, he refers to the other as "the Most High" to evoke the other's transcendence and eminence, yet he also speaks of the other's lowliness and destitution—"the stranger, the widow, and the orphan." The other is both the "Most High," the Holy One, and the face of the neighbor—the stranger and the vulnerable one. When speaking to Christian audiences, he often referred to chapter 25 of Matthew's Gospel, "in so far as you did this to one of the least . . ." He writes, "The relation to God is presented there as a relation to another person. It is not a metaphor; in the other, there is a real presence of God. In my relation to the other, I hear the word of God. It is not a metaphor. It is not only extremely important; it is literally true. I'm not saying that the other is God, but that in his or her face I hear the word of God" (*IRB*, 171).

---

11. Blanchot, *Writing of the Disaster*, 47.

"Jerusalem Writings"

In 1998 I traveled to Jerusalem with Mary and our four sons. We rented an apartment on a hill in a neighborhood called Ramat Eshkol. We arrived late at night and our hosts were there to greet us. They had made up our beds and even decorated the children's bedroom with colorful quilts and cartoon characters. There was food in the fridge and a specially baked cake. We had arrived in the land of Abraham and Sarah and Jewish hospitality. A rabbinic legend says that Abraham's tent had no less than four entrances in order to welcome a guest approaching from any direction (*NTR*, 99).

The morning brought a marvel that remains ingrained in our memories to this day. We awoke to the view from our third-floor balcony. Stretching before us was the ancient land of Israel, the distant desert hills, the newly forested valley, and rock-hewn buildings rising distinctly from the landscape. In the foreground, a flock of goats and a lone Bedouin shepherd. Then, late at night, the haunting cry of the call to prayer from a distant minaret: "Allahu Akbar . . ."

On Friday afternoons, the whole neighborhood would prepare for the first evening star and welcoming Shabbat, the "bride" of Israel—*Lecha dodi likrat kallah*—"Come, my beloved, to greet the bride." It was tradition to tidy the home in preparation and to purchase flowers from one of the many vendors on the streets. We always knew when Shabbat officially began because a siren would sound out across the city. From our balcony, we watched the sun go down over the hills and then blessed bread and wine together. This was the Sabbath day of rest, instituted since the creation of the world. It felt good to live in a city that publicly recognized and celebrated this time without labor, without crass economics, without measures of success or failure.

Our lives were suddenly thrown into an ancient and foreign landscape, into strange patterns of time and rhythm. Sunday was no longer Sunday, but the day when our sons would wake up and complain, "It's Sunday, do we have to go to school?" Our weekend no longer ended on Sunday, for this was now the beginning of the week. Our day no longer ended at night, for the first star in the night sky was now the beginning of the day. Our normal cycles of measuring time were thrown into a different framework—where a new day begins at night and the calendar revolves around the moon rather than the sun. We were living in a different world; we were living in Jerusalem.

For You Alone

As a Golda Meir Fellow at the Hebrew University of Jerusalem, I received a small stipend that allowed my family and I to spend this year living together in Jerusalem. After a while, we no longer felt like tourists and began to absorb the culture and patterns of this biblical land. Our sons attended the local Hebrew school. I caught the bus each day to the university's Mount Scopus campus. Mary worked in the Old City with the Sisters of Sion, a Catholic women's religious order devoted to improving relations between Jews and Christians.

On Saturdays, when traditional Sabbath law forbade the use of cars and buses, we often relied on Isam, a Palestinian taxi driver, to take us on various outings—for a picnic or to the zoo or to the Old City; he even drove us to the Dead Sea on one occasion, some 110 kilometers away.

When Christmas arrived, there wasn't the slightest hype or interest. The shops were bereft of the Christmas paraphernalia we were used to—decorations, lights, and Christmas trees. We went to the Old City and found an Arab shop that was selling a whole array of Christmas decorations. We bought some tinsel, lights, and a musical Santa. I went with my young sons to the nearby forest valley, cut a small pine branch, and returned home to erect our "tree," with the boys crafting homemade decorations. On Christmas morning we felt somewhat bereft—no one else was celebrating. We were alone in our apartment, making long-distance calls to Australia, trying to capture the spirit of Christmas.

"Why do you worship a baby?" one of our close Jewish friends asked. She was intrigued by our celebration of Christmas. Later, when Passover arrived, we too expressed our intrigue, asking, "Why can't we buy bread or beer or anything with yeast?"

I recall our local trip to the nonkosher delicatessen. We would buy ham and bacon, wrapped in brown paper bags, and leave the store with this sense of having purchased something illegal, like contraband. When our sons' Orthodox friends came to visit, we provided paper plates and cups so they could observe the requirement to keep milk and meat products separate. We had entered a strange land, yet we relished and absorbed it as something fresh and new, unknown and yet full of surprising attraction.

It was during this time that I began my writing on the works of Emmanuel Levinas. My "study" in our apartment was a small loft. I had already begun reading Levinas, but now I had some dedicated time to put pen to paper, to begin digesting and clarifying Levinas' works for myself— and to do this in the very land of Israel, the land of Moses and the prophets, the land of biblical and rabbinic tradition. What better place, I now think, to spend time with a great Jewish thinker of the twentieth century.

This is how my "Jerusalem writings" (as I affectionately call them) began: sitting in a loft in an apartment overlooking Jerusalem, attending each day the university where Martin Buber spent much of his career, and living in the land where God called and entered into a covenant with humanity.

It has been some sixteen years since I first commenced those writings. Since then, I have continued to write and teach on the works of Emmanuel Levinas and to be inspired by his thought.[12] It feels right at this current time of my life to return to those days, those days of Jewish living in the company of a great Jewish thinker.

Reading from Right to Left

When we read (that is, for those of us reading now), we read from left to right. Yet there is another way of reading—a Jewish way, for example—that begins from the other side, reversing direction, reading from right to left.

"Reading," as I am using it here, is a metaphor for *interpreting*—that perennial activity of human understanding that seeks a way of knowing, relating, and acting in the world. How do we "read" life? How do we attend to the world in which we live? What matters? What counts? How should we respond? The question of how we *live* life is closely connected to the question of how we *read* life.

The metaphor of "reading from right to left" suggests another way of reading that cuts across our familiar patterns of understanding. It is a disorienting experience to encounter this other way of reading, particularly for those of us who are deeply shaped by a culture that is largely Western-Greek-Christian in its orientation, rather than Jewish-Hebraic.

In a major essay on Levinas, Jacques Derrida begins by citing a passage from Matthew Arnold that reads, "Hebraism and Hellenism—between these two points of influence moves our world. At one time it feels more powerfully the attraction of one of them, at another time of the other; and it ought to be, though it never is, evenly and happily balanced between them."[13]

---

12. Chapters 3 and 7 in this book are modified versions that have appeared in my earlier work, *Practical Theology*, 77–97, 115–35.

13. Derrida, *Writing and Difference*, 79. For an evaluation of the relationship between Levinas' philosophical ("Greek") and Jewish ("Hebrew") writings, see Gibbs, *Correlations*

Jewish thinkers such as Emmanuel Levinas, Jacques Derrida, Martin Buber, and Abraham Heschel (to name a few) straddle both Greek and Jewish worlds. Their thought represents "something in the twentieth century that probably has not been seen since the thirteenth: Jewish individuals highly learned in the texts both of Jewish tradition *and* of Western philosophy."[14] Their writings are an attempt to reclaim a Judaic, rabbinic wisdom that has lain buried throughout much of Western history, a recovery of Hebraic experience submerged in Greek thought, yet that nevertheless maintains a resilient resistance to ruling Western exemplars.[15]

When encountering a great body of work, Paul Ricoeur says that one of the most important aims of interpretation is to enter the "proposed world" of the text.[16] There is little doubt that Levinas proposes a distinctly unique world for us to live in, a world in which relationships between people are characterized by profound ethical and divine concern. My hope is that the following work can bring the interested (though not necessarily academically schooled) reader into the "proposed world" of Levinas. As Walter Kaufmann suggests, "most books die unnoticed; fewer live for a year or two."[17] However, there are other works, such as those of Levinas, that endure and require our attention: "We must learn to feel addressed by a book, by the human being behind it, as if a person spoke directly to us. A good book or essay or poem is not primarily an object to be put to use, or an object of experience: it is the voice of You speaking to me, requiring a response."[18]

According to Hélène Cixous, living a life of truth means "being in touch with the more-than-me," and our greatest writers have always been those "bent on directing their writing toward this *truth*-over-there."[19] Similarly, Levinas says that the desire for truth "is turned toward the 'elsewhere' and the 'otherwise' and the 'other'" (*TI*, 33). It is the desire to cross over toward the other, or to turn around and face the other, which means that

---

in Rosenzweig and Levinas, 156–75, and Meir, "Hellenic and Jew in Levinas's Writings." On Levinas' "Jew-Greek" heritage, see Aronowicz's "Introduction" to *NTR*, x–xv, and Peperzak's biographical note on the Jewish-Russian-European-Greek-Christian context of Levinas' life and work in *To the Other*, 8–9.

14. Meskin, "Jewish Transformation of Modern Thought," 513–14.

15. Handelman, *Slayers of Moses*. See also Chalier, "Philosophy of Emmanuel Levinas and the Hebraic Tradition," in Peperzak, *Ethics as First Philosophy*, 3–12.

16. Ricoeur, *Hermeneutics and the Human Sciences*, 131–44.

17. Kaufmann, "I and You: A Prologue," 20.

18. Ibid., 39.

19. Cixous, *Coming to Writing*, 44; Cixous, *Three Steps on the Ladder of Writing*, 6.

Introduction: "Jerusalem Writings"

to read from right to left is to read and interpret life "otherwise," from the "other side," from over "there," which is a very difficult thing to do. Our social patterns and cultural norms, our routine "habits of the heart," are often difficult to break with or break through.[20] Contemporary concerns come and go, but sometimes they hang around long enough to form cultural "habits," and sometimes we need a good prophet/thinker to jolt us from our cultural habits. Levinas is a thinker who can speak to the broader cultural makeup of Western society in a very prophetic way. A culture, for example, that has "habits" that privilege the individual's quest for autonomy, freedom, and self-authenticity. A culture that can be indifferent to the "other" in our very midst—the neighbor, the stranger, the refugee. And a culture where "postmodernity" leaves many people anxious and unsure about what religious expression and ethical commitment could possibly mean anymore.

To read against our habits is to encounter a reading that "reads differently," in a different direction—like words fighting the direction of words, stepping over words that have for too long held sway, taking words in other directions, reading against the grain, reading from right to left. Levinas tracks a way of reading and responding to life that resounds with the prophetic message of the Hebraic tradition, a tradition that has never found a comfortable place in the dominant streams of Western thought. "At this level," writes Derrida, "the thought of Emmanuel Levinas can make us tremble."[21] It would not be wrong to call Levinas' writings profoundly counter-cultural, yet even this seems too familiar a description, as though we would know how to identify an Amos should he again stand in our midst.

Responsibility before freedom, obligation before choice, infinity before totality, the other before me, passivity before power, alterity before identity, "Thou art" before "I am": These are the counter-directional concerns of Levinas' other way of reading. These are the readings that move across the page from the other margin, beginning "over there"—on the other side—rather than from "here," on this side. Contrary readings, starting from a place we least expect, leading in a direction that takes us elsewhere, away from ourselves, cutting across our accustomed paths, forcing us to open the book the other way around.

---

20. Bellah et al., *Habits of the Heart*.
21. Derrida, *Writing and Difference*, 82.

If you can imagine what it is like attempting to speak of "reading from right to left" (the "Hebrew" way), while at the same time having no other means to do so except by writing from left to right (the "Greek" way), then you may understand something of Levinas' difficulty. He is trying to write in a language that is "otherwise than being" while all the time feeling caught in the very sway of "being's language." The language of being is primarily concerned with the language of unity and presence—the confidence of the self to think itself, to be itself—so that this "being I" is also "Being's being," a perfect match between knowing and being grounded in the "I am." Thus, reading in a Greek way (from left to right) would be to say, for example, "I think, therefore I am." This is a quintessential expression of Western thought, one that places the *I* as the point of convergence and centerpiece of all reality. The very vocation of Western philosophy, according to Levinas, is to harmonize and secure my own being with Being's being (*GCM*, 43–51, 137–43). It is the ability to say *I* in such a way that "to think being is to think on one's own scale, to coincide with oneself." It is to place the human subject on a plane that is equal to reality, "miraculously equal to the knowledge that sought it, marvelously *made to measure* for that knowledge." According to Levinas, this ability to say *I*, "which equals itself in equaling being, without anything being able to remain outside this adequate knowledge to weigh it down, is called *freedom*" (*OS*, 30).

The *I* triumphs in freedom and autonomy. This leads to a formula that summarizes the whole of Western philosophy: "Every philosophy is an egology," Levinas says (*TI*, 44). The *I* possesses, domesticates, takes to itself all that is foreign and other, and makes of it a knowledge, a comprehension, a fit with itself. Anything foreign to the self, anything strange or different, anything unfamiliar, anything that threatens to dislocate the self, is gathered up, unified, "brought home," secured, possessed, made the same. In short, Western (and Greek) philosophy is continually "engaged in reducing to the Same all that is opposed to it as *other*" (PI, 91). "Freedom, autonomy, *the reduction of the Other to the Same*"—here, says Levinas, is where "every power begins" (PI, 97).

It is not too difficult, beneath the density of Levinas' language, to discern how much of our Western culture is dominated by a celebration of the self, the autonomous individual, and the quest for self-fulfillment and freedom. "Examine an average mind, " writes Abraham Heschel, "and you will find that it is dominated by an effort to cut reality to the measure of the ego, as if the world existed for the sake of pleasing one's ego."[22] One of the great ideals of Western freedom is the "unencumbered self"—independent, self-reliant, and free.[23] Over and over again, we strive to imagine ourselves as free—without constraint, where nothing binds or weighs, nothing rubs or irritates—always looking for a perfect match between our desire to be and the fulfillment of that desire. We are always seeking "my place in the sun" (DwEL, 24). We live in a culture and a society that continually tells us that autonomy is the most important thing to achieve—my place in the world, my security, my future, my happiness. Of course, it is natural that we would seek a place to dwell in the world and to find a measure of happiness and enjoyment. However, what is at issue here is the level of primacy we give to this quest to lead authentic, secure, self-fulfilled lives—and, moreover, the level of violence we extend in this urge "to be."

In an age of "auto-nomy" (self-rule) and "auto-affection" (self-love), Levinas wants to speak instead of "hetero-affection" (OB, 121), "other love"—love that opens itself toward the other, love that divests the ego of its imperialism, love that dethrones the self in service of the neighbor (the "nigh one") and the stranger (the "far one"). He wants to speak (in other words) in the name of the Other, which is a move not atypical of prophetic language, a language that speaks "from on high" in defense of "the stranger, the widow, and the orphan" with a judgment and an appeal that questions our self-made worlds (TI, 76–77). Prophetic language reminds us that whenever we turn our energies primarily to the task of "being"—of securing our presence in the world—we are immediately captured by the other's accusation: "What right do you have to be over against me? Why do you take up so much room in the world?"

Levinas does not shy from using extreme motifs that radically call into question and upset the power and status of the *I*. He is trying to read life otherwise, "otherwise than being," to read against the all-powerful desire of the ego to be and to secure its presence in the world. He is trying to read in a counter-directional way that begins from the other side, from the other point of view, "to separate oneself from a whole philosophical tradition that sought the foundations of the self in the self" (TI, 88). He is reading from right to left, across the grain of a prevalent Western philosophy and culture. He wants to expose this tradition to the intrusion and revelation of the other, such that "the essence of reason does not consist in securing for man a foundation and powers, but in calling him in question and in inviting him

22. Heschel, *Between God and Man*, 136.
23. Bellah et al., *Habits of the Heart*, 152.

to justice" (*TI*, 88). As Susan Handelman suggests, Levinas' writing is like a "battering, an obsession . . . it parallels the language (and aim) of the biblical prophets—as urgent appeal, imperative demand, anguished rhetorical questioning."[24]

In an insipid, narcissistic culture, Levinas helps us feel again *what it is to be addressed*. His writing comes to us as a prophetic appeal that is deeply shaped by the Hebraic tradition. According to this tradition, freedom does not reside in my authentic subjectivity; rather, freedom is *subjected* to an exteriority—the exteriority of God and neighbor. A self that is founded on autonomous subjectivity—free and above all constraints—knows and is bound only to itself, is a "self-sameness," an *egoism* (or, even worse, a potential nationalism or "totalitarianism"). For Levinas, existence *for itself* is not the ultimate meaning; rather, it is existence *for the other* (*TI*, 88).

What matters is not so much the "Here I am" that is the declaration and assertion of my existence, but the "Here I am" that is the *response* of my existence to the call and claim of the other. "The word *I* means *here I am*," writes Levinas (*OB*, 114). The priority here is not with the *I* constituting itself, but with the call of the other who asks after me, who asks me to be, not for myself alone, but also for "the stranger, the widow, and the orphan." This calling into question of my existence by the presence of the other is, according to Levinas, the very call of justice (*TI*, 43). It is this call that comes first, that is always prior, that is always before me, and that constitutes my identity as a response-ability and answer-ability. As Adriaan Peperzak suggests, "In the ethical 'experience', the ego of *I think* discovers itself as *I am obliged* . . . not *I think, I see, I will, I want, I can*, but *'me voici'* (Here I am)."[25]

Levinas is converting the "I think, therefore I am" of modern, Western thought into the "Here I am" of biblical, prophetic response. "The *I* loses its hold before the absolutely Other, before the human Other, and can no longer be powerful" (*BPW*, 17). Relinquishing the power to say *I*, however, is not the annihilation of the *I*; rather, it is the "election" of the *I* as chosen and responsible before the face of God and neighbor. "I am," says Levinas, "as if I had been chosen" (*OS*, 35).

To speak of these themes—the love of God and the love of neighbor—is to recognize that although "philosophy is essentially Greek, it is not exclusively so. It also has sources and roots that are non-Greek . . . [such

---

24. Handelman, *Fragments of Redemption*, 180–81.

25. Peperzak, "Some Remarks on Hegel, Kant, and Levinas," in Cohen, *Face to Face with Levinas*, 211–12.

as] the Judeo-Christian tradition that proposes an alternative approach to meaning and truth" (*DF*, 19). It may be surprising to imagine the Jewish and Christian traditions as alternatives in this "postmodern age," an age that now sees *itself* as the alternative, leading the way in the wake of God's death and the loss of traditional religious concepts. Yet there is another way of reading our times signalled by the metaphor of "reading otherwise" or "reading from right to left." This alternative reading draws upon age-old biblical themes: invoking the name of God, the love of God and the love of neighbor, care for the "orphan, widow, and stranger," the desire for justice to flow like water over the land, the beatitude of mercy, and the yearning for the coming of God's kingdom and the messianic age.

In the background, as I write, a track by Van Morrison is playing with the refrain, "I'm carrying a torch for you."[26] What does it mean to carry a torch in the world, not for myself alone, but also for "you"? The works of Emmanuel Levinas are striking in the constancy of their thought and the strength of their appeal—we are here on this spinning blue planet not by chance, but by a bond that urges us to be one-for-the-other, to carry each other, to escape the narrow confines of our small egoism. Here is "transcendence" par excellence. Here is what the name of God signifies, the relational and ethical bond that takes us outside ourselves toward the other in our midst. According to Levinas, this turning toward, this face-to-face, is the essential divine and ethical relation:

> Perhaps the spiritual only shows, only reveals its specificity when being's routine is interrupted: in the strangeness of humans vis-à-vis one another, but of humans capable of a sociality in which the bond is no longer the integration of parts in a whole.
>
> Perhaps the spiritual bond lies in the non-indifference of persons toward one another that is also called love, but that does not absorb the difference and strangeness and is possible only on the basis of a spoken word or order coming, through the human face, from most high outside the world. (*OS*, 102–3)

A Thinker of "Great Size"

"In the name of the Father, and the Son, and the Holy Spirit. Amen." So goes the prayer that has been with me since my childhood (in Latin: *In nomine Patris, et Filii, et Spiritus Sancti. Amen*).

26. Morrison, "Carrying a Torch."

"Hear O Israel, the Lord our God, the Lord is One." So goes the Shema that was inscribed on every doorpost in my Jerusalem apartment (in Hebrew: *Shema Yisra'el Adonai Eloheinu Adonai echad*).

These are beautiful prayers, and sometimes I find myself caught in a quandary. "Where flames a word for which both can vow?" asks Paul Celan. Where is this flaming word, this word of avowal, which burns in both these traditions? Celan's poem continues, first with the image of the crucified one: "I know you, the one pierced-through." Then with the image of the holy one: "I know you—wholly, wholly real"—and I, "wholly illusion."[27] The crucified one of the Christian tradition and the holy one of the Jewish tradition—my avowal. I cannot pretend to have found a way of reconciling these two traditions, nor any desire or need to do so. I am in accord with Levinas, who refers to the relationship between Judaism and Christianity as a "symbiosis," a "privileged neighborliness," a "shared life," whose destinies are "incontestably and essentially entwined" (*IRB*, 95).

With a body of work as vast and deep as Levinas', it is inevitable that there will be a plurality of readings. Mine is only one such reading and I make no claim to definitiveness. As Levinas himself says, referring to textual study, "revelation has a particular way of producing meaning, which lies in its calling upon the unique within me" (*LR*, 195). Each person, by virtue of his or her own uniqueness, is required in the act of reading and interpreting in order that various facets of a text's meaning may shine forth. A multiplicity of persons is required to reveal the plentitude of textual meaning. A revered text is never so revered as when it engenders sincere engagement and innovative commentary.

In writing this work, my aim is not to add yet another authoritative text on Levinas. My aim is to pay homage to Levinas by offering my own unique reading, born of many years of engaging his texts in the conditions of my own life. Moreover, while I am aware that Levinas is not beyond critique, my aim is not to parse Levinas' texts through a labyrinth of critical appraisal. Whatever the shortcomings of Levinas' work—and I do not know any thinker who is free of them—I am more interested in highlighting the positive value of his message.

I approach Levinas as a thinker of "great size," and to this day I remain indebted to him as someone who has taught me much in my life and given me a renewed sense of voice and vocation. To be taught—that is enough

---

27. The verses from Celan are cited in Gadamer, *Gadamer on Celan*, 122.

Introduction: "Jerusalem Writings"

for me, that is enough to place Levinas in the ranks of a "teacher" in whose company I am happy to be a student.

In this work there are occasions of repetition. Where such repetition seems beneficial, I have purposefully allowed it to remain. Repetition is common in many religious traditions—for example, in liturgical rituals and cycles of readings. It is rare that great teachings are learned on one reading alone. The early rabbinic teachers (the *tannaim*) were sometimes known as "repeaters."[28] Repetition is required for all learning—very few people learn things "once and for all." Rather, their learning is many times over. Repetition need not be a bad thing; it can also help us attend, over and over again, to the thing we are trying to learn and to practice. Levinas himself certainly "repeats" many of his key themes in various ways. One could even say that he is a "repeater" of tradition and stands in a long line of repeaters: "Hear, O Israel . . . repeat these words . . ." (Deut 6).

> The Talmud asks the question: "How do we know about the resurrection of the dead?" The rabbis discuss the issue over a dozen pages or so, wielding arguments, citations and allusions. And among the allusions, a reference is made to a passage from the Song of Songs where there is mention of "one who makes the dead move their lips." This is given as proof that the dead are resurrected. But in what situation does this happen? When one quotes someone who is dead, when something is said in his name, when what he said is now relevant. Levinas may not have left any disciples behind, but thousands of students are still able to make his lips move.[29]

I hope that I too, in writing this work, may be able "to make his lips move."

---

28. The name *tanna* means one who studies, repeats, and hands down what he has learned from his teachers. See Steinsaltz, *Essential Talmud*, 24.

29. Malka, *Emmanuel Levinas*, 105–6 (citing Simon Hazan).

Part One

For You Alone

2

Indifference

Nobody Asks after You

Indifference

> it's like being sick all the time, I think, coming home from work,
> sick in that low-grade continuous way that makes you forget
> what it's like to be well. we have never in our lives known
> what it is to be well. what if I were coming home, I think,
> from doing work that I loved and that was for us all, what
> if I looked at the houses and the air and the streets, knowing
> they were in accord, not set against us, what if we knew the powers
> of this country moved to provide for us and for all people—
> how would that be—how would we feel and think
> and what would we create?
>
> —KAREN BRODINE[1]

This is a poem I know. I suspect that the seeming ordinariness of the sickness it describes is not disconnected from the deeper wounds that injure our collective lives as human beings. Like the poet, I too want to know what it is like to be well, to feel a healthy "well-being" (*shalom*) circulating in our relational worlds—in our families, in our neighborhoods,

---

1. Brodine, "June 1978," in *Illegal Assembly*.

Part One—For You Alone

in our workplaces, in our communities, in our cities, in the *polis* that comprises our shared, public life ("to provide for us and for all people").

And yet, there is this anxiety within me that is constant and inescapable ("it's like being sick all the time"). Levinas calls it "there is" (*il y a*). Nothing else. It just is. Neutrality. Indifference. Just a dull murmur or rumbling—"the muffled rustling of nothingness back unto which the elements flow and are lost" (*TI*, 146). This is a world without concern, without care, impersonal, indifferent, care-less—it just is. It is this stark, oblivious indifference that Søren Kierkegaard writes about in his *Fear and Trembling*:

> If underlying everything there were only a wild, fermenting power that writhing in dark passions produced everything, be it significant or insignificant, if a vast, never appeased emptiness hid beneath everything . . . if there were no sacred bond that knit humankind together, if one generation emerged after another like forest foliage, if one generation succeeded another like the singing of birds in the forest, if a generation passed through the world like a ship through the sea, as wind through the desert, an unthinking and unproductive performance, if an eternal oblivion, perpetually hungry, lurked for its prey and there were no power strong enough to wrench that away from it . . .[2]

In a less passionate way, the definitional pages of the Oxford dictionary put it this way:

> *Indifferent*: neither good nor bad; not especially good; fairly bad; having no partiality for or against; having no interest in or sympathy for; neutral.
>
> *Indifference*: lack of interest or attention, unimportance, neutrality.

The poet Paul Celan, however, puts it best:[3]

> Nowhere
>   does anyone ask after you—

This is the void, the coldness of the stars that just stare, the heaving of the ocean that just rumbles and roars, the emptiness of the streets where a woman feels sick with the indifference of the world. Nowhere does anyone pay any attention, even though *there you are*, in our very midst, burdened and seeking the relief of compassion and a sense of human connection and

---

2. Kierkegaard, *Fear and Trembling*, 15.
3. Celan, "The Straitening," in *Selected Poems*, 141.

solidarity. Yet nowhere does anyone ask after you, unable even to recognize that "the love of neighbor in all its fullness simply means being able to say, 'What are you going through?'"[4] To live in a world without response—a response-less world, a world devoid of responsibility—is to live in a world of indifference and disregard. Levinas refers to this dread-filled experience simply as "there is" (*LR*, 29–36). Nothing matters, nothing calls, nothing answers, nothing counts. There is. Nothing other.

Levinas began writing his reflections on the horror of the *there is* while imprisoned in a German camp during World War II. In *Existence and Existents*, "written down for the most part in captivity" (*EE*, 15), he reflects on the terrifying impersonality and anonymity of "being," as though nothing in the grand sweep of *existence* really cared about a personal and individual *existent*. It was as if he felt unable to escape the terror of reality, the "impossibility of escaping from an anonymous and uncorruptible existence . . . the *there is* has no exits." Like a chained prisoner, he felt chained to "the fatality of irremissible being" (*LR*, 33). For Levinas, "being in general" carried no quality of life's vital essence or openness; rather, it carried all the horror of a constrained and claustrophobic prison existence. This is in sharp contrast to Martin Heidegger, for whom the German expression *es gibt* (there is/it gives) marked the generosity of Being that confers light and truth and mystery to all things.[5] For Levinas, however, there is little comfort in the lightness of being that simply bestows itself freely and indiscriminately. The "there is/it gives" strikes him as chaotic, shapeless, anonymous, impersonal, and it is from this "unbearable lightness of being" that he seeks to find an exit.[6]

Levinas is not trying to escape from a fear of death or nothingness. It is not finitude that frightens him. Indeed, it is futile trying to escape the limitations of our finitude; we have no chance of getting away. Even when we seek a refuge from the world and its onslaught, Being is still *there*—it tracks us wherever we go. Levinas' difficulty is not with nothingness, but with the very fact of Being, this "inexpungeable *something*."[7] Faced with the droning, anonymous, impersonal forces of Being, "the likeable game of life loses its gamelike quality." Instead, it becomes a marker for unremitting suf-

---

4. Weil, *Waiting on God*, 115.

5. Heidegger, *Being and Time*, 255. See Peperzak, "On Levinas's Criticism of Heidegger," in *Beyond*, 204–17.

6. The reference here is to Kundera, *Unbearable Lightness of Being*.

7. Moyn, "Judaism against Paganism," 43.

fering and the "sharp feeling of being fixed," with no chance of interrupting or transcending the suffocating immanence of "pure Being itself."[8]

Levinas feels little sympathy for this gamelike Being that is nothing but a "play of influences and impulses," a game "without players, or stakes," a "game without a subject," a "gracious disorder of simple glints of being." All this, for Levinas, is but the "irresponsibility of a game," a perverse frivolity, a "human fiasco" (*GCM*, 48). He wants to break with this "philosophy of the Neuter: with Heideggerian Being [and] impersonal neutrality" (*TI*, 298). He wants to argue for something "otherwise than being," to think beyond the totalizing confines of Being that holds everything in its capricious power, to move against the incessant and unbearable lightness of "pure being" to the urgent and weighty concern of "being-for." As he says in an interview reflecting on his initial musings in the stalag, "being-for-the-other seemed to me, as early as that time, to stop the anonymous and senseless rumbling of being" (*EI*, 52). It is as if we can imagine Levinas, chained to existence and locked in his barracks, saying, along with Celan, "With all my thoughts I went out of the world: and there you were . . ."[9]

From within the prison house of being, Levinas glimpsed a way out of the all-encompassing immanence of being-in-the-world. He found an exit from self-enclosed being that allowed him to move toward being-open-to-the-other. What he perceived in this radical movement of transcendence he later named the "face"—the one who is suddenly there, outside my world, the one who is other than me and exterior to myself. With the revelation of the face, Levinas no longer felt trapped by the anonymous *there is*. Rather, "there you were"—and he realized that the world is not structured by indifference and impersonality, but by the "gleam of exteriority or of transcendence in the face of the Other" (*TI*, 24). It is not the impersonal *there is* that marks our struggles—it is you, the other, who claim our existence: "I do not struggle with a faceless god, but I respond to his expression, to his revelation" (*TI*, 197).

The woman on the street, "coming home from work" (a widow? a single parent? a stranger nevertheless)—she is the one whose face is revelation. She is the one whose face exposes the indifference of the world. As though we finally went out of our fenced-off houses and saw her coming, saw her walking toward us—"and there you are," in our very midst, appealing

---

8. Ibid., 41–43.
9. Celan, "With all my thoughts," in *Selected Poems*, 171.

against our indifference, summoning us to *non*-indifference, to response and responsibility. "My neighbor," not the impersonal *there is*, "is the being par excellence" (*BPW*, 10). Her face is the absolute resistance to indifference, the extraordinary relation of another's looking at me and speaking to me, refusing to be absorbed by the gathering forces of impersonal Being. From the depths of Celan's devastating plea—"Nowhere / does anyone ask after you"—Levinas brings us face to face with the Other who cries out and asks after us: "The Other becomes my neighbor precisely through the way the face summons me, calls for me, begs for me, and in so doing recalls my responsibility, calls me into question" (*LR*, 83). It is the ethical relation of being-for-the-other that breaks up the immanence of being-in-the-world: "Ethics begins before the exteriority of the *other*, before other people, and, as I like to put it, before the face of the other, which engages my responsibility by its human expression . . . An ethics of heteronomy that is not a servitude, but the service of God through responsibility for the neighbor, in which I am irreplaceable" (*OS*, 35).

The world is not structured by indifference; rather, it is constantly charged with the call/demand/obligation to respond, to answer, to say "here I am" (*EI*, 109). This is the human vocation par excellence—the act of answerability. It is a vocation that is desperately needed in our society, in which so much energy is expended in the maintenance of faceless, bureaucratic structures, in the useless creation of consumer needs and shopping malls, in the withdrawal of anguished lives into the security of their private worlds. Is this what we mean by our freedom, our autonomy, our independence? Or is it rather, as Abraham Heschel says, that we are "thirsty for what is more than existence"? And who or what makes us thirst? Who or what is the bearer of this "more than," this "excedence," this transcendence? Heschel writes,

> We are all in search of a conviction that there is something which is worth the toil of living. There is not a soul which has not felt a craving to know of something that outlasts [exceeds, transcends] life, strife and agony . . . Who has made us thirsty for what is more than existence? There is only one way to fumigate the obnoxious air of the world: to live beyond our own needs and interests . . . It is a most significant fact that the human person is not sufficient unto themselves, that life is not meaningful to me unless it is serving an end beyond itself, unless it is of value to someone else.[10]

10. Heschel, *Between God and Man*, 132–35.

Part One—For You Alone

In a similar vein, Martin Buber brought to the world his essential philosophy of the "I-Thou" relation.[11] It is as though Buber finally broke through the Western tradition's obsession with the *I*, exposing it to the alterity of the other, to the transcendence of the Thou. Like Levinas and Heschel, Buber rallied against the indifference of the world that fails to recognize the other in our very midst. His writings continually plead that we "ask after you," that we keep you in mind, that we come in support of you—to be your ally, to confirm your existence.[12] For Buber, "the basis of our lives together is twofold, and it is one—the wish of everyone to be confirmed as what they are, even what they can become, by others; and the capacity in us to confirm others in this way."[13]

The singular emphasis on relationality in Jewish writers such as Heschel, Buber, and Levinas is quite remarkable at times. In his own reflections on "being," Heschel is also concerned to avoid generic, abstract descriptions of life that leave the face of the other person lost in anonymity or reduced to the horizon of the self-same. In a phrase that resonates with both Levinas and Buber, Heschel says, "to *be* is to *stand for.*"[14] "To be" is to confirm the existence of the other person—to be for the other—to shift the focus from myself alone toward the claims and needs of the other in the face-to-face relation. Heschel writes, "How rarely do we face a person as a person. We are all dominated by the desire to appropriate and to own. Only a free person knows that the true meaning of existence is experienced in giving, in endowing, in meeting a person face to face, in fulfilling other people's needs."[15]

While both Heschel and Levinas offer strong critiques of the pervasive individualism of our era—the dominance of the ego that keeps everything in its power and reduces all otherness to the self-same—they also offer strong critiques of totalizing systems that sacrifice the individual to impersonal, anonymous structures. According to Heschel, "it is always one person at a time whom we keep in mind . . . when trying to fulfill: 'Love thy neighbor as thyself.'" A human being is not valuable because he or she is a member of the human race; "it is rather the opposite: the human race is

---

11. Buber, *I and Thou.*
12. Buber, "Buber's Reply," *PN*, 39.
13. Buber, *Between Man and Man*, 61.
14. Heschel, *Between God and Man*, 151.
15. Ibid., 136.

valuable because it is composed of human beings."[16] Similarly for Levinas, the face of the other is the face of the exceptionally *singular one*—the one who refuses to be contained and absorbed by totalizing systems or schemas, but who stands against these systems as a singular claim of justice and compassion.

It is important to recall that Levinas' life and philosophy were deeply marked by the horror of the Nazi genocide. As one commentator says of him, "Levinas is a prophet of the murdered people . . . He is not simply a theorist, but a person responding to the trauma of our time. His ethic is at once an intellectual edifice *and* an extended prayer."[17] From his initial wrestling in the prison camps with an anonymous, impersonal, indifferent universe, he came to perceive the great danger of subordinating individual "existents" to "existence," that is, to anonymous "Being," to an absolutized "Whole," to a grand "System"—or, as Levinas says, to a "Totality." Long before the postmodern critique of "metanarratives," Levinas already perceived the danger of totalizing narratives that suppress/oppress/murder everything that is other and different to the all-powerful system: "Individuals are reduced to being bearers of forces that command them unbeknown to themselves" (*TI*, 21). It is not difficult to hear in this sentence the haunting, marching echoes of the Third Reich.

Susan Handelman reminds us that there is a close connection in Levinas' thought between the violence of political totalitarianism and the "ontological totalitarianism" of Western philosophy that reduces all otherness to the Same.[18] Against Heidegger's "Being" that simply "gives itself," Levinas wrote, "None of the generosity which the German term *es gibt* is said to contain revealed itself between 1933 and 1945 . . . Enlightenment and meaning dawn only with the existent beings rising up and establishing themselves in this horrible neutrality of the *there is*" (*DF*, 292). Ontological thinking is an attempt to bleach out the existence of the other into the all-absorbing coalescence of the Same, of reducing "beings" to "Being"—the singular face of revelation to the anonymous, faceless system that thereby permits terror and tyranny to go unnoticed and unchecked. According to Levinas, totalizing thought that gathers everything into the immanence of Being engenders totalizing systems of behavior that have real historical impacts: "One has to respond to one's right to be, not by referring to some

16. Ibid., 133.
17. Gottlieb, "Ethics and Trauma," 232–33.
18. Handelman, *Fragments of Redemption*, 189.

abstract and anonymous law . . . but because of one's fear for the Other. My being-in-the-world or my 'place in the sun,' my being at home, have these not also been the usurpation of spaces of belonging to the other man whom I have already oppressed or starved, or driven out into a third world; are they not acts of repulsing, excluding, exiling, stripping, killing?" (*LR*, 82)

Levinas insists that the first word of the face is this: "You shall not commit murder" (*TI*, 199).

Saving God's Name

> My heart is moved by all I cannot save:
> so much has been destroyed
>
> I have to cast my lot with those
> who age after age, perversely,
>
> with no extraordinary power,
> reconstitute the world.
>
> —ADRIENNE RICH[19]

How can Levinas maintain that love and "being-for-the-other" is fundamentally structured into life when he has witnessed a century of unbounded suffering and evil? "It might astonish some," writes Levinas, "that faced with so many unleashed forces, so many violent and voracious acts that fill our history, our societies and our souls—that I should turn to the *I-Thou* or the responsibility-of-one-person-for-the-other to find the categories of the Human" (*OS*, 42). When we survey the history of the twentieth century we may indeed wonder whether this "being-for-the-other" is indeed the case—and it certainly amazes me that Levinas can claim this is the case after his experiences with Nazism in the war. Levinas is sometimes critiqued for being a "utopian" thinker. Being-for-the-other is simply too high-minded. It posits an ideal world, an impotent moral demand that none of us can live up to. Maybe it can work in the "city of God" or the "kingdom of God," but certainly not among us who dwell on earth. When Levinas was asked whether his thought was utopian and unrealistic, he replied,

---

19. Rich, "Natural Resources," in *Dream of a Common Language*, 67.

Indifference

> This is the great objection to my thought. "Where did you ever see the ethical relation practiced?" people say to me. I reply that its being utopian does not prevent it from investing our everyday actions of generosity and goodwill towards the other: even the smallest and most commonplace gestures, such as saying "after you" ... bear witness to the ethical. This concern for the other remains utopian in the sense that it is always "out of place" (*u-topos*) in this world, always other than the "ways of the world"; but there are many examples of it in the world. (DwEL, 32)

"Hatred of the other" is the root of all evil, and "being-for-the-other" is the sign of all goodness, even the "small goodness" enacted every day in the world, yet often unnoticed and unreported. To save the name of God, or to hallow God's name, is to save the name of this "being for." It is to save the name of goodness, love, grace, and compassion. To save the name of God is to save the name of humanity. It is not to save the name of a faceless God, a God of impersonal Being, a God of the swirling cosmos. Rather, it is to save the face of ethical relation, the life of each other in relation to each other, bound and responsible one-for-the-other. To save the name of God is to save the name of the other, every other, each other.

We live in a world that cares too much about idols that are just dead things—idols that cannot speak, cannot feel, cannot touch, idols that have no soul, no sense of the human, the living, the life of speaking, touching, responding, of healing, giving, and forgiving. To save the name of God is to save the name of the one who speaks, who sees, who hears, who touches— against all the dead and lifeless idols of our world:

> ... their idols, in silver and gold,
> products of human skill,
> have mouths, but never speak,
> eyes, but never see,
> ears, but never hear,
> noses, but never smell,
> hands, but never touch,
> feet, but never walk
> and no sound rises from their throats.
> Their makers will end up like them,
> and so will anyone who relies on them.
> (Ps 115:4–8)

To save the name of God is to save the name of life, to save the name of the other, lest we end up worshipping our own selves, our own technologies, our own economic systems, our own constructed worlds, our own carvings and Wall Streets—relying too much upon them, becoming too much like them: dead, lifeless, inhuman. To save God's name is to recognize that the name is important—the name of the other—the one who has a mouth that speaks, who has eyes that look, who has ears that listen—not a faceless God, but the God who is face-to-face, the God of the living.

"I offer you the choice of life or death, blessing or curse. Choose life, then, so that you and your descendants may live" (Deut 30:19). What will we choose—"being-for-the-other," which spells life, or "hatred of the other," which spells death? One wonders whether the Deuteronomic writer offers such a stark and "simplistic" choice out of frustration. What appears so "simple" is usually that which is most ignored, or dismissed as a remote, impractical ideal. And yet,

> It is not beyond your strength or beyond your reach. It is not in heaven, so that you need to wonder, "Who will go up to heaven for us and bring it down to us, so that we may hear and keep it?" Nor is it beyond the seas, so that you need to wonder, "Who will cross the seas for us and bring it back to us, so that we may hear it and keep it?" No, the Word is very near to you, it is in your mouth and in your heart for your observance. (Deut 30:11–14)

We can speak words of despair. We can speak words of hope. We can speak words that destroy, or words that heal. Which of these two shall we privilege? Which will claim priority? The unimaginable takes two forms, that of grace and that of disaster. At every moment existence confronts us with the choice between life and death; at every moment we are asked to respond, to give an answer. Theology carries the burden of disaster's unimaginable despair, and salvation's unimaginable hope. Every word of theology is thus weighed on the scales of disaster and grace. Which weighs more? What will tilt the balance? In this struggle with heavy words that matter, theology takes a risk. It makes a judgment: grace, hope, love—these words are heavier, they weigh more, they matter most. According to Levinas, it is this love, this "being-for," this goodness, that is written into the very fabric of life:

> It is this attention to the suffering of the other that, through the cruelties of our century (despite these cruelties, because of these cruelties) can be affirmed as the very nexus of human subjectivity, to the point of being raised to a supreme ethical principle—the only one it is impossible to question—shaping

> the hopes and commanding the practical discipline of vast human groups. (*EN*, 94)
>
> The only absolute value is the human possibility of giving the other priority over oneself. I don't think there is a human group that can take exception to that ideal, even if it is declared as an ideal of holiness. (*EN*, 109)
>
> It is in view of the Good that "every soul does all that it does." (*EN*, 204)
>
> Love is originary. (*EN*, 108)

Love is originary. The Good is primary. Life is on the side of love, on the side of goodness. It is not being-in-itself, it is not sheer being, indifferent being—it is "being-for." It may be easy to dismiss Levinas' thought as utopian, excessive, or unrealistic. Yet this may also be its attraction, because it speaks with such prophetic excess: "If you do away with the yoke, the clenched fist, the wicked word, if you give . . . then your light will shine like the dawn and your wound be quickly healed over" (Isa 58:9–11). We are confronted with a truth and a goodness that seem impossible and unbelievable in the wake of a century of cruelty. Yet it is strange the way we are often attracted to "unbelievable truths" rather than those that seem too "believable," how we sense that there is always more to life than what we see, more than what we understand, more than what is given. This is the type of world Levinas brings before us: a world of amazing grace, unbelievable love, generous self-giving, beyond the realms of being, outside the realms of thought, more than the realms of the containable—infinite. Indeed, "infinity" is the very realm of the unbelievable, whereas "totality" is the realm of what is contained and controlled as "believable."

To argue for the possible is an easy thing. It is much more difficult, and yet maybe more necessary, to argue beyond the realm of the foreseeable and the possible, to argue instead and more daringly for what is impossible, which is like arguing on the side of "amazing grace," or arguing for a strange, impossible "kingdom of God" where a different logic of love is operative, where a different "rule" applies. It is odd to encounter a type of thinking that rarely talks of faith or belief, yet that all the time seems to be asking us to adopt an enormous faith that life is otherwise, that it spins in an orbit of otherness that compels a gravitational love. Especially when the world in which we live seems to be spinning around an axis of egocentrism and disregard of the other, Levinas asks us to believe that it is spinning

Part One—For You Alone

otherwise, that it is tied to a gravitational "being-for" of gratuitous love and response and self-donation . . . Unbelievable! Even more so given what we know of Levinas' wrenching background. The unimaginable takes two forms, that of grace and that of disaster—blessing and curse, life and death, being-for-the-other and hatred-of-the-other. For Levinas, the capacity to be-for-the-other is much larger and more primordial than the capacity for hatred. It is this "capacity," this "great size," this generous being-for-the-other that we need to hallow in life. It is this hope of salvation that requires our response, our "yes," our "amen."

3

Under Your Gaze

> Here I am under your gaze, obliged to you, your servant.
> In the name of God.
>
> —Emmanuel Levinas

"About Face"

*P*ostmodernity is a word that is often used in academic circles and increasingly in popular circles as well. According to David Tracy, it is a complex word with many "faces," yet its most salient feature is the call to turn around and to "face the other": "The turn to the other is the quintessential turn of postmodernity itself. It is that turn, above all, that defines the intellectual as well as the ethical meaning of postmodernity. The other and the different come forward now as central intellectual categories across the major disciplines, including theology . . . Part of that return to otherness is the return of biblical Judaism and Christianity to undo the complacencies of modernity, including modern theology."[1]

One of the reasons Levinas seeks to refocus our attention toward the face of the other is his concern that we have enclosed ourselves in a world of "immanence." In other words, we have reduced everything to our being-in-the-world, and we no longer know how to speak of transcendence—the desire of infinity, the voice of otherness, the God of revelation who addresses

---

1. Tracy, "Theology and the Many Faces of Postmodernity," 108.

our lives. He wants to speak against the complacencies of an age that thinks itself free of everything that is other than itself and beyond the embarrassment of a relationship with an unknown God.

Levinas introduces his *Of God Who Comes to Mind* with a question: How can we speak of God "without striking a blow against the absoluteness that his word seems to signify?" How can we speak of "the infinity or alterity or novelty of the absolute" without giving it back into immanence? In other words, if we bring God too quickly and too readily into the ambit of our understanding and our grasp, don't we thereby miss God altogether, the God of transcendence and otherness? It seems, then, that speaking of God requires "impossible requirements!" (*GCM*, xii). For if we want to respect the concentration and absoluteness of God's revelation, if we want to expose ourselves to the transcendence of God's word, if we want this word to come to us with a "power of speech" that addresses our lives, then it must, somehow, be a word that comes "from on high"—a revelation that is nowhere already known by us, that is nowhere the same as us, that is not a knowledge we already possess or a god already within us. Otherwise, how could we speak of *revelation*?

In "Revelation in the Jewish Tradition" (*LR*, 190–210), Levinas begins with a similar question: How do we connect the world we inhabit with something that is no longer "of this world"? How can we make sense of the exteriority of the truths and signs of revelation? How do we speak of an otherness that comes "from outside," from somewhere else? How is this thinkable? Truths from outside? From somewhere else? From where?

Haven't sociologists told us that our truths are the products of our own social constructions of reality? Haven't psychologists reminded us that many of our truths are reflections or projections of our own inner desires and conflicts? Wasn't it Heidegger who revealed that all our knowing reflects the ontological condition of being-in-the-world? And hasn't postmodernism (or at least a certain type of postmodernism) confidently pronounced that there are no metanarratives, that there is "nothing outside the text"?

All this, for Levinas, is so much immanence, and it only serves to dull the voice of revelation, of that which comes from outside, from somewhere else, from somewhere otherwise, from beyond being. In the midst of "the magnificent funeral celebrations held in honor of a dead god" (*LR*, 193), Levinas arrives with news that turns everyone's head, that leaves everyone somewhat stunned, for all of sudden here is a philosopher who dares speak again of revelation, of truths from outside, of an Other that is "otherwise than being."

Levinas begins his first major work, *Totality and Infinity*, with the statement "The true life is absent" (*TI*, 33). Isn't this something we all experience? Isn't it the case that, at rock bottom, we always feel an "absence" (or as Augustine said, a "restlessness"), that we never seem to find the perfect match between our desires and their fulfilment, that we always experience a basic uneasiness in life, never a sense of total well-being and peace? Somehow, we always feel a separation, a gap, a rift, a rupture, never a feeling of completeness, harmony, perfect unity, never a feeling of "totality," but rather one of "infinity"—of desires that are infinite, questions that open out endlessly, yearnings that are never quenched. For Levinas, this experience is a first indicator of an otherness that we are always turned toward, of an "elsewhere" and an "otherwise," of a fundamental movement "from an 'at home' which we inhabit, toward an alien outside-of-oneself, toward a yonder" (*TI*, 33).

In the Greek philosophical tradition, this experience has generated whole systems of thought that attempt to close this gap, that have sought to correlate the structures of our thinking (epistemology) with the structures of being (ontology). It is the destiny of knowledge to search out and adhere to being, and it is the destiny of being to disclose itself, to be known. The two (knowledge and being) share a common destiny, are entwined, are a harmonious whole, are fully present because always present to each other. As Levinas says, the whole trajectory of Greek philosophy is its "equation of truth with an *intelligibility of presence* . . . an intelligibility that considers truth to be that which is present or co-present, that which can be gathered or synchronized into a totality that we would call the world or *cosmos*" (DwEL, 19).

In contrast to this search for harmony, unity and presence, Levinas prefers to speak of that "which cuts through and perforates the totality of presence and points towards the absolutely other" (DwEL, 21). He prefers to stay with the experience of rupture, because this experience opens us to the address of the other—that which speaks from outside, that which refuses to be tamed and domesticated into our harmonious worlds of rest and repose. Indeed, the philosopher's desire to get a good night's sleep where all is well in the world, a drowsy self-satisfied presence where there is no interruptive other, where everything is unified into a comfortable Sameness— this experience is contrasted by Levinas with the state of "vigilant insomnia" where the other haunts our ontological existence and keeps us awake, keeps us vulnerable and exposed to the revelation of God (DwEL, 28).

Part One—For You Alone

In comparing the Greek tradition of speculative contemplation with the biblical tradition of revelation, Levinas says,

> [For the Greek tradition], the opposites of repose—worry, questioning, seeking, Desire—are all taken to be a waste of repose, an absence of response, a privation, a pure insufficiency of identity, a mark of self-inequality. We have wondered whether the Revelation might not lead us to precisely this idea of inequality, difference and irreducible alterity which is "uncontainable" . . . a mode of thought which is not knowledge but which, exceeding knowledge, is in relation with the Infinite or God . . . Perhaps the attitudes of seeking, desiring and questioning do not represent the emptiness of need but the explosion of the "more within the less". . . (*LR*, 208)

And again:

> Should we not go beyond the consciousness which is equal to itself, seeking always to assimilate the Other, and emphasize instead the act of deference to the other in his alterity, which can only come about through the awakening of the Same—drowsy in his identity—by the Other? (*LR*, 209)

Levinas disturbs our quest for a self-satisfied harmony and wholeness. He is trying to wake us up lest we fall asleep in our own drowsy, comfortable worlds. Attitudes of "seeking, desiring and questioning," rather than "rest and repose," provide the best environment for the revelation of the other. "Within the vision I am developing," he writes, "human emotion and spirituality begin in the for-the-other, in being affected by the other" (*IRB*, 53). In this sense, Levinas doesn't have a lot of time for the peace and serenity of contemplation or mysticism—at least contemplation or mysticism of the "cheap" kind, where everything is played out in the depths of my self. "The mystical event," he says, "is always very suspect to me, unless it is a metaphor of something else, of a perfect accord with Him" (*IRB*, 58). According to Levinas, losing myself in prayer and contemplation, being absorbed into the mystery, entering the space of mystical tranquility—this is the last thing revelation is meant to do. Union with God is not a mystical fusion; rather, it is an "accord" with God's will. The other is the prophetic voice of revelation, not the disclosive voice of being. God is otherwise than being, not the ground of being. And our problem is not that we have been forgetful of being; our problem is rather that we have been forgetful of the other. He writes, "Ethical responsibility is . . . a *wakefulness* precisely because it is a perpetual duty of vigilance and effort that can never slumber.

Ontology as a state of affairs can afford to sleep. But love cannot sleep, can never be peaceful or permanent. Love is the incessant watching over the other; it can never be satisfied or content with the bourgeois ideal of love as domestic comfort" (DwEL, 30).

Much of today's popular spirituality goes in search of something that will give our lives a deeper sense of meaning, that will fulfill our desires and yearnings, that will absorb our fragmented, isolated selves into a larger, more integrated whole. For Levinas, this is reflective of an existential need that is too tied to the self and what the self lacks, rather than a Desire that reaches beyond the self toward the Other (DwEL, 31). To be an *I*, to secure my identity, to feel my own authentic subjectivity—this, for Levinas, will only lead us circling back into the Same. The subject is always trying to secure its identity in terms of itself.

According to Levinas, we need to start elsewhere, outside our selves, "outside the subject" (*OS*). This strikes me as an amazing thought, particularly for our Western culture that is often dominated by a quest for self-authenticity and that so highly prizes the autonomous, free, self-sufficient individual. Our "enlightened" culture is often suspicious of anything that might impose itself on our lives or threaten our individual freedom. We like to stay in "control" of the world as critical, independent, self-empowered subjects. I have noticed in my own teaching that, when dealing with Levinas' texts, our class often bristles in the face of the priority Levinas gives to responsibility rather than freedom, obligation rather than choice, self-giving rather than self-agency, passivity rather than assertiveness, "exterior-to-me" rather than "interior-to-me." Levinas rubs against our cultural habits. We find ourselves protesting, "What about me?"

What, then, does Levinas propose? What I find rather startling is his ability to speak in the name of the absolutely transcendent, the infinitely other, yet to do so by speaking of a very simple, concrete relation: that of the face-to-face (*TI*, 185–219). Every face we encounter is a face of otherness. Every face says, "I am other to you." Every face says, "I am not you." Every face says, "Don't kill me; don't absorb me into your world; don't assimilate me by making me the same as you. I am other. I am different. I am not you."

It is important to note that Levinas is talking here about the naked face, the face that is not masked by the whole social apparatus of roles and status. Rather, this is the naked face that stands before me, completely exposed, completely vulnerable, infinitely other, absolutely singular. "The skin of the face is the most naked, most destitute . . . there is an essential poverty in the face" (*EI*, 86). This is the face of you, and you are vulnerable and dependent on me. Yet you also face me with an "uprightness"—face-to-face. The unique, singular face stands opposed to the indifference of "impersonal, anonymous Being." Rather, the face is "expression"—it is not just "something" that I look upon, that I hold in my gaze. The face "faces" me, and this "toward me" is both a profound appeal against my indifference to your naked vulnerability and an accusation that prohibits my violence toward you. The face of the other "is a double expression of weakness and demand." The face is both "lordship and that which is without defense." "Exposed in its nudity," it is also "the supreme authority that commands . . . the face is the site of the word of God" (*IRB*, 170, 215).

The face of the other breaks into my world and calls out to me. I am not an *I* unto myself, but an *I* standing before the other. The other calls forth my response, commands my attention, refuses to be ignored, makes a claim on my existence, tells me I am responsible. And this always. I will never be freed from the face of the other. So much so, that Levinas says we are always held "hostage" to the other, that we are never released from the other's speaking to us and calling forth our response: "It is impossible to evade the appeal of the neighbor, to move away" (*OB*, 128). The other says, "I am here," and appeals to us, commands us: "Thou shalt not kill"—which is one of the commandments that Levinas often cites.

What matters for Levinas is not so much the question of meaning in life, but the question of ethics or holiness: "The concern for the other," he says, "breaks the concern for the self. This is what I call holiness" (*IRB*, 55). What matters is not so much our separation from God and the desire for mystical participation; rather, what matters is our disregard for each other, and the desire for sociality, for ethical responsibility. What matters is not so much the declaration of my existence that says, "Here I am," but the "Here I am" that is the response of my existence to the call of the other.

According to Levinas, this responsive "Here I am" is testimony itself to the revelation that comes from outside, from elsewhere, from otherwise than my being (*EI*, 106). Wherever we find people saying "Here I am"—not as an assertion or declaration of their existence, but as a response—then we are witnessing a testimony to the voice of the Other that calls from beyond. For Levinas, this is Revelation, and this is how "God comes to mind" (*GCM*, 168):

> We said right at the beginning: the subject of our enquiry is the very fact of Revelation, and the relation it establishes within

exteriority. This exteriority . . . cannot be transformed into a content within interiority; it remains "uncontainable," infinite, and yet the relation is maintained. The path I am led to follow, in solving the paradox of Revelation, is one that claims we may find a model for this relation in the attitude of non-indifference towards the Other, in the responsibility towards him; and that it is precisely through this relation that a person becomes his "self," designated without any possibility of escape, chosen, unique, not interchangeable, and—in this sense—free. Ethics provides the model worthy of transcendence and it is as an ethical kerygma that the Bible is Revelation. (*LR*, 207)

To turn around, to face the other—this is the conversion required of philosophy and theology. As David Tracy notes, "surely, on the central question of transcendence, this ethical route to the Absolute Other only by way of the interrelationships of human others is Levinas' most original, and daring, and for Jewish and Christian theology, both promising . . . and controversial move."[2] There are some who might question whether Levinas is merely "reducing" religion to ethics. Yet this is a question that probably troubles the "theologically comfortable" more than those who know what is at stake in the world of real historical pain and suffering. The initial reception of liberation theology, for example, was dogged by the accusation that it was a "political reduction of the Gospel."[3] Yet liberation theology has continually insisted that the truth of theology will always be judged by the practice of ethical action and the demands of justice and mercy. "Any attempt to separate the love of God from the love of neighbor," Gustavo Gutiérrez says, "gives rise to attitudes which impoverish the one or the other."[4]

If, for Levinas, "ethics provides the model worthy of transcendence," it is because he is a little nervous about theology providing the "model," particularly when it is a "worn-out theology . . . with its transcendence that can be stepped over like a fence" (*PN*, 92). In other words, if there is any "reduction" to be spoken of, it is theology's complacent reduction of "the Most High God," the God who commands our attention toward "the widow, the orphan, the stranger and the beggar" (*LR*, 251). This is the transcendence of God that can never be scaled, the height of the Other that rises above

2. Tracy, "Response to Adriaan Peperzak on Transcendence," in Peperzak, *Ethics as First Philosophy*, 194.
3. Geffré and Gutiérrez, *Mystical and Political Dimension of the Christian Faith*, 11.
4. Ibid., 63.

us—demanding our attention, commanding our response, requiring our love. As though we could ever finally "jump the fence" and say to ourselves, "no more is required of me," when all the time we are faced with that most demanding of the Gospel sayings: "The poor you will always have with you" (Matt 26:11). The neighbor will always be there. I cannot escape the Other; I will always be hostage to the height of the Other who asks after me. "There will never cease to be poor in the land; I command you, therefore: Always be open-handed with your neighbor, and with anyone in your country who is in need and poor" (Deut 15:11).

Levinas proposes no secular humanism; rather, he protests the domesticating of the divine. The "low fence" of theology is the fence that reduces God to a "theme" for myself, as though God were simply "there" to be grasped and known by us, present to us, when all the time "divinity keeps its distances" (*TI*, 297). As though theology were all about my identification with God, when it is often about God's identification with the other. Like the sensibilities of liberation theology, Levinas wants to keep the human neighbor between me and God, such that we cannot too readily approach the invisible God without first encountering the height of our neighbor. "Is divinity possible without relation to a human Other?" asks Levinas (*LR*, 247). Or as St. John says, how can we say we love God, whom we have not seen, unless we love a brother or a sister whom we have seen? (1 John 4:20–21). Or as Gutiérrez says, "We stand before something which challenges our categories, the mystery of God who will not be *reduced* to our mode of thinking, and who judges us on the basis of our concrete, historical actions toward the poor . . . Now we face a God who blocks the path of a false love which forgets sisters and brothers while claiming to direct itself spiritually toward God, more to domesticate God than to feel itself questioned by God's word."[5]

"Being Faced"

> I tremble at what exceeds my seeing and my knowing . . . although it concerns the inner-most parts of me, right down to my soul, down to the bone, as we say . . . It is the gift of infinite love, the dissymmetry that exists between the divine regard that sees me, and myself, who doesn't see what is looking at me . . .
>
> —Jacques Derrida[6]

---

5. Gutiérrez, *Essential Writings*, 105.
6. Derrida, *Gift of Death*, 54–56.

> An ethical meaning of the relation to the other, answering, in the form of responsibility before the face, to the *invisible that requires me*; answering to a demand that puts me in question and comes to me from *I know not where*, nor when, nor why.
>
> —Emmanuel Levinas (*OS*, 92)

It is difficult to talk about the experience of "being faced." It is more common and familiar to talk about the experience of "facing being." Indeed, many of us resonate with this phrase because we continually find ourselves "facing things." We face life's uncertainty and we wonder about the future. We face life's difficulty and we wonder whether we will ever find a measure of peace. We face life's profound ambiguity and we wonder whether it will ever become clear to us. Facing being primarily means that our own being is a matter of concern for us. "We consider our being, question it, are troubled and afflicted by it, laden with it . . . We do not engender our being; it is given to us, laid upon us; we are burdened with it and have to bear it. We do not exist, simply; we have to be."[7]

We face our lives—and at the same time we face our limitations. We wonder what life is about and what it all means. We find ourselves facing questions that are of concern to us—about the shape of our lives, the shape of the world around us, questions about our future, our hopes for happiness, questions about pain and suffering. Facing being, we face the finitude of our existence and the vastness of our questions, and we feel caught up in life's great mystery or, more darkly, in its stark futility. Either way, we are lost in questions about life—its meaning, its purpose, its reason, its mystery, its elusiveness.

Mostly, we hold this experience and these questions in secret. Who can ever say to another what I feel when I find myself "facing being"? Philosophers, theologians, and other writers are probably the ones who most "break with secrecy" to talk about this experience. They think deeply about this question and give us all a certain vocabulary to talk about the experience of "facing being." They break with secrecy, such that "facing being" is filled with a multitude of responses. It "means" this. It is "about" this. These are the "reasons." This is "why." This is "how it happens" or "fails to happen." The secret need no longer be secretive, and we are overwhelmed with these gallant and noble voices—all "facing being" together.

---

7. Lingis, "The Sensuality and the Sensitvity," in Cohen, *Face to Face with Emmanuel Levinas*, 225.

"Being faced," however, is different. The intuition in this phrase shifts attention from *my gaze*, which tries to bring everything under its surveillance, to *the gaze of the other*, which sees me without my knowing who is looking at me. The question of "facing being" *turns around* to become the question of "being faced"—"with the gaze, look, request, love, command, or call of the other."[8] It is no longer I who face being, but the other who faces me. I am looked upon. I am asked after. Here, I lose a certain hold over myself and find that I am no longer the one who interrogates and questions; rather, I am the one who is faced by the other's interrogation and questioning. This is not unlike the "resolution" to the book of Job, when all those questioners suddenly find themselves placed in question ("Where were you when . . . ?"). God questions more than God answers. The Jewish poet Edmond Jabès, for example, links God intrinsically to *The Book of Questions*.[9] Levinas goes so far as to say that God is an "abusive word" (*OB*, 156). Rather than our facing God, God faces us and we are left feeling "abused" and subjected. In the midst of all our questions and anxiety, God dares yet to face us and hold us in question, as though we were the ones accused, questioned, held responsible—as though we were meant to answer, not God.

Throughout his second major work, *Otherwise Than Being or Beyond Essence*, Levinas uses some very extreme words to describe the exposure we undergo in "being faced." He speaks of our being persecuted and held hostage by the face of the other. Rather than the notion of a free ego that chooses its commitments, Levinas speaks of the prior condition of being hostage to the other, a condition that is not rooted in our freedom or our choice, but in our being chosen or bound or tied to the other. Perhaps this is why Luke's Gospel has Jesus "sweating blood" when it comes to the moment of that most difficult of prayers: "Not my will but yours be done" (22:42).

Prior to any choice or intentionality on our part, we are already exposed to the other. It is almost as if the other holds me against my will, against my ravenous desire to be the center of the universe. Prior to any decision on my part, I am born into a world where the other is always asking after me. I am bound and tied to you—to every you—from my first breath till my last. I am invested with responsibility even when I do not want to be: "The condition of being hostage is not chosen; if there had been a choice, the subject would have kept his as-for-me" (*OB*, 136). I am always

8. Derrida, *Gift of Death*, 68.
9. Jabès, *Book of Questions*.

and already obligated to you—chosen—even before I choose. "The self is a *sub-jectum*; it is under the weight of the universe, responsible for everything" (*OB*, 116).

Levinas cites a well-known passage from the Talmud: "All in Israel are responsible for one another" (*OS*, 35; Tractate *Shevuo*t, 39a). We can read "Israel" as shorthand for "humanity," which means that being-for-the-other is written into the very fabric of life, is the way life is fundamentally structured. Levinas is also fond of quoting a passage from Dostoyevsky's *Brothers Karamazov*: "Each of us is guilty before everyone and for everyone, and I more than the others" (*OB*, 146). To which we could add the following words of Derrida: "This guilt is originary, like original sin. Before any fault is determined, I am guilty inasmuch as I am responsible . . . Guilt is inherent in responsibility because responsibility is always unequal to itself: one is never responsible enough."[10]

"Being faced" means finding ourselves faced by a continual requirement of obligation and responsibility to and for the other. Even a casual reflection on our lives will reveal how bound we are to others, how constantly we are beset by the demands of obligation and the requirements of love—to family and friends, to those we work with, to neighbors and strangers, to those in our society whom we do not know yet whose claim on our lives we feel nevertheless. "Being faced" is another way (maybe the exemplary way) of speaking of transcendence. As John Caputo notes, "We cannot transcend it, because it is transcendence itself. We are the ones transcended, overcome, lifted up or put down, overtaken, thrown. Obligation is the sphere of what I did not constitute . . . Obligations come over us from the other whose transcendence shocks our freedom and autonomy."[11]

While "facing being" turns us inward upon our selves, to our own questioning and anxiety ("where our own being is a matter of concern for us"), "being faced" places us before the other who "opposes" me with the "absolute frankness of his gaze." The other addresses me, speaks to me, asks after me. The face of the other is "the epiphany of what can thus present itself directly, and therefore also exteriorly, to an I" (*PI*, 110). Being faced means I am no longer able to stay within the realms of my own "being"; rather, I am exposed to another who calls out from beyond my existence. "It is as though I were destined to the other before being destined to myself," Levinas says (*GCM*, 165). The presence of "me to myself" is broken, and I

---

10. Derrida, *Gift of Death*, 51.
11. Caputo, *Against Ethics*, 27.

am no longer able to persevere in my being, in the project of myself. "*I am no longer able to have power* . . . true exteriority is in this gaze which forbids me my conquest" (PI, 110). In a crystalline phrase of diamondlike insight, Levinas writes, "The Other must be closer to God than I" (PI, 111).

We may wonder about the excessive rhetoric that Levinas' language forces upon us. To be so bound to the other is indeed to be held hostage. Yet who of us has not known countless times in our lives when, faced with love's requirements, we have taken the very form "of worrying about the other, a spending without counting, a generosity, goodness, love, obligation to others. A generosity without recompense, a love unconcerned with reciprocity, duty performed without the 'salary' of a good-conscience-for-duty-performed . . ." (OS, 87). How else would we describe the condition of responsibility if not in this way? How else would we describe the requirements of love if not in this way? What else could obligation mean if it did not mean this *kenosis*? "Is that not what the self emptying itself of itself would mean?" Levinas asks. "It is being divesting itself, emptying itself of its being, turning itself inside out, and if it can be put this way, the fact of 'otherwise than being' . . . It is through the condition of being hostage that there can be in the world pity, compassion, pardon and proximity—even the little there is, even the simple 'After you' . . ." (OB, 111, 117).

Sometimes, as Franz Kafka once wrote, we need texts that wound us and in the process transform us: "A book must be the axe for the frozen sea inside us."[12] Levinas knows what he is up against in trying to break the hold of our own self-absorption and self-obsession. Unlike the ethical theories of "social contract" or "rational agency" that attempt to *adjudicate* self-interest, Levinas is concerned with delimiting and even *renouncing* self-interest. Indeed, he leaves the reader feeling both inundated by and resistant to the radical otherness he announces. It is quite amazing, really, how much it takes to convince me of the "real presence" of the Other, how much I am always blocking this announcement, resisting this impingement on my life. As Peperzak says, "*The Other* halts the movement through which the I tries to unfold." I do not belong to myself, not because I am a mysterious essence, but because "my essence consists in a being *toward* and *for the Other*." There is quite a real sense in which the Other "makes me

---

12. Kafka, *Letters to Friends*, 16.

suffer by urging me to endlessly detach myself from the desire to return to myself as a ravenous center of the universe."[13]

In her book *Saints and Postmodernism*, Edith Wyschogrod reminds us that this language of extremity and excess (of self-denial and self-giving, self-sacrifice and self-donation) has always been the language of the saints. Saintly life has always been connected to the compassion, mercy, and love of the great religious traditions—for example, "the *kuruna* or compassion of Buddhism, the *rachamim* or mercy of Judaism, or the *agape* of Christianity."[14] Saints are not people of moderation, reasonableness, or nuanced argument. Rather, "the saintly desire for the Other is excessive and wild" (255). According to Wyschogrod, "a saintly life is defined as one in which compassion for the Other, irrespective of cost to the saint, is the primary trait" (xxiii). The world's religious traditions have always "addressed the problems of the wretched of the earth in the person of saints, those who put themselves totally at the disposal of the Other" (xiv). Saints are "fleshly signifiers of compassion, generosity, self-sacrifice" (59). "The vocation of saintliness is recognized by all human beings as a value," Levinas says. This "for-the-other of saintliness defines the human" (*AT*, 171).

And lest we wonder whether the life of the saint is still a real and living presence for us today, lest we too readily dismiss the extremity and excess of Levinas' philosophy, John Caputo remind us that

> From time to time, here and there, it happens that men and women respond, answer a call, spend themselves, using themselves up entirely for the Other. They spend years, maybe a lifetime, serving others, giving themselves up for the good of others . . . Fools spend their lives working to feed and house the poor, or teaching in crime-ridden schools, or protecting defenseless wildlife; they lead a celibate life serving the peasants in Central America, only to be dragged out of bed one night and shot to death by right-wing gangsters; they spend the better part of their adult life in prison, refusing to cut a deal with a racist government, trying to make a point.[15]

Saints are exemplary people whose exemplary stories we tell over and over again because their extraordinary lives are testimonies to the divine.

---

13. Peperzak, *Beyond*, 184–85.

14. Wyschogrod, *Saints and Postmodernism*, 186 (subsequent references provided in parentheses).

15. Caputo, *Against Ethics*, 126–27.

Their lives are full of "insatiable compassion," which is a desire that is also a "diaconate." They place themselves in service, in the "welcome of the absolutely other" (TO, 351, 353). Their lives are testimony to the transcendence of "being faced by the other." As Levinas says, the witness of an answerability that says "Here I am" is the very "glory of the Infinite," because it witnesses to that which is before us, prior to us, that which is first and foremost and facing us because always engendering our response. "The glory of the Infinite is glorified in this responsibility" (OB, 144). It is not to us, but to the Other, to your Name, that glory is given (cf. Ps 115:1). Levinas writes,

> When in the presence of the Other, I say "Here I am!", this "Here I am" is the place through which the Infinite enters into language, but without giving itself to be seen ... The subject who says "Here I am!" *testifies* to the Infinite. It is through this testimony ... that the revelation of the Infinite occurs. It is through this testimony that the very glory of the Infinite glorifies *itself*. (EI, 106–7)

"Here I am" is a "prophetic signification" that recalls the Hebrew phrase of the Scriptures, *hineni*. Abraham says *hineni* when called to offer his son Isaac (Gen 22:1); Moses says *hineni* when standing before the burning bush (Exod 3:4); Isaiah says *hineni* when God asks whom he shall send (Isa 6:8). Hineni—"here I am"—is the very sign of "the-one-for-the-other" (OB, 151). Here I am, for You. This for-the-other is often perceived as "a seed of folly," an obsession, a "sickness" ("I am sick with love," Song 2:5), yet for Levinas, *hineni* is "a marvelous accusative: here I am under your gaze, obliged to you, your servant. In the name of God" (GCM, 75).

"Here I am ... for you ... in the Name of God" expresses the deeply felt religious sensibility that when we clothe the naked or respond to the one in need, when we welcome the stranger or answer for the defenseless, we are "testifying" to God's presence. It is as if we sense that in these gestures of human response and love toward the other, we feel "the *passing itself* of the Infinite" (OB, 150). As though a touch of infinite goodness, a hint of immeasurable love, a trace of divinity *itself* passed this way. Indeed, this very passing of God, which can neither be contained nor caught nor stilled (nor least, "thematized" as a presence belonging to me)—"this is how God comes to mind."

"Here I am under your gaze." Merold Westphal writes that when speaking of the experience we undergo in being faced by the other, "Levinas employs a vocabulary so deeply religious as to awaken even the sleepiest reader that something unusual is going on."[16] Indeed, as Levinas himself says, "one is tempted to call the plot religious" (*OB*, 147). One such "religious plot" can be found in the story of Abraham welcoming the three strangers (Gen 18:1–15). When we read what the rabbis have to say about this story, it is striking how their commentary lingers at some length in the "space" between verse 1 and verse 2.[17] Verse 1 says, "The Lord appeared to him at the Oak of Mamre while he was sitting by the entrance of the tent during the hottest part of the day." Verse 2 says, "He looked up and there he saw three men standing near him. As soon as he saw them he ran from the entrance of the tent to meet them, and bowed to the ground." A large question looms in the "gap" between verse 1 and verse 2 that engages the rabbis' interpretive attention. They offer at least two possible readings, to which I will add Levinas' own voice.

The first reading follows these lines: verse 1 suggests a revelation of God, and verse 2 that this revelation is "interrupted" by the appearance of three wandering strangers. According to this reading, the rabbis say, "The deed of hospitality is greater than the welcoming of the Divine Presence."[18] In other words, Abraham does not linger to enjoy communion between himself and God (v. 1), but runs in haste to attend to the needs of three desert travelers who require food, shelter, and rest (v. 2). Abraham becomes an exemplary model of true service and hospitality toward the stranger, one that has inspired generations of Jewish tradition: "The stranger did not lodge in the street; my doors I opened to the roadside" (Job 31:32). In the space between verse 1 and verse 2, the rabbis suggest that Abraham rightly interrupts his own peace and communion with God to attend to the real, concrete needs of tired and weary strangers. In a similar fashion, Levinas accords some sympathy with this reading when he writes: "To give, to-be-for-another, despite oneself, but in interrupting the for-oneself, is to take the bread out of one's mouth, to nourish the hunger of another with one's own fasting" (*OB*, 56). (When Levinas speaks of taking the bread out of one's own mouth, he may well be alluding to those inmates of the camps who gave their very own meager portion of bread, from their very mouths, to help keep another alive.)

---

16. Westphal, "Levinas' Teleological Suspension of the Religious," in Peperzak, *Ethics as First Philosophy*, 152.

17. I am relying here on Leibowitz, *Studies in Bereshit (Genesis)*, 161ff.

18. Ibid., 161.

The second reading (interpretation) seeks to understand the confusion evident in the opening verses (and much of chapter 18) between the speech of God and the speech of the strangers addressed to Abraham. According to this reading, the rabbis suggest that the strangers *are the way* in which God appears to Abraham. In this sense, the "gap" between verse 1 and verse 2 holds these two verses together, rather than separating and distinguishing them. As Levinas suggests in one of his own Talmudic readings, "The respect for the stranger and the sanctification of the name of the Eternal are strangely equivalent. And all the rest is a dead letter" (*NTR*, 27). According to this reading, there is a certain confluence between the voice of "the Most High" and the arrival of three strangers requiring Abraham's attention. The "gap" between verse 1 and verse 2 suggests the very passing of God, of which Levinas says, "Is not this imposition on me, this devolving-upon-me of the stranger, the way by which there 'arrives on the scene,' or comes to mind, a God who loves the stranger who puts me in question by his demand, and to which my 'here I am' bears witness?" (*GCM*, 167).

These are only two possible readings of the opening verses of Genesis 18. In the story of Abraham and the strangers, the rabbis wonder about the experience we undergo in being faced by the other, standing "under your gaze." Perhaps Levinas captures a sense of both these readings of God's revelation to Abraham when he writes, "The Justice rendered to the Other, to my neighbor, gives me an unsurpassable proximity to God . . . One follows the Most High God, above all by drawing near to one's neighbor, and showing concern for 'the widow, the orphan, the stranger and the beggar,' an approach that must not be made 'with empty hands'" (*DF*, 18, 26).

Let me conclude with a story. One afternoon I walked along the streets of Jerusalem. Like other major cities, Jerusalem has many beggars on its streets. It was easy to pass them by, just as I passed by so many other strangers. However, on this particular afternoon, I was suddenly gripped by the face of a woman who was begging—or rather, I felt her gaze. Her face pressed up against me, and against the myriad other faces in a bustling street. She stood out, singularly, and I felt the "absolute frankness" of her gaze. Though she sat on a cobble-paved street in a pool of squalor—ragged, dirty, nursing an infant, her hand outstretched, pleading, with completely "defenseless eyes"—she nevertheless looked at me with such commanding authority, such "height," such strength of appeal. She was the destitute one who nevertheless rises above me as the one "for whom I can do all and to whom I owe all" (*EI*, 89).

Under Your Gaze

    Though I knew that a handout to an outstretched hand was but a small charity, I nevertheless could not pass her by. I made my way through the crowded street and gave her some money, placing it in her empty hand—and she smiled and said, in a language I did not understand, "Thank you." This incident is undoubtedly minor, less than a mite, yet I felt as though in that place, on the streets of Jerusalem, "the Most High" was facing me.

4

For You Alone

The Miracle of Exteriority

> I am you, when
> I am I.
>
> To stand-for-no-one-and-nothing.
> Unrecognized,
> for you
> alone.
>
> —Paul Celan[1]

Who?

Who? is an unusual question. It is not a question that typically springs to mind. Rather, questions like "what?" or "why?" or "how?" claim much of our attention. These questions tend toward things and concepts, whereas *who?* is a question that draws us toward the personal and the relational. *Who?* is a thoughtful and thought-provoking question that calls upon the intersubjective or dialogical contours of life. *Who?* reminds me of *You*.

Questions are persistent in their hold on us. Questions of any significance are such that we are never finally finished with them, nor they with us. As Hans-Georg Gadamer suggests, it is not we who raise questions;

---

1. *Ich bin du, wenn / ich ich bin.* ("I am you, when I am I"). It is with these lines from Celan that Levinas introduces his key chapter, "Substitution" (*OB*, 99). The verse is from Celan's poem "Praise of Distance" (*Selected Poems and Prose of Paul Celan*, 25). The second verse is from *"To Stand"* (*Selected Poems*, 233).

rather, questions arise or present themselves to us: "A question presses itself on us; we can no longer avoid it and persist in our accustomed opinion."[2] Questions are often unsettling; they rarely let us settle down. *Who?* is particularly unique in this regard because it is a question that never leaves me alone. It never leaves me just to myself, never lets me be *just me*. Rather, *who?* is a question that always places the other before me. "Here above all," Levinas says, "is the situation in which one is not alone" (PI, 118). There is always someone else, someone other than me. This is a deep intuition of *who?*—that I am never left alone, never just myself, that my existence is always implicated, always tied to an other, always in relation.

Who? is a question that is central to Martin Buber's work. Rather than "what?" or "why?" Buber brought this question back to life. He took our gaze off ourselves and turned it toward the face of the other. Indeed, Buber saw this as the primary task of the question *who?*—to turn our gaze from ourselves to *You*—because he knew that *who?* and *You* are inseparable. He joined them this way: I-Thou, I-You.[3]

Who? always places me in relationship with "thou," with *You*. It is a question that is impossible to ask in a vacuum or a void; rather, *who?* always ties me to the presence of the other. *Who?* persists because of *You*. In other words, whenever I ask the question *who?*, I know that you are there facing me, before me.

In ways similar to Buber, Levinas kept hearing and asking *who?* against the murmuring indifference of "there is." Life is more than the brute reality of raw existence—not just "there is," but *who?* is there. And if *who?* is there, then I am called to respond. My existence is heavy with necessity in the face of this question. *Who?* always unsettles indifference. *Who?* is the question of my responsibility, my answerability. *Who?* takes me from a world of impersonal indifference to a world charged with non-indifference. I feel compelled to respond, to answer, to open, to turn around, to say, "Here I am."

Who? is not a question that can be satisfied within the realms of my own being. Rather, it is a question that opens out to the "miracle of exteriority . . . to have an outside, to listen to what comes from outside" (DF, 29). *Who?* always leads *toward You*. *Who?* introduces the face of the other that calls into question every attempt at self-possession. Rather than appropriation or possession, *Who?* attracts desire and passion. It fills me with desire for relationship, yet guards this relationship against

---

2. Gadamer, *Truth and Method*, 366.
3. As Buber says, the "primary word is *I-Thou*," *I and Thou*, 3.

the contrivance of too close an identification. Thus it is both distance and proximity: taking me outside of my world and away from myself, yet moving toward *You* who are always there before me. Another way of saying this is that *who?* is the question of transcendence that is always close to me, or as Levinas says, "transcendence has no meaning except by way of an I saying You" (*GCM*, 147).

The openness of *who?* welcomes the other's transcendent exteriority. Against the tranquilized world of immanence (where everything plays out "within the same"), I find myself awakened to the voice of the other who calls from beyond. "I tremble," writes Jacques Derrida, "at what exceeds my seeing and my knowing although it concerns the inner-most parts of me, right down to my soul, down to the bone, as we say."[4] Even with the one closest to me, I find myself saying, "I will never fully understand my relationship with you. It forever eludes me. In this sense, you are a stranger and you are infinite. Yet, even though I do not fully understand, I know that *you matter*."

It is not meaning alone that makes things matter, but *You*—the other. You make it matter. Not "why?"—a question tied to reasoning and grand meaning—but "*who?*"—a question tied to me-in-relation-to-the-other. This is what matters. Again and again I have encountered this in various thinkers of our times:

"You who will never be me or mine"

No manner of speaking about desire is valid without this muted question: "Who are you who will never be me or mine, you who will always remain transcendent to me, even if I touch you, since the word is made flesh in you in one way, and in me in another?"

—Luce Irigaray[5]

The question "Who?" is the question of transcendence ... The question "Who?" is *the* religious question. It is the question about the other man or woman and the claim the other makes, about the other being, the other authority. It is the question about love for one's neighbor.

—Dietrich Bonhoeffer[6]

---

4. Derrida, *Gift of Death*, 54.
5. Irigaray, *To Be Two*, 19.
6. Bonhoeffer, *Christology*, 30–31.

There is always someone else, you know... Even if the name of the other does not appear, even if it remains secret, it is there, it teems and maneuvers, it screams sometimes, it makes itself all the more authoritarian.

—Jacques Derrida[7]

Something of this call of the other must remain nonreappropriable, nonsubjectivable, and in a certain way nonidentifiable, so as to remain *other*, a *singular* call to response or to responsibility. This is why the question "Who?" remains forever problematic. And it *should* remain so. This obligation to protect the other's otherness is not merely a theoretical imperative... This question of the subject and the living "who" is at the heart of the most pressing concerns of modern societies.

—Jacques Derrida[8]

In relation to whom, to what other, is the subject exposed? Who is the "neighbor" dwelling in the very proximity of transcendence?

—Jacques Derrida[9]

I will never be you, you will never be mine. A gap remains between me and you, between you and me. I will never be capable of perceiving you completely, and not even of loving you, or of speaking to you completely... My perception must remain a path towards you, towards us, an us which is always disunited, distanced, always a "two" irreducible to one.

—Luce Irigaray[10]

Another? The other! Ah, the other, here is the name of the mystery, the name of You, the desired one... The other to love. The other who puts love to the test: How to love the other, the strange, the unknown, the not-me-at-all?

—Hélène Cixous[11]

"Thou art" precedes "I am." I am because I am called upon to be.

—Abraham Heschel[12]

---

7. Derrida, *Points,* 353–54
8. Ibid., 276, 283 (adapted).
9. Ibid., 283 (adapted).
10. Irigaray, *To Be Two,* 42–43.
11. Cixous, *"Coming to Writing",* 140.
12. Heschel, *Who Is Man?,* 98

Part One—For You Alone

This is the most important experience in the life of every human being: something is asked of me... there is a calling, a demanding, a waiting, an expectation. There is a question that follows me wherever I turn: What is expected of me? What is demanded of me?... I am because I am called upon to answer. We are not left alone... We know ourselves as exposed, challenged, judged, encountered.

—Abraham Heschel[13]

"You who are not and will never be me or mine" are transcendent to me in body and in words, in so far as you are an incarnation that cannot be appropriated by me... Rather than grasping you—with my hand, with my gaze, with my intellect—I must stop before the inappropriable, leaving the transcendence between us to be... I respect you because you are transcendent to me... But this not being *I*, not being *me*, or *mine*, makes speech possible and necessary between us.

—Luce Irigaray[14]

And who shall I say is calling?

—Leonard Cohen[15]

The Miracle of Exteriority

Levinas was suspicious of mysticism, as though a "mystic" were some sort of "inner person." It is a misnomer to think that artists and poets and philosophers are only concerned with the interior world. Rather, they are often captivated and taken by the exterior world—so much so that they realize their own interiority is no match.

"Transcendence is what turns its face toward us" (*EN*, 34). Levinas refers to "exteriority" (the one who faces me) as a "miracle" or a "marvel"— "a relationship with an unassumed exteriority... man is the one for whom the exterior world exists" (*EN*, 15). "Such a situation is the gleam of exteriority or of transcendence in the face of the other" (*TI*, 24).

It is as if transcendence magnetizes relation, always attracting and drawing me toward you, yet also resisting and refusing my assimilation of you. "Oh, the miracle of exteriority!" Levinas exclaims (*DF*, 29).

Reflecting on his work during a conversation, Levinas says the following: "The principal task behind all these efforts consists in thinking

---

13. Ibid., 108, 104–5 (adapted).
14. Irigaray, *To Be Two*, 18–19.
15. Cohen, "Who By Fire?", in *Stranger Music*, 207.

the Other-in-the-Same . . . without thinking the Other as an other Same . . . The *in* does not signify an assimilation: the Other disturbs or awakens the Same; the Other troubles the Same, or inspires the Same, or the Same desires the Other, or awaits him" (*GCM*, 80).

In other words, the principal task consists in thinking of You-who-are-in-my-world—without thinking of You as simply another Me, as though You were the same . . . The *in* does not mean assimilation. Rather, You disturb or awaken Me; You trouble Me, or You inspire Me, or I desire You, or I await You.

When I drift into myself, you come to disturb me, and I am awakened by your call to respond, to be-for-you. When I think all is well, you come to trouble me, and I find myself worrying and concerned for you. When I am caught in despair or indifference, you come to inspire me and I am opened to a world of non-indifference. When I find myself coiled in anxiety, you come to arouse my desire, and I find myself yearning and waiting for you to come.

I am drawn by an inseparability that keeps me and you forever in relationship, what Levinas calls an "unrelenting relation" (*TI*, 295). I am "connected" by this inseparability that binds me to you, but this connection is never one of fusion, identification, or assimilation. Rather, it is marked by a separation, or a difference, or an asymmetry between you and me. This asymmetrical character of the relational encounter is a key concern in Levinas' writings. "If there is not this dissymmetry," he says, "then no line of what I have written can hold" (*GCM*, 91). Levinas wants to preserve the other as unique and singular, while at the same time maintaining a relation between the other and myself. And so we are led to wonder: what could it mean to speak of a relation that is marked at one and the same time by a separation and an inseparability? Or, what could it mean to speak of a relation between you and me that is also a nonrelation? In *Totality and Infinity* (which is "an essay on exteriority"), Levinas says, "the description of this relation is the central issue of the present research" (*TI*, 42).

Even though I know the experience of nonrelation, I have tended to view it as a negative, that is, relation is good, nonrelation is bad. However, Levinas has helped me understand that nonrelation is not necessarily negative, that it can hold a surprising positivity—especially when relation and nonrelation are not pitted against each other in opposition, as though one term were good and the other bad. The problem, I suspect, is that relation gets all the kudos and nonrelation never gets a chance to voice its insight.

In conversations with a measure of depth and intimacy, I often become aware of how distinct and separate the other is from me. I don't mean this in a negative sense, because this separateness is the very thing that provokes or lies at the foundation of our relation. After all, if we were all "one" and "the same" we would know nothing of the other who is unique and distinct. However, we are not all one and the same—which means that, even in our most intimate relationships, there is still this undeniable and fundamental separateness that lies at the heart of our relational life. Without separation there would be no truth, no truth of you or me; there would be only the neutrality of an all-absorbing "oneness."

"Truth," Levinas says, "does not undo 'distance,' does not result in the union of the knower and the known, does not issue in totality" (*TI*, 60). Separation is important in the encounter with the other because it preserves the other from assimilation or fusion. Instead of the idea of totality, "there must be substituted the idea of separation resistant to synthesis" (*TI*, 293).

And yet, we often crave "oneness," harmony, peace. We crave an existence in which there is no separation, no unsettlement, no rupture. All is well, we think, when all is One. All is well when all is at peace, at rest, at-one-ment. All is well when all is together, when there is no rupture or dissatisfaction between me and you—when we can say, in effect, that "I am" and "You are" such that there is no distinction or separation between us, such that we are, finally—totally—One and the Same.

We hold in great esteem words such as *mutuality, reciprocity, equality, inclusivity, one-ness*. Maybe we need to also pay attention to words such as *separateness, asymmetry, difference, otherness*. Not as words of negativity (that is, contrary to all those "positives" previously named), but as words of excess and beyond, of "excedence" and "transcendence," of *more than* and *other than*—words that transcend the selfsame quest for unity and sameness, that open a gap or space between us, that signal the other's refusal to be tamed by all-encompassing concepts such as oneness, identity, sameness, totality. Rather, to be always left uncertain about ourselves, always implicated by what is other-than-me, always entangled by you and (in this sense) unfree and without autonomy, always marked and defined by the singular, the separate, the other one.

According to Levinas, the ontology of Western thought has typically deadened the voice of the Other in preference for schemas of participation and totality:

> Greek ontology . . . expressed the strong sentiment that the last word is unity, the many becoming one, the truth as synthesis. Hence Plato defined love—*eros*—as only *half*-divine, insofar as it lacks the full coincidence or unification of differences that he defined as divinity. [According to] this platonic ontology . . . love is perfect when two people become *one*. I am trying to work against this identification of the divine with unification or totality. Man's relationship with the other is *better* as difference than as unity: sociality is better than fusion. The very value of love is the impossibility of reducing the other to myself, of coinciding in sameness. (DwEL, 22)

Levinas is not interested in abstract thought that generalizes, envelops, and assimilates. This type of thinking only serves to diminish or reduce *relation* by dissolving the singularity of the other, and yet it is this singularity that lies at the heart of the relational encounter. Only the singular, the separate, the unique, "the other" can defy the all-absorbing grasp of totalities. For Levinas, every totalizing move is a move against relation and toward assimilation.

The words that are most familiar to us in describing healthy relational encounters—*mutuality, reciprocity, participation, identification with*—these words are held in suspicion by Levinas because he fears they are not striking enough to describe the relational encounter. They do not let us hear the singular word spoken to me from a "separateness" that I am not a part of. Levinas inserts into our relational vocabulary words we least expect—*separation, otherness, difference, singularity, alterity*—words that do not fit comfortably within our relational repertoire.

Suppose we take for granted that mutuality and reciprocity are important in every relationship. We know in our bones they are important. We know how difficult it is to work toward healthy relationships that are mutual and reciprocal. Even though we can't (and shouldn't) take these words for granted, let's suppose we could. I am suggesting this because I doubt we will hear Levinas' word, *separation* (or *asymmetry*), if we are all the time asking in the back of our minds, "What about mutuality, reciprocity?" I want to give Levinas' thought its best chance to influence our relational vocabulary, and if our relational vocabulary is linked in a fundamental way to our spiritual vocabulary, then this makes our listening to Levinas doubly important.

We can begin with one of Levinas' typically dense and evocative sentences: "The same and the other maintain themselves in relationship and absolve themselves from this relation, remain absolutely separated" (*TI*, 102). Or again: "A relation in which the terms absolve themselves from the relation, yet remain absolute within the relation" (*TI*, 64). The key words here (aside from relation) are *absolve* and *absolute*. If I were to translate these sentences, I would say something like, "I am in relation with you. I am in relation with you because of you. If you were not there, if you were not you, there would be no relation. Absolutely. You count, pre-eminently." As Levinas says, "The face is meaning all by itself. You are you" (*EI*, 86).

If I am in relation with you only for my sake, then we have no relation—there is only the selfsame. However, because I desire so much to be in relation to you, it is important that you are you. Therefore, I *absolve* you from myself, from having to fulfill the conditions of *my* relationship with you. I *absolve* you from having to be reciprocal. I *absolve* you from having to make this relationship turn back on me, because I want it to turn on you—absolutely.

It has taken me numerous lines to say what Levinas says in one line. If I were to attempt a one-liner, I would say something like, "Every true relationship is structured by love." Of course, we all know this, so it doesn't really say much, just as we all know that relationships are structured by mutuality and reciprocity. Yet it seems to me that Levinas is holding the word *love* to its own flame—stretching love to see how far it will go, testing love to see if it really is love, holding love close to the flame of its own word to see if it really ignites. In other words, is my relationship to you so absolutely gratuitous that I absolve you from the relation, from the circle of exchange, from compensation or mutuality, from reciprocity toward me? This question sounds to me like it is hovering around a "definition" of the theological word *grace*—absolutely amazing grace. It evokes the language of gift and self-donation, a self-giving that gives absolutely and absolves or *for-gives* the other's indebtedness.

Levinas draws appreciatively on Martin Buber's philosophy of dialogue and relation. However, he was also critical of Buber's account of the "I-Thou" relation that is mutual, symmetrical, and reciprocal.[16] While there are differences between these two great Jewish thinkers, I tend to see these as differences of emphasis rather than differences of focus or intent. Buber, for example, writes, "This person is other, essentially other than myself, and

---

16. Levinas' reflections on Buber can be found in *OS*, 4–48; *TI*, 68–69; *PN*, 17–39; *GCM*, 137–51. See also Atterton, Calarco, and Friedman, *Levinas and Buber*.

this otherness of his is what I mean, because I mean him; I confirm it; I wish his otherness to exist, because I wish his particular being to exist."[17]

Buber respects otherness, and Levinas is not totally against mutuality in relationship. He speaks of our need to confirm one another, of the fundamental respect that characterizes every real and honest relation. "How does the face of the other affect me?" Levinas asks. His answer: "I recognize him, that is, I believe in him." Similarly, "the face that looks at me affirms me." This is a condition of *respect* in which we "reciprocally affirm one another" (*EN*, 34–35).

The miracle of exteriority is the miracle of having another to love; it is the miracle of relation, the miracle of living in each other's presence. "In ethical and religious terms: you will have someone to love, you will have someone for whom to exist, you cannot be just for yourself" (*EN*, 113).

"The Most High"

> I question myself only in You.
> I measure myself only against You.
> I am only a word at the heart of Your words.
> I am only vocabulary where You are written.
>
> —EDMOND JABÈS[18]

Levinas suffers little embarrassment linking the word *God* to the relational encounter. Indeed, this is where the word *God* counts most, rather than in the realms of belief or nonbelief, theology or speculation, grand schemas or totalities. He writes, "We propose to call 'religion' the bond that is established between the same and the other without constituting a totality" (*TI*, 40). Or again: "For the relation between the being here below and the transcendent being that results in no community or concept or totality—a relation without relation—we reserve the term religion" (*TI*, 80).

According to Levinas, we have become so accustomed to living in an experiential and contextualized world that we no longer know how to hear a transcendent word. Secular disciplines such as psychology and sociology are relativizing disciplines in which any truth or "exteriority" is reduced to one's own context such that "what I take as true is defined by what I am."

17. Buber, *Between Man and Man*, 61.
18. Jabès, *Book of Resemblances*, 1:90–91.

When truth is reduced to conditions or context, then "a living man would not differ from a dead one. Generalization is death" (*EN*, 26–27). The contextual world is bound to the world of experience, "in which a subject always thematizes what he equals," whereas the exterior world opens to the world of transcendence, "in which the subject answers for that which his intentions have not encompassed" (*DF*, 295). According to Levinas, sociology and psychology are "deaf to exteriority. Man as Other comes to us from outside, a separated—or holy—face. His exteriority, that is, his appeal to me, is his truth" (*TI*, 291).

Levinas links transcendence with infinity or exteriority. These terms find their *apex* in the word *God* (*OB*, 156). Transcendence, however, should not be read as the "more than" of the numinous or otherworldly (out-there or behind-there somewhere) but as the "more than" of relation. Relation is driven by what exceeds relation—what Levinas calls "desire"—"the more within the less" (*LR*, 208). "The relation to the Infinite is not a knowledge, but a Desire" (*EI*, 92).

Transcendence evokes in an exemplary way the experience of relation/nonrelation or inseparability/separability. Levinas is seeking a "nonallergic relation with alterity" (*TI*, 47). He says that all his efforts to speak in the name of God are efforts to speak in the name of "uncontaminated" transcendence—"transcendence that does not close over into a totality" or "transcendence that refuses totality" (*TI*, 293).

Perhaps it is not surprising that "the Most High" is a significant metaphor for Levinas, one that is linked to desire, separateness, and holiness. He writes, "Desire is desire for the absolutely other . . . A desire without satisfaction which, precisely, understands the remoteness, the alterity, and the exteriority of the other . . . the very dimension of Height: the Most High" (*TI*, 34).

"Height" is linked to desire and holiness, that is, as "separation" that is not absorbed into the world of immanence or the selfsame. Indeed, as Susan Handelman notes, "*separation* is the root meaning of the Hebrew word for holiness—*kedusha*." The rabbis refer to God as *Ha-Shem*, or "the Name," or "The Holy One Blessed be He" (*ha-kadosh baruch-hu*).[19] The invocation of God's name expresses the holiness of God as the one who maintains relation and yet resists union or identification.

---

19. Handelman, *Fragments of Redemption*, 294, 282. See also Levinas, "The Name of God According to a Few Talmudic Texts," in *BV*, 116–28.

"Exteriority," Levinas says, "is not a negation, but a marvel" (*TI*, 292). "The emphasis of exteriority is excellency. Height is heaven. The kingdom of heaven is ethical" (*OB*, 183). *Exteriority, separation, height*—Levinas places these words in service of the ethical relation. While they come to him from a religious sensibility steeped in the Jewish people's relation to God, they nevertheless always refer to the relational and ethical encounter between human beings. "The privilege of the Other in relation to the I—or moral consciousness—is the very opening to exteriority, which is also an opening to Highness" (*DF*, 294). The other comes to me from "on high" and calls out to me, breaks into my world, as the singular one to whom I can respond and offer myself. Whereas "possession is preeminently the form whereby the other becomes the same by becoming mine" (*TI*, 46), transcendence suggests an inability to possess, to own, or to dominate.

The other is "higher" than I, where height means this separation that resists reciprocity or symmetry between us. "To recognize the Other is to give. But it is to give to the master . . . to him whom one approaches as 'You' in a dimension of height" (*TI*, 75). Yet height is not power, as in "the high and mighty." Rather, height is encountered in the other person's lowliness and destitution that nevertheless rises above me with an ethical demand.

Philippe Nemo asks Levinas, "In the face of the Other you say there is an 'elevation,' a 'height.' The Other is higher than I am. What do you mean by that?" Levinas replies, "The first word of the face is the 'Thou shalt not kill.' It is an order. There is a commandment in the appearance of the face, as if a master spoke to me. However, at the same time, the face of the Other is destitute; it is the poor for whom I can do all and to whom I owe all. And me, whoever I may be, but as 'first person,' I am he who finds the resources to respond to the call" (*EI*, 88–89).

Levinas links transcendence and height with the vulnerable or poor one who stands outside my closely hugged truths, "who disturbs the being at home with oneself" (*TI*, 39). While I can ignore this disturbance, the other nevertheless remains higher than I as the one who places me in the position of the "accused" or the "questioned." "True exteriority is in this gaze which forbids me my conquest" (PI, 110). I lose the power of my own proud subjectivity and become instead the one who is called to respond, placed in the role of the servant, rather than the master. I lose the power to say "I am" and am placed instead in the more receptive and responsive position of "Here I am"—"for you."

Levinas' religious metaphors gain all their power and vividness as ethical urgings. All his efforts to sing God's praises are efforts to remind me of the presence of the other, to remind me of You. He speaks of God only because he knows that this word is inextricably inscribed in ancient stirrings that have to do with our salvation, with healing and redemption in the world, with relations of love and justice between us, with *shalom*. Without enlisting religious metaphors that serve to agitate our lives toward the other (such as "holiness," "transcendence," the "Most High"), Levinas' ethical urgings would be but thin veneers lacking any sense of veracity or visitation upon us. As Levinas' friend Maurice Blanchot notes, "The greatest transcendence, the transcendence of transcendence, is ultimately the immanence, or the perpetual referral, of the one to the other. Transcendence within immanence: Levinas is the first to devote himself to this strange structure . . . and not to let himself be satisfied by the shock value of such contrarieties."[20] Not to be satisfied, particularly in an age that is "drugged by immanence," an age in which self-awareness, self-sufficiency, self-autonomy, and self-fulfillment have become the new opium of the people. We have sufficiently inoculated ourselves against the allergy of transcendence. Levinas writes,

> The crisis inscribed in Ecclesiastes is not found in sin but in boredom. Everything is absorbed, sucked down and walled up in the Same . . . Vanity of vanities: the echo of our own voices, taken for a response to the few prayers that still remain to us; everywhere we have fallen back upon our own feet, as after the ecstasies of a drug. Except the other whom, in all this boredom, we cannot let go . . . It is because responsibility for the Other is transcendence that there can be something new under the sun. (*GCM*, 12–13)

Contrary to the opiates of immanence, Levinas wants to speak of the prescription of the divine: "The overflowing exteriority . . . precisely constitutes the dimension of height or the divinity of exteriority. Divinity keeps its distances. Discourse is discourse with God and not with equals" (*TI*, 296–97). Levinas continues: "The absolutely foreign alone can instruct us. And it is only man who could be absolutely foreign to me" (*TI*, 73). In what sense? Because "the relationship between men is certainly the non-synthesizable par excellence" (*EI*, 77). The other is separate and holy, unique and singular, a command and an appeal. The other is what I cannot possess or dominate, assimilate or absorb, domesticate or colonize. The other is what

---

20. Blanchot, "Our Clandestine Companion," 48.

I cannot synthesize with myself, what I cannot know or appropriate, what I cannot blend or fuse with myself. "*Correlation does not suffice as a category of transcendence*" (*TI*, 53). The other is the holy one—a "nonrelation"—and yet, a nonrelation that maintains a relation, "precisely the *idea of the Infinite* . . . as though the *in* of the Infinite signified at once the *non-* and the *within*" (*GCM*, 63).

"All that Matters Is My Relationship to You"

> Even in your arms I know
> I'll never get it right;
> even when you bend
> to give me comfort in the night.
> I've got to have your word on this
> or none of it is true,
> and all I've said was just instead of
> *coming back to you.*
>
> —Leonard Cohen[21]

We are not entirely sure who Cohen is referring to when he speaks of *you*, or rather, *to you*. There are many modes of speaking to you. Is he speaking intimately to his lover? Or is this religious expression? Or both? Or the inner conversation of the soul? Whom is he writing to? Whom is he addressing? It is difficult to clarify who the other is. We are not entirely sure because it is dialogical rather than logical. With a poem like Cohen's, we intuitively "fill in" the meaning, because we all fundamentally know what it is to be in relationship with an other—with *you*.

When it comes to poets and songwriters, or artists and writers, or prophets and saints, we find multifarious expressions of relationships bound to an "other," tied to *you*. "There is language, there is art," George Steiner writes, "because there is 'the other.'"[22] We can think, for example, of St. Augustine's *Confessions*, perhaps one of our finest testimonies of an "I saying you." The word *you* occurs in 381 of the 453 paragraphs of Augustine's

---

21. Cohen, "Coming Back to You," in *Stranger Music*, 340.
22. Steiner, *Real Presences*, 137.

Part One—For You Alone

Confessions.[23] All his meditations, his questions, and his searching come down to this mysterious *you,* this presence of another-than-myself.

There are many things in life that vie for our attention and absorb our energies, yet all that ultimately matters, as Van Morrison suggests, "is my relationship to you."[24]

The experience of *you* is the experience of encounter. Our lives are made up of millions of moments of encounter—with the natural world, with people and events, with art and music, with texts and traditions, with silence and prayer. Sometimes these encounters offer us a deep sense of communion; at other times they expose us to life's suffering and fragility. Life is full of joyous, sorrowful, and glorious mysteries. We can never fully define these moments, yet we know they are real—really real.

There is speech and thought, listening and response, conversation and relationship, because there is an other—because there is you—written in the signs of life, reminding us that we are living, personal, relational beings.

There is no limit to the innumerable ways that *you* can address our lives. Our hearts are always restless, St. Augustine said, until we realize that they do not rest inside us; rather, "they rest in you."[25]

There is no rest within myself alone, because my life is all the time called into existence by you. You do not leave me to simply be myself—an "I" without you. Rather, you speak to me and require me. You address me and implicate me. My life carries meaning because it is meant; it has purpose because it is required; it bears significance because it is implicated. We do not find this meaning or this purpose or this significance solely within our own selves or from our own resources. We find it in relationship with you—with "you and you-again."[26]

All of life, each and every life, is tied to another life. We do not exist—can not exist—on our own. We are bundled together in life—with all that is living and shares time with us. We are bundled together with every living creature, with all the natural world. We are bundled together with friends and family, with neighbors and strangers, with the rich and the poor, with the just and the unjust. We are bundled together with writers and artists, texts and traditions, saints and prophets. We are bundled together on this beautiful blue earth, under a night sky—the wheat and the chaff together.

23. Caputo, *Prayers and Tears of Jacques Derrida,* 295.
24. Morrison, "Town Called Paradise."
25. Augustine, *Confessions,* 21.
26. Celan, "Zurich: The Stork Inn," in *Selected Poems,* 161.

And in the midst of all this life, there is an abiding mystery, there is "my relationship to you."

You is a very large word, a sizeable word. It is a sizeable word because without the presence of you, life would be fatally reduced to solitary egos, disconnected monads, enclosed identities, and mystery-less existence. Without you, there would be no poetry or art, no religious expression, no prayer, no desire, no reaching out to one another. There would not even be the simple bonds of human love.

What could be more natural, or more human, or more divine, than to speak of the relational quality of life? It is in my nature to seek you. It is in my nature to want to know you. It is in my nature to desire you. Perhaps it is in my nature because I am not made solely for myself, simply to be me; rather, I am made for you. It is in my nature *because of you*.

Whether I strike you down or lift you up, whether I shut myself off or open myself up, whether I love or hate—all this takes its course in the presence of you. This is why *you* is a very large word, because everything that happens—for good or for ill—happens between us, between you and me.

Martin Buber reminded us that our world would grow dark and "eclipsed" if we could no longer recognize and respond to the presence of you.[27] He spent most of his life trying to prompt us to become more aware—more sensitive, more responsive, more attentive—to the "other" in our lives, although he preferred to speak of the personal you (*Du* in German) rather than an impersonal "other."[28] Buber kept pressing questions like this: what would life mean if we were all the time simply saying "I"—"I think, I will, I want, I can, I am"—without ever noticing you or responding to you? Where would we be, and in what way would life matter, if it wasn't for you? And why does it take such continual effort and constant reminder to convince me of your real presence?

According to Levinas, much of the religious soul in the West has been captured by a type of "immanentism," whereby any talk of God's otherness or revelation or transcendence seems offensive to our intelligence. We are allergic to transcendence. "But the paradox of faith," writes Jacques Derrida, "is that interiority remains 'incommensurable with exteriority.'"[29] The inner world is no match for the transcendence of exteriority. If the event of religious faith is not to be dissolved into psychology, withdrawn

---

27. Buber, *Eclipse of God*.
28. Kaufmann, "I and You: A Prologue," 14.
29. Derrida, *Gift of Death*, 63.

into inwardness, deadened by sameness, reduced to the innate processes of socialization, or lost in an all-absorbing immanence, then it must be aligned with an elsewhere and an otherwise, with "revelation." Rather than relinquish mystery and revelation to the world of being or the swirl of the cosmos, the religious event "fractures the immanence of that world by positing something that it could not accommodate."[30] Revelation punctures the circle of immanence and arrives instead as a magnificent message. Especially for the prophetic traditions of Judaism and Christianity, attention to the voice of the other is always a pivotal moment in the announcement and advent of God. "Theology should guard the radical transcendence of God," writes Hans Jonas, "whose voice comes not out of being but breaks into the kingdom of being from without."[31]

Much attention in spiritual life is given to the "interior life." No doubt this is important. Yet Levinas also brings a deep appreciation for the "exterior life." He writes, "The exteriority of discourse cannot be converted into interiority. The interlocutor can have no place in an inwardness; he is forever outside. The relationship between separated beings does not totalize them; it is an 'unrelenting relation,' which no one can encompass or thematize... For no concept lays hold of exteriority" (*TI*, 295).

Revelation establishes a relation with exteriority. "This exteriority—unlike the exteriority which surrounds man whenever he seeks knowledge—cannot be transformed into a content with interiority; it remains 'uncontainable,' infinite, and yet the relation is maintained" (*LR*, 207).

Levinas privileges you before me, you above me, you in front of me. Paul Ricoeur evokes similar associations: *anteriority*—"before me"; *superiority*—"above me"; *exteriority*—"in front of me." According to Ricoeur, these three references delineate the religious. It is interesting that he does not speak of *interiority* or "within me."[32]

"Being is exteriority," Levinas says (*TI*, 290). Our interior worlds will never be the full measure of all that lies outside ourselves, "in front of us" and "beyond us."

Monotheism is not afraid or embarrassed to speak in the name of "thou," "you," the "Most High," "the orphan, widow, stranger." Monotheism is a vigorous and infinite exposure to what is other in our life—God,

---

30. Moyn, "Judaism against Paganism," 49. See also Levinas' essays in *GCM*, Part 1, "A Rupture of Immanence."

31. Moyn, "Judaism against Paganism," 49 (citing Hans Jonas).

32. Ricoeur, *Critique and Conviction*, 170.

neighbor, creation—none of which originates in me or is purely internal to me. Exteriority is necessary if we are ever to experience what is required of us or what we are called to serve and dedicate our lives to. Exteriority is necessary even to know that we are loved, that *another* loves me. Our twofold lives (call and response, commandment and obedience, being chosen and choosing) are directly attributable to the monotheistic insight that "the Lord our God, the Lord, is one"—unique, irreplaceable, original, existing—the "singular one" who binds us in relation rather than the "all-absorbing one" who assimilates us in sameness. Levinas writes, "Forty centuries of monotheism have had no other goal than to liberate humanity from their own obsessive grip" (*EN*, 31). "*Shema Yisraël!*"

In rabbinic thought, God is commonly referred to as "Master of the World," "Our Father in Heaven," "the Merciful and Gracious," "the Long Suffering," "the One Abounding in Kindness." As Levinas notes, all these names express *relations*, not essence (*BV*, 118–19). He goes on to say that "the God revealed in his Names is given a meaning from out of the human situations, of misery or happiness, in which he is invoked" (*BV*, 123).

In the Christian tradition, the prayer that Jesus taught begins with this same recognition and dedication—"Hallowed be your Name." This hallowing takes place on earth, here among us, as the only way to honor the appeal of heaven. The name of *you* is a sizeable word because it is the only word that can be hallowed—held holy—or disparaged. It is the only word that can enlist relations of love and forgiveness, or hatred and abuse. The way we live together—what we create or destroy, what we respect or disregard—has everything to do with how we respond, or fail to respond, to the presence of each other, to the presence of you. This is why we should pay attention to those thinkers among us who place *you* at the center of their thought, who hallow God's Name, and who seek the holiness of life in the relations between us.

"God cannot be spoken of, but God can be spoken to. God cannot be seen, but God can be listened to. The only possible relation with God is to address him and to be addressed by him, here and now."[33] For most people of faith, God is not a theory or a problem, a treatise or a dogma, a speculation or a doctrine, a *this* or a *that*. God is the one who hears our prayers, more than the one we talk about. It is more important to speak to God rather than about God. "Go into your room and shut the door and pray to your Father who is in secret" (Matt 6:26). For many people, God is their

---

33. Kaufmann, "I and You: A Prologue," 26.

deepest and most secret hope, the one they talk to, the one they pray to, the one who listens and understands. In speech, as also in prayer, "we do not just think of the interlocutor, we speak to him" (*EN*, 32).

Amidst the hardships of life, God is the miraculous one. God can do what seems impossible, can change what seems hopeless, can soften even the hardest heart. God is personal, relational, mysterious, and intimate. Levinas writes, "I do not wish to talk in terms of belief and non-belief. *Believe* is not a verb to be employed in the first person singular. Nobody can really say *I believe*—or *I do not believe* for that matter—that God exists. The existence of God is not a question of an individual's soul uttering logical syllogisms. It cannot be proved. The existence of God . . . is the sacredness of man's relation to man through which God may pass" (DwEL, 18).

Drawing on Franz Rosenzweig's *Star of Redemption*, Levinas muses that God did not create religion; God created the world. "The separation of men into the religious and non-religious does not get us very far. It is not at all a question of a special disposition which some possess and others lack" (*DF*, 186–87). Rather, religion is a matter of living relations that all humans engage in.

The fact that *I* learn to say *You*—this is religion.[34]

> And you:
> you, you, you
> my later of roses
> daily worn true and
> more true—
>
> —Paul Celan[35]

---

34. This is an adaption of a quote from Rosenzweig, cited by Levinas in *DF*, 192.

35. Celan, ". . . Plashes the Fountain," in *Selected Poems*, 187.

5

Sociality

More than One, Every One

The Question of Sociality

Even though Levinas lived in Paris and mixed with some of the Parisian intellectuals of his time, Salomon Malka notes that he was never actually seen in a Parisian café.[1] Indeed, in one of his Talmudic lectures, Levinas offers the following critique of Parisian café culture:

> The café is a place of casual social intercourse, without mutual responsibility. One goes in without needing to. One sits down without being tired. One drinks without being thirsty . . . The café is not a place. It is a non-place for a non-society, for a society without solidarity, without commitment, without common interests, a game society . . . Society without yesterday or tomorrow, without responsibility, without seriousness—distraction, dissolution.
>
> Here you are, each at your own little table with your cup or your glass. You relax completely to the point of not being obligated to anyone or anything, and it is because it is possible to go and relax in a café that one tolerates the horrors and injustices of a world without soul. (*NTR*, 111–12)

The image of the café suggests urban relations that are free, pleasurable, anonymous, and noncommittal. We live our lives separately and side by side, lives of freedom, tolerance, and togetherness—without any great

---

1. Malka, *Emmanuel Levinas,* 134.

encroachment or demand. In our public relations, we generally embrace a cultural discourse of "universal acceptance" that speaks of tolerance and inclusiveness. Yet such a universal acceptance runs the risk of never really noticing or encountering the unique singularity of the face of the other. Sitting in our cafés, we are never really grasped by the other who stands out against the neutrality of city streets and public civility.

Even though the café scene held no interest for Levinas, he nevertheless upheld the value of interpersonal and social relationships. "One of the blessings of multiplicity," he says, "is that there are many more relations of love in the world when there is plurality . . . How much better it is to be two than to be alone . . . There is an excellence intrinsic to the social" (IwEL, 106, 108). Even God prefers another to himself, which is why he "withdrew" so that creation could emerge, or why he "descended" so that creation could be affirmed. God is "bored to be alone," and also recognizes that it is "not good for man to be alone" (Gen 2:18). Levinas writes,

> I am thinking in effect of a God who is bored to be alone. It is Christian too. I do not say that it is uniquely Jewish. It is a God whose grandeur, whose justice and *rachamim* [mercy] you see everywhere. You see his humility; it is a God who comes down . . . It is a God who has not negated the finite and who has entered into the finite . . . This means it is a God who has sent you the other human being . . . It is the constitution of society . . . there is a human being sent toward the other human being. That is my central thesis and consequently it is this structure that is divinity. (IwEL, 107)

According to Levinas, the face-to-face ethical relation of being-for-the-other is written into the very fabric of life. It is the most primordial datum in human experience. "It is the presupposed in all human relationships," Levinas says. "If it were not that, we would not even say, before an open door, 'After you, sir!' It is an original 'After you, sir!' that I have tried to describe" (*EI*, 89). Indeed, "the face to face is a final and irreducible relation" that "makes possible the pluralism of society" (*TI*, 291).

Given Levinas' primary concern for the fundamental ethical relation between the other and me, the question nevertheless arises concerning relations that extend into the larger concerns of society, that is, "forms of togetherness" that are implicated in more than the immediacies of the face-to-face relation. Whereas Levinas posits the face-to-face relation of responsibility against a "café culture" that pays little regard to the other, we still need to ask how this "face-to-face" ethics can help us with the necessary questions engendered by the conditions of *social* existence. Social existence means existence with *more than one*, which brings before us questions concerned with *every one*—forms of togetherness that necessarily involve questions of politics, society, equality, just laws, and so on. In other words, how does Levinas' insistence on the singular call to responsibility—the face-to-face relation, the one-for-the-other—also address the social and political dimensions of human existence, the "many-faced otherness"? Or, as Levinas himself asks, "What about humanity in its multiplicity? What about the one next to the other—the third, and along with him all the others? Can that responsibility toward the other who faces me, that response to the face of my fellow man ignore the third party who is also my other? Does he not also concern me?" (*EN*, 202). Or again: "If proximity ordered to me only the other alone, there would not be any problem . . . It is troubled and becomes a problem when a third party enters" (*OB*, 157).

"How is it that there is justice?" Levinas asks. He replies that it is "the multiplicity of men and the presence of someone else next to the Other, which condition the laws and establish justice." He continues: "If I am alone with the Other, I owe him everything"; but I am never alone with the Other; there is always "someone else" (*EI*, 89–90). This "someone else" means that "the interpersonal relation I establish with the Other, I must also establish with other men" (*EI*, 90). Multiplicity means more than one. Multiplicity means every one. "And thus comes justice," Levinas says, which requires the extension of love into the conditions of sociality. This extension of love into society—into multiplicity—is what we generally call "justice" or "social justice." It requires dealing with more than one, and yet Levinas insists, "Justice, exercised through institutions, which are inevitable, must always be held in check by the initial interpersonal relation" (*EI*, 90). In other words, the face-to-face relation inspires and elicits, rather than impedes, the many-faced otherness that forms the social body. "My relation with the other as neighbor gives meaning to my relation with all others" (*OB*, 159).

Levinas does not ignore the questions and concerns of politics and social existence. He is wary, though, of moving too quickly into theories of collective existence that run the risk of forgetting the human other in the name of grander political schemas or universal generalizations. It is important to remember that Levinas' major works were written after World War II and the devastation of the Shoah, in which a ruthlessly planned

Part One—For You Alone

death machine was orchestrated by a barbaric leader of a civilized, Western, Christian nation of great thinkers, poets, and musicians. Where does this leave the status of our great ethical codes and traditions? Indeed, Levinas introduces his first major work by wondering whether or not we have been "duped by morality" (*TI*, 21). Our ethical philosophies and social frameworks seem to have failed us terribly. One of the reasons for this failure, Levinas suggests, is that we have not recognized the prior, fundamental, primordial ethical relation of being-for-the-other and responsibility for the other. Like a red-hot iron, Levinas purposefully intensifies and burns into our thinking the axiomatic ethical import of the face-to-face relation as that which lies at the very source of every human endeavor, every human reflection, and every human encounter.

I am reminded of an attempt I made to express Levinas' thought as a teacher in an undergraduate class. I placed on the floor a dozen or so black-and-white photographs of various faces. The faces represented the plurality of our world, each one expressing different cultural backgrounds and conditions of human existence. They were stark, engaging photographs. Then I took a huge blanket and threw it over all these singularly expressive faces so that they were completely covered. The blanket represents what Levinas fears most—the totality of thinking that attempts to "cover" everything. It is like a "metanarrative" or a "grand narrative" that is big enough and large enough to contain and encompass everything, to have it all "covered"—with nothing left outside its all-encompassing "worldview." However, the blanket, which strives to cast its narrative hold over everything, actually smothers, covers and obliterates the faces. The Levinasian moment happens when this smothering blanket is actually lifted and removed, and all of a sudden the faces appear—exposed, radiant, revealed, open, upright, facing. When the blanket is removed, there is openness, exposure, and the face to face—there is "revelation." Indeed, this lifting of the blanket is the revelatory moment for Levinas. It is when the face of the other "appears" and the call to ethical relationship "happens"—when the singularity of the face stands out against totalizing narratives that cover, smother, encompass.

Levinas' insistence on the face-to-face relation is not an apolitical stance; rather, it is the very prompting of a transformed conception of politics and society, one that keeps before us the face of the human other who is irreducible to any form of totalizing politics. "The social relation engenders the surplus of the Good over being, multiplicity over the One" (*TI*, 292). Levinas is suspicious of philosophical systems that strive for all-encompassing frameworks, blankets of thought that are large enough to cover it all. Into this blanketing system he introduces the "other"—who escapes, refuses, transcends, interrupts, exposes, questions the system (the "same"). Levinas brings the singular, vulnerable face of the other as witness and judge against the all-powerful system. In this sense, the other is "outside" the system as exteriority and transcendence. He writes,

> The history of modern Europe attests to an obsession with . . . an order to be established on universal but abstract rules—i.e., political rules, while underestimating or forgetting the uniqueness of the other person, whose right is, after all, at the origin of rights, yet always a new calling. The history of modern Europe is the permanent temptation of an ideological rationalism, and of experiments carried out through the rigor of deduction, administration and violence. A philosophy of history, a dialectic leading to peace among men—is such a thing possible after the Gulag and Auschwitz? (*TN*, 121)

Morality is not a subset of truth. Rather, "morality presides over the work of truth." It is "not a branch of philosophy, but first philosophy" (*TI*, 304). Ethics should not be understood as a secondary discipline based on a theoretical philosophy. As Peperzak notes, "The thesis defended by Levinas insists that every philosophy that is true to authentic experience, must be ethical from the outset, and that it is totally impossible to think seriously and fundamentally if the moral perspective is placed in parenthesis, even if only provisionally."[2]

The "Love of Wisdom" and the "Wisdom of Love"

Levinas addresses the relationship between politics and ethics in a dense and yet evocative essay written in 1984, "Peace and Proximity" (*BPW*, 161–69). He begins with a critique of the Western European tradition that attempts to establish peace on the basis of "the True," that is, on the basis of a "Greek wisdom" that seeks to reconcile differences through reason and discourse, to find agreement among diversities in a common identity, to establish the peaceful unity of the One among the many. Levinas refers to this as "peace on the basis of the state"—"which would be a gathering of humans participating in the same ideal truths . . . which governs them or gathers them together . . . where the other is reconciled with the identity

---

2. Peperzak, *Beyond*, 207.

of the identical in everyone" (*BPW*, 162). However, Levinas continues, this European liberal tradition now suffers a "guilty conscience" that recognizes its own failure and even how often its political order led to the violence of imperialism, colonialism, and genocide. He writes,

> This history of peace, freedom, and well-being promised on the basis of a light projected by a universal knowledge on the world and human society—and even on religious teachings that seek justification in the truths of knowledge—this history does not recognize itself in its millennia of fratricidal, political, and bloody struggles, of imperialism, of human hatred and exploitation, up to our century of world wars, genocides, the Holocaust, and terrorism; of unemployment, the continuing poverty of the Third World; of the pitiless doctrines and cruelties of fascism and National Socialism, up to the supreme paradox where the defense of the human and its rights is inverted into Stalinism. (*BPW*, 163)

Levinas worries about the overriding attachment of European politics to a Greek wisdom that too often seeks peace on the basis of the "One" and the "True" whereby this "unity" and "truth" becomes instead a quest for domination and a pursuit of power. "The great empires which, to such a large extent, decide the destiny of our planet," Levinas writes, "issue from a European politics, economy, science, and technology and from their power of expansion" (*BPW*, 163).

Rather than seek peace on the basis of truth and unity, whereby everything is gathered together in the *sameness* of "the One," Levinas wonders whether peace can only be found in the *surplus* of the "one"—that is, not an all-embracing "Oneness" that gathers into a totality, but rather the *singular one* that *exceeds* these assimilating efforts.

The singular one does not always need or want to be integrated into the whole, but often stands as an other who is "more than" or "other than" our systems of integration. In other words, the *surplus* of the other need not be seen as a failure or absence of unity; rather, the surplus of the other is the "excellence of love" that asks us to be-for-the-other without needing to integrate the other into the Same (*BPW*, 158).

The quest for common identities can create those who are "in" and those who are "out," leading to exclusionary and excommunicative practices. Even the phrase "unity in diversity" (*E pluribus unum*), while a noble sentiment, can nevertheless suggest that strangeness, difference, and diversity are welcomed and celebrated, but only if there is "unity"—as though there were a secret fear that the stranger might actually disrupt or threaten the gathering-together of a community or a society or a nation. Welcome is extended, but only insofar as unity is preserved and not threatened. Perhaps this is why immigration policy is always such a controversial subject, because people fear the breakdown of society. We tend to prefer unified and harmonious worlds of peace and oneness, which is not always good news for the alien or for the one who doesn't fit.

It is worth citing Levinas' own words as he attempts to speak of a peace that is different from the peace of unity and truth:

> One can ask oneself if peace has not to respond to a call more urgent than that of truth . . . It would no longer be a matter of peace conforming to the ideal of the *unity of the One* which every alterity disturbs . . . Instead of being the result of an absorption or disappearance of alterity, peace would be the *fraternal* mode of a proximity of the other, which would not simply be the failure to coincide with the other but would signify precisely the *surplus* of sociality . . . the *surplus* of love.
>
> Peace as a relation with an alterity . . . independent, then, of any belonging to a system, irreducible to a totality and refractory to synthesis. A project of peace different from political peace . . . Here, on the contrary, in ethical peace, the relation is with the inassimilable other, the irreducible other, the unique . . . Peace different from the simple unity of the diverse integrated by synthesis . . . Rather, peace as an incessant watching over the unique and the other . . . the mysterious surplus of the beloved. (*BPW*, 165–66)

Levinas is evoking here the biblical tradition that speaks of peace "as love of the neighbor, which is not a matter of peace as pure rest that confirms one's identity but of always placing in question this very identity, its limitless freedom and its power" (*BPW*, 167). The Greek heritage of Western thought, which seeks the truth and the unity of the one and the same, needs to be supplemented by the biblical heritage, a heritage that founds peace on the "whole gravity of love" and fellowship with the other human. We need to know, Levinas asks, "if the egalitarian and just state in which man is fulfilled . . . proceeds from a war of all against all, or from the irreducible responsibility of the one for all, and if it can do without friendship and faces?" (*OB*, 159–60). In other words, ethics must continue to inspire the social and political order as the call of the other and the face-to-face relation of friendship and ethical intersubjectivity.

Nevertheless, Levinas concludes his essay by recognizing that the Greek philosophical heritage also plays a necessary role. While the face of the other is the face of the *unique and incomparable one*, there are nevertheless times when we must make comparisons, weigh issues, think about questions of equality, give attention to questions of fairness, frame laws with a certain universal applicability, structure society according to the democracy of discourse between equals. "Must not human beings, who are incomparable, be compared?" (*EN*, 104). Levinas acknowledges that there is a certain "necessity of thinking together under a synthetic theme the multiplicity and the unity of the world" (*BPW*, 168). Justice "calls for judgment and comparison, a comparison of what is in principle incomparable, for every being is unique, every other is unique" (*EN*, 104). However, Levinas insists that this Greek wisdom of ordering, thematizing, and synthesizing must always be attentive to the "extravagant generosity of the for-the-other." Its wisdom must become more than philosophy's love of wisdom, but also the very biblical "wisdom of love at the service of love" (*BPW*, 169; *OB*, 162).

Love Watches Over Justice: "The Little Act of Goodness"

"Politics left to itself," writes Levinas, "bears a tyranny within itself; it deforms the I and the other who have given rise to it, for it judges them according to universal rules, and thus *in absentia*" (*TI*, 300). The workings and determinations of justice are often conducted in the great halls of the law, in the manner of a "politics left to itself" and its own devices, as though politics had no other concern than its own concern, whereas all the time it should be concerned with the well-being of the *polis* and the common good. And all too often, rules and legislation and judgments are made in the absence of the one who stands outside—"*in absentia*"—as though the law didn't really care about those left standing outside its gates, whereas all the time it is meant to be concerned for the welfare of all, even and especially for the least of all.

Left to itself, the wheels of politics and the laws of justice can turn with unrelenting power—"oh, the violence of administration!" Levinas cries (*IRB*, 51). The processes and systems of management are everywhere in our lives. Knowingly or unknowingly, we are entangled in procedures of power, policy, and paperwork. Hannah Arendt calls it our "infinitely complex red-tape existence."[3] "Every attempt to organize humanity fails," writes Levinas (*IRB*, 217). Many a system has been tried, and many a system has failed. Even the much-lauded system of "democracy" has not yet achieved what it seeks, as Martin Luther King Jr.'s "I Have a Dream" speech powerfully attests.[4]

Certain strains of Catholic social teaching express a suspicion toward grandiose and yet vain political programs. In his encyclical *A Call to Action*, for example, Pope Paul VI worries about the ambiguity inherent in every social ideology:

> Sometimes it leads political or social activity to be simply the application of an abstract, purely theoretical idea . . . There is also the danger of giving adherence to an ideology which does not rest on a true and organic doctrine, to take refuge in it as a final and sufficient explanation of everything, and thus to build a new idol, accepting, at times without being aware of doing so, its totalitarian and coercive character. And people imagine they find in it a justification for their activity, even violent activity, and an adequate response to a desire to serve. The desire remains but it allows itself to be consumed by an ideology which, even if it suggests certain paths to man's liberation, ends up by making him a slave.[5]

Like Levinas, Paul VI worries that "politics left to itself" holds the inherent danger, even under the banner of a desire to serve, of turning the law and politics into an idol. Even democracy can be turned into an idol—as when, for example, it is invoked by those who seek a justification for the "war on terror." Violence can spread even in the name of democracy and freedom, especially if these are taken as "a final and sufficient explanation of everything." Paul VI offers the following caution: "Politics are a demanding manner—but not the only one—of living the Christian commitment to service to others . . . The domain of politics is wide and comprehensive, but it is not exclusive. An attitude of encroachment which would tend to set up politics as an absolute value would bring serious danger."[6]

This is a concern that Levinas also shares, for he has personally witnessed and suffered the dangers of social and political systems that can all too easily assume the tyranny of coercive and totalitarian practices. "A state

3. Arendt, *Portable Hannah Arendt*, 25.
4. King, *Testament of Hope*, 217–20.
5. Paul VI, *Octogesima Adveniens: A Call to Action*, 27–28.
6. Ibid., 46.

in which the interpersonal relationship is impossible," writes Levinas, "is a totalitarian state" (*EN*, 105). And again: "The State issued from the proximity of the neighbor is always on the verge of integrating him into a we, which congeals both me and the neighbor" (*OB*, 161). Levinas is suggesting that a purely theorized or impersonal public—even under the banner of "civil society"—is really no public at all. Unless public life is underwritten by the personal, then its collective structures are always in danger of forgetting or repressing the very relation that "gives rise" to political activity, namely, the "I and the other" of human fraternity and ethical responsibility. As Roger Burggraeve notes, "Coming from his experience of the Holocaust, Levinas is extremely apprehensive at the suggestion that politics and the State would have the last word in our human relations."[7] "Left to itself," politics "deforms the I and the other." In other words, the ethical relation must continually inspire the social and political order. Paul VI writes, "Human rights are still too often disregarded, if not scoffed at, or else they receive only formal recognition. In many cases legislation does not keep up with real situations. Legislation is necessary, but it is not sufficient for setting up true relationships of justice and equality . . . If, beyond legal rules, there is really no deeper feeling of respect for and service to others, then even equality before the law can serve as an alibi for flagrant discrimination, continued exploitation, and actual contempt."[8]

One of the cardinal points of Catholic social teaching is that the human person is "the foundation, the cause and the end of every social institution."[9] While we must necessarily attend to the social fabric of our institutional structures, political administrations, and judicial systems, we must recognize that all these social institutions are not the *foundation* or basis of ethical relations, but the *consequences* or "guardianships" of the more originary ethical relation that comes to us, not from our well-constructed social theories or ethical codes, but from the fundamental relationship of the "I and the other." If our social and political frameworks are not directed toward or inspired by this fundamental ethical relation, then our "collective measures lose their human meaning because they have forgotten or masked real faces and real speech. This forgetfulness is the beginning of tyranny."[10] As Burggraeve notes, Levinas makes it exceptionally clear that

---

7. Burggraeve, *Wisdom of Love in the Service of Love*, 145.
8. Paul VI, *Octogesima Adveniens: A Call to Action*, 23.
9. John XXIII, *Mater et Magistra: Christianity and Social Progress*, 219.
10. Peperzak, *To the Other*, 31.

"the interpersonal relation serves as the basic norm for a society of many . . . Nothing—neither politics, law, the State, institutions and society, nor labor, technology, money, business and all other forms of 'exchange'— can exempt itself from responsibility of one-for-the-Other."[11] This means that those who design, operate, and maintain our social structures must themselves be inspired by this fundamental ethical responsibility. If we are teachers, pastors, or health care workers; if we hold positions of authority as lawyers, police officers, or government officials; if we are members of one another—parents, neighbors, citizens—then we need to ensure that everyone who comes our way is given access to the dignity of human relationships in the *polis* of our shared life together.

The true aim of all social and political activity "should be to help individual members of the social body, but never to destroy or absorb them."[12] Levinas notes, however, that there is a "ceaseless deep remorse of justice" (*IRB*, 206), for while the dignity of each and every person is *unique* and *incomparable*, there are nevertheless times when it is necessary for the law to calculate and make comparisons, to weigh and to measure. Justice that seeks to be true and good is always saddened by its inability to be truly just for each and every person who comes before the law, because it knows that it must necessarily weigh individual cases according to universal principles, and yet it also knows that no universal principle is ever adequate to deal with each and every human particularity that comes before it in all its special instance and circumstance. "Legislation is always unfinished, always resumed," Levinas says. While the law aims to approximate the justice due to every person, it is nevertheless "distanced by the necessary calculations imposed by a multiple sociality, calculations constantly starting over again" (*IRB*, 206). In other words, the law—when it is functioning well, or as best it can—is nevertheless painfully and "remorsefully" aware of its own pitfalls and shortcomings.

"Justice is necessary," Levinas says, "that is, comparison, coexistence, assembling, order, thematization . . . the intelligibility of a system, and thence also a copresence on an equal footing as before a court of justice" (*OB*, 157). However, this "reasonable justice" that is based on fairness and equality and universal principles is nevertheless "bound by legal strictures and cannot equal the goodness that solicits and inspires it" (*IRB*, 207). Underlying all quests for justice stands "the whole gravity of love"—a love that

---

11. Burggraeve, *Wisdom of Love in the Service of Love*, 146.
12. Paul VI, *Octogesima Adveniens: A Call to Action*, 46.

does not measure or boast but "bears all things" (1 Cor 13:7). In the name of this love, Levinas prefers to "reserve another word: *miséricorde*, mercy, when one assumes responsibility for the suffering of another" (*IRB*, 146). He even goes so far as to suggest that "the little act of goodness [*la petite bonté*] from one person to his neighbor is lost and deformed as soon as it seeks organization and universality and system, as soon as it opts for doctrine, a treatise of politics and theology, a party, a state, and even a church. Yet it remains the sole refuge of the good in being. Unbeaten, it undergoes violence and evil, which, as little goodness, it can neither vanquish nor drive out" (*IRB*, 206–7).

"Justice itself is born of charity" (*IRB*, 168). If it is inspired by goodness, if it is founded on charity, if it is chastened and softened by mercy, then it may be possible for justice to best approximate what it seeks. Otherwise, it will always be deformed and wounded—unable to rise to the heights of justice, which always wells up from mercy's appeal of loving-kindness. "God is the God of justice, but his principle attribute is mercy" (*IRB*, 169). Love disarms justice, unsettles justice, and watches over justice. We should "never forget," Levinas says, "that justice comes from *chesed*—favor, goodness, loving-kindness" (IwEL, 106).

According to Martha Nussbaum, a politics "inclined to mercy" recognizes "how pervasive the obstacles to goodness are, how deeply rooted, how much a part of oneself as well as others." A politics of mercy diverges from strictness toward forbearance, from cruelty toward "a slow gentle fostering of what good there may be." A politics of mercy recognizes that "the human world is held together by pity and fellow-feeling."[13]

Acts of charity and mercy may seem small in the face of the huge demands of social justice and the necessary concerns of politics in the world. However, it is often these small and fragile acts of love that ultimately watch over justice. Just as the parent watches over a child who is sick, or the lover watches for the beloved, sitting up through the night—"faint with love" (Song 5:8)—unable to sleep but rather full of concern and solicitude, so too "love must watch over justice" (*IRB*, 169). Mercy not only crowns or seasons justice, but ultimately even supplants it. Seemingly fragile acts of tenderness and love—acts of social mercy—should not be considered mere "band-aids." Rather, they are the very sign of God's goodness in the world. A rabbinic parable speaks of the Messiah who is found at the city gates, attending to the afflicted and the suffering, "binding up their wounds," and

---

13. Nussbaum, *Love's Knowledge*, 213, 375.

Sociality

says that while "others bind an *entire* area covering *several* wounds with one bandage, the Messiah dresses *each wound separately*."[14] Often, acts of mercy and charity may seem to be mere supplements to the grander works of justice; they may even seem "foolish" in the eyes of the world. And yet St. Paul says,

> God chose what is foolish in the world to shame the wise; God chose what is weak in the world to shame the strong; God chose what is low and despised in the world, things that are not, to reduce to nothing things that are . . . None of the rulers of this age have understood this. (1 Cor 1:17–18; 2:8)

According to Paul VI, various political models have been tried, "but none of them gives complete satisfaction." Nevertheless, "the Christian has the duty to take part in this search and in the organization and life of political society."[15] This leads me to wonder: must the practical and ethical sphere of society always operate under the auspices of justice? Or, as Paul Ricoeur suggests, along with the demands of justice, do we not need a "poetics of love"?[16] Could it be that an "excess of justice"—lacking in love or mercy—is dangerously close to becoming an injustice? On the other hand, is it possible that an "excess of love" could ever jeopardize or fail the requirements of justice? Isn't it rather the case that the practices of love and mercy keep justice from becoming unjust, such that the conditions of justice are always tested against the superabundance of merciful and unconditional love? In other words, justice's "logic of equivalence" needs to be constantly supplemented or watched over by love's "logic of superabundance."[17]

Mercy is "the sole refuge of the good in being." While justice is imperative—a mutual indebtedness—mercy nevertheless remains as the sole refuge in life, the sole refuge in our relationships and our society. Mercy is refuge for the immigrant, relief for the overburdened, rescue for the afflicted. Social mercy is crucial to our society; without it we could not even claim *to be* a society—a society, that is, of any human or humane proportion, where our bonds are always ones of friendship and fraternity, forgiveness and forbearance—knowing that we are all in this boat together, and only mercy can sustain us.

---

14. Pearl, *Theology in Rabbinic Stories*, 145 (citing *Sanhedrin* 98a).
15. Paul IV, *Octogesima Adveniens: A Call to Action*, 24.
16. Ricoeur, "Love and Justice," in Ricoeur, *Figuring the Sacred*, 315–29.
17. Ibid., 329.

Part One—For You Alone

Social Mercy

According to Levinas, hidden within the quest for justice in the world (especially in Western cultures) "there is a memory of the Bible." In our efforts to create a just society, this ancient memory provokes "the endless requirement of justice hidden behind justice, the requirement of an even juster justice, more faithful to its original imperative in the face of the other" (*TN*, xx). In other words, our quest for justice finds its original inspiration in the memory of the biblical tradition. This tradition serves as a constant "corrective" to our attempts to secure justice in the world, a corrective that reminds us of "the uniqueness of the other" and "the mercy that uniqueness appeals to," over against our systems of justice (*TN*, 121). "The inter-human perspective can subsist, but can also be lost, in the political order of the City," Levinas says. The *I* is not simply a "citizen born of the City" or a product of "civil society." Rather, "the inter-human is also the recourse that people have to one another for help . . ." (*EN*, 100–101).

Jacques Derrida, famously known for coining the word *deconstruction*, had a long-standing interest in questions concerning justice and interacted closely with Levinas' work. In a celebrated essay he makes the bold claim that "justice in itself, if such a thing exists, outside or beyond the law, is not deconstructible."[18] Derrida draws a distinction between justice and "the law." By "law" he means all the legal systems, codes, rights, and institutions that exist in an effort to ensure that the claims of justice are met. The law exists for the sake of justice, and yet "justice in itself" is never fully realized. Because of this, the law must be continually deconstructed—critiqued, revised, reformed—so that it can better approximate the justice that it seeks, yet always falls short of. If laws were not deconstructible, we would end up in a fixed system, and any hope of achieving justice would be lost to us. However, it is "justice in itself" that prompts the revision and critique of the law, that prevents the law from thinking that it is *in itself* undeconstructible, that it is *in itself* justice—whereas the law is only a means to justice which always stands "outside or beyond the law" as the undeconstructible "test" of the law. In a roundtable discussion, Derrida makes his case this way:

> There is a history of legal systems, of rights, of laws, and this history is the history of the transformation of laws. You can improve the law, you can replace one law by another one . . . So, the law as such can be deconstructed and has to be deconstructed. That is the

18. Derrida, "Force of the Law," 14.

> condition of historicity, revolution, morals, ethics, and progress. But justice is not the law. Justice is what gives the impulse, the drive, or the movement to improve the law, that is, to deconstruct the law. Without a call for justice we would not have any interest in deconstructing the law . . . Deconstruction is a call for justice. Justice is not reducible to the law, to a given system of legal structures . . . That is why the call for justice is never, never fully answered. That is why no one can say "I am just."[19]

Derrida establishes justice—or the call of justice—as that which forever prevents us from thinking that our laws and moral codes are "just" or that they are equal to "justice." This strikes me as a persuasive argument—and yet I find myself wondering whether it is justice alone that is "beyond the law" and undeconstructible, or whether it is mercy ("kindly love") that rises even higher than justice as that which cannot be deconstructed. My own sense is that it is mercy that remains as the everlasting appeal that keeps *even justice itself* from becoming the final arbiter or test of our laws and our moral codes. When we seek to be just, it is not only justice that we seek, it is also mercy. Without mercy, even justice itself cannot save us.

Perhaps it is because no one can say "I am just" that the call of mercy rises above justice as the highest appeal. For if no one can claim to be just, then each of us will be continually dependent on mercy's appeal ("forgive us our debts, as we forgive those who are in debt to us" [Matt 6:12]). Mercy stands "outside or beyond the law" as the ultimate appeal that keeps even *justice itself* answerable to a higher call, the call of mercy—"the *rahamim* of the Bible" (*TN*, 121).

There is much that is unjust in our society, yet I have often wondered whether it is the lack of mercy and charity that causes injustice to prevail. Or rather that, without mercy, justice is perilously close to becoming unjust. This leads me to conclude that mercy is not the opposite of justice—or the complement of justice—but its very condition.[20] Justice on its own never suffices. As Burggraeve notes, "The charity of one-for-the-Other is never completely fulfilled by public justice or any socio-political system. This is why justice has constant need of review, reform and renewal."[21]

Levinas shared a friendship over many years with Pope John Paul II. In his encyclical *Dives in Misericordia* (*On the Mercy of God*), Pope John

---

19. Derrida, *Deconstruction in a Nutshell*, 16–17.
20. Veling, *Beatitude of Mercy*.
21. Burggraeve, *Wisdom of Love in the Service of Love*, 148, 150.

Paul II notes that mercy is "the greatest of the attributes and perfections of God."[22] God's faithfulness is always demonstrated, not in strict justice, but in mercy (*rahamim*):

> Love, so to speak, conditions justice and, in the final analysis, justice serves love. The primacy and superiority of love vis-à-vis justice—this is a mark of the whole of revelation—are *revealed precisely through mercy*. This seemed so obvious to the psalmists and the prophets that the very term *justice* ended up meaning the salvation accomplished by the Lord and his mercy. *Mercy differs from justice, but is not in opposition to it* . . . Indeed, *true mercy is the most profound source of justice*. (26, 68)

This is not an escape from the demands of justice. Rather, this is a heightening of justice's concerns to the very pinnacle where we recognize that only mercy can ultimately perfect the justice that we seek. Mercy is love. Mercy is compassion. Mercy is solidarity. Mercy is good news for justice, not bad news.

John Paul II notes that "human action can *deviate from justice itself*, even when it is being undertaken in the name of justice"(58; my italics). We can easily deceive ourselves into thinking that we are acting justly, and for this reason John Paul II suggests that without mercy justice cannot be established. "The experience of the past and of our own time demonstrates that justice alone is not enough, that it can even lead to the negation of itself, if *that deeper power, which is love,* is not allowed to shape human life in its various dimensions" (58–59; my italics). The pope refers to the ancient saying, attributed to Cicero, *summum ius, summa iniuria*, which can be translated as "the more justice, the more injury" or "the extreme law is the greatest injustice" (59). Justice requires mercy to ensure that our practices of judgment and justice are not harsh or severe, so that we can act *humanely* with tolerance and restraint, "bearing with one another in love" (Eph 4:2). The pope writes,

> Society can become ever more human only if we introduce into the many-sided setting of interpersonal and social relationships, not merely justice, but also that "merciful love" which constitutes the messianic message of the Gospel . . . A world from which forgiveness was eliminated would be nothing but a world of cold and unfeeling justice, in the name of which each person would claim his or her own rights vis-à-vis others; the various kinds of

---

22. John Paul II, *Dives in Misericordia*, 61 (subsequent references in parentheses).

Sociality

selfishness latent in man would transform life and human society into an arena of permanent strife between one group and another. (70–71)

According to Simone Weil, this "cold and unfeeling justice" is often narrowly associated with the language of rights. Whenever someone cries out, "Why am I being hurt?" we are in the realm of evil and injustice. This is in contrast, Weil suggests, to another cry that is all too often heard: "Why has somebody else got more than I have?"[23] This is the "cry of rights," of which she says, "The notion of rights is linked with the notion of sharing out, of exchange, of measured quantity. It has a commercial flavor, essentially evocative of legal claims and arguments. Rights are always asserted in a tone of contention; and when this tone is adopted, it must rely upon force."[24] There is a latent violence associated with the language of rights, especially when these are asserted in a narrowly self-interested manner of "what is owed to me." According to Weil,

> Every time we put forth some effort and the equivalent of this effort does not come back to us in the form of some visible fruit, we have a sense of false balance which makes us think that we have been cheated. The effort of suffering from some offence causes us to expect the punishment or apologies of the offender, the effort of doing good makes us expect the gratitude of the person we have helped . . . Every time we give anything out we have an absolute need that at least the equivalent should come back to us, and because we need this we think we have a right to it. Our debtors comprise all beings and all things; they are the entire universe. We think we have claims everywhere.[25]

John Paull II writes of the importance of mercy over against seizing my rights and claiming "my place under the sun" (DwEL, 24):

> Mercy is an indispensible element for *shaping* mutual relationships between people, in a spirit of deepest respect for what is human, and in a spirit of mutual brotherhood. It is impossible to establish this bond between people, if they wish to regulate their mutual relationships solely according to the measure of justice. In every sphere of interpersonal relationships justice must, so to speak, *be "corrected" to a considerable extent by merciful love*, which is so much of the essence of the Gospel. (69)

23. Weil, *Simone Weil*, 93.
24. Ibid., 81.
25. Weil, *Waiting on God*, 141.

John Paul II notes that sometimes mercy is dubiously presented as a relationship of inequality between the one who offers mercy and the one who receives it, such that mercy belittles or humiliates the receiver. However, "mercy is manifested in its true and proper aspect when it restores to value, promotes and *draws good from all the forms of evil* existing in the world and in the person" (36). Mercy does not diminish human value and dignity; rather, it acts to restore the dignity that is proper to human life. "In reciprocal relationships between persons, merciful love is never a unilateral act or process . . . An act of merciful love is only really such when we are *deeply convinced* . . . that we are at the same time *receiving* mercy from the people who are accepting it from us" (66–67).

Solidarity is perhaps the word that comes closest to mercy. The word *merciful* is derived from "suffering with" the fate of another's misery; from this *misericordia* is named, since the misery of the suffering person makes the merciful person's heart suffer, *miserum cor*. Mercy means that I stand in solidarity with the one who suffers, that I stand in solidarity with God who loves, that I stand in solidarity with "sinners" who are, like myself, always dependent on a love that outstrips judgment and is even stronger than death. St. Thomas Aquinas writes that "a person is said to be merciful [*misericors*], as being sorrowful at heart [*miserum cor*]; in other words, as being affected with sorrow at the misery of another as though it were his own. Hence it follows that he endeavors to dispel the misery of this other, as if it were his; and this is the effect of mercy."[26]

Taking on the suffering and sorrow of another "as though it were my own" expresses the conviction that we are bound together as human beings—in our joys and our hopes, and also in our sin and our distress. "For the other" is "for the joy of the other" and also "for the fault of the other."

Levinas suggests that when we are addressed by the gaze of the singular face in all its vulnerability and uprightness, there is a sense in which "the whole of humanity looks at us" (*TI*, 213). "My relation with the other as my neighbor gives meaning to my relations with all others" (*OB*, 159). In the face of the other I see the face of every other, such that each face "attests . . . to the whole of humanity, in the eyes that look at me" (*TI*, 213). "In a certain sense, all others are present in the face of the other" (*EN*, 106). If we can speak at all of a universality or equality, then it is founded upon this fraternity of human beings exposed to the vulnerability of each other's nakedness

---

26. Aquinas, *Summa Theologica* 1, q.21, art. 3.

and suffering. It is founded upon the solidarity of human compassion that binds us to be one-for-the-other.

Merciful deeds are works that God loves; they divinize those who practice them and mold them into the likeness of divine goodness. Mercy is an act of healing and love. It is healing because it seeks to help those in its care realize that we need not be condemned to hatred—love is possible. We need not be condemned to cycles of violence—forgiveness is possible. We need not be condemned to conflict and division—understanding is possible. If we could be more aware of the need for social mercy, if we could speak more readily of social mercy, if we could let the language and the sentiments of social mercy hold greater sway in our society, our institutions, and our social structures, we would in no way jeopardize our quest for social justice. Rather, we would enhance this quest. Mercy is the very foundation of justice, such that without social mercy our quest for social justice will always be misguided and thwarted.

"In spite of its excesses, only love is just," wrote Reb Emri.

Reb Ziré replied: "What can we conclude but that love is as vulnerable as the lover, and justice, as the judge?"
And he added: "Caution the just against his own justice."

"Love forgives justice for distrusting love" (Reb Kamri).
—EDMOND JABÉS[27]

"Only the excess of beatitude will respond to the excess of evil."
—PHILIPPE NEMO[28]

---

27. Jabès, *Book of Resemblances*, 3:52–53.
28. Cited by Levinas in *GCM*, 132.

Part Two

The Talmudic Ocean

6

The Talmudic Ocean

A Mysterious Teacher

In his biography of Levinas, Salomon Malka notes that Levinas suffered two alarming "shocks" or "jolts" in his life—"1933 with Hitler's rise to power, and 1945 with his encounter with Chouchani."[1]

Very little is known about Chouchani—where he was born, where he grew up, where he gained his immense knowledge. "It was as if he fell from the sky," Levinas says (*IRB*, 87). Chouchani is not even his real name, which nobody knows. Malka writes, "Levinas never had much to say when we tried to get him to talk about Chouchani. He came to know him in the years following the war, invited him to stay in his home . . . and spent many nights, for almost four years, under his tutelage."[2]

Chouchani was gifted with an exceptional memory and intelligence. He "knew by heart the entire oral tradition to which the Scripture gave rise. He knew by heart the Talmud and its commentaries, and the commentaries on the commentaries" (*IRB*, 74). Along with an almost perfect mastery of the Bible, the Talmud, and Jewish philosophy, he also had an immense knowledge of literature, the sciences, and mathematics. Moreover, he spoke virtually all the languages familiar to the Jews of Europe. He was a wandering teacher who "resembled a hobo," with no fixed address, passing from New York to Strasbourg, from Paris to Jerusalem. He would give lessons on the Bible or Talmud in exchange for room and board, and across the globe

---

1. Malka, *Emmanuel Levinas*, 159.
2. Ibid., 155.

Part Two—The Talmudic Ocean

he gained many students, including Elie Wiesel.³ His last days were spent in South America, where he died in anonymity, in 1968, with these words inscribed on his tombstone: "His birth and his life are bound up in secret."⁴

When Levinas encountered Chouchani, he was still a "career-less philosopher" on the margins of university life. Levinas' son, Michael, recalls of this time: "He ceased all philosophical work between 1947 and 1952, from the time he received Chouchani at home. He said that he spent as much time writing his dissertation as he did being trained by Chouchani."⁵ Levinas recalls how he would often be up late at night, until two or three in the morning, listening to Chouchani's lessons. Studying Talmud with Chouchani was a very special apprenticeship:

> He turned over to me neither his immense knowledge nor certainly his incomparable intelligence, but he did show me how one should approach these texts—this unattainable level. Next to him, what I do is nothing, and I am nothing. He was a terrifying dialectician. He could, when he wished to, defend one day to the same students almost the contrary of what he had taught the day before. With an extraordinary virtuosity but also, each time, with new dimensions of meaning! I conserved from him an unforgettable and incommunicable recollection of the life of the spirit. (*IRB*, 286)

"From Chouchani I learned the method," Levinas recounts, "to take the Talmud in all its facets, not as a doctrine but simply as open possibilities."⁶ Like the hidden life of his teacher, Levinas learned that studying Talmud means "lighting up the hidden horizons of the text, the forgotten, the ignored, the obfuscated."⁷

Chouchani is "the great master" whom Levinas often mentions in his Talmudic commentaries. "I owe him everything I publish on Talmud," Levinas says (*IRB*, 160). "It was this post-war encounter that reactivated my latent—I might even say dormant—interest in the Judaic tradition" (*DwEL*, 18). It was through Chouchani that Levinas came into deeper contact with the Talmudic texts. "Although educated since early youth in the

---

3. Wiesel, "The Wandering Jew," in Wiesel, *Legends of Our Time*, 87–109.

4. Malka, *Emmanuel Levinas*, 155–56. See also Aronowicz's introduction to Levinas' *Nine Talmudic Readings*, xiii. Levinas refers to Chouchani's death in *NTR*, 8.

5. Malka, *Emmanuel Levinas*, 265.

6. Ibid., 239–40.

7. Ibid., 125.

square letters, I have come late—and on the fringe of purely philosophical studies—to Talmudic texts, which cannot be practiced in amateur fashion" (*NTR*, 9).

Levinas was among those who established, in 1957, an annual colloquium of Jewish intellectuals meeting in France. The program of the colloquia, Levinas notes, "always envisioned a Talmudic commentary, next to a biblical commentary, to be related to the general theme suggested to its members" (*NTR*, 3). With only a few exceptions, Levinas participated in all the colloquia, from his first Talmudic lecture in 1960 to his last in 1989. He gave twenty-three "lectures" or "readings" in all. They held a very great place in his life and his work.[8] While he often credits Chouchani in his Talmudic lectures, his references are typically oblique and indirect. In very few places does he actually spell out "the method" he learned from his teacher. However, it is possible to distill certain "principles" or hermeneutical practices that lay at the heart of Levinas' approach to navigating the "talmudic sea," to reading these "old tractates" (*NTR*, 9). In this chapter, I explore these principles or practices under the following seven headings:

1. The Four Compass Points: The Written and Oral Torah, the Halakhah and Aggadah
2. Beyond History: The Harmonics of Talmud
3. Memory and Association
4. Spirit-Letter
5. The Universal in the Particular
6. Obedience and Instruction: Texts that Teach
7. Application: "I Am Required"

These are not distinct or separable practices; as such, it is inevitable that some repetition or similarity occurs between them. If anything holds them together, it is the searching and the questioning, the teaching and the learning, the listening and the responding. For the rabbinic interpreters, "what matters is that they belong to the Book, and through the Book they belong together. The Book is the world and the world is the Book; to live is to interpret, and to interpret is to live. But they can only do it together,

---

8. Ibid., 125–43. Levinas' Talmudic lectures can be found in the following works: *Difficult Freedom, Nine Talmudic Readings, Beyond the Verse, In the Time of the Nations, New Talmudic Readings*.

Part Two—The Talmudic Ocean

not alone."⁹ The Mishnah says, "If two sit together and words of Torah are between them, the Divine Presence rests between them."¹⁰ Similarly, Matthew's Gospel says, "Where two are three are gathered in my name, I am there among them" (18:20).

1. The Four Compass Points

The Talmud has no page one. Every tractate of Talmud begins on page two, so that you know from the very beginning that you are dealing with a book that is of divine origin—without beginning, and infinitely open—without end.

"I don't know if you have ever seen a page or a treatise of the Talmud," Levinas says in an interview. He continues: "The text of the Mishnah, written down in the second century, debated in the Gemara, written down toward the end of the fifth century, commentaries by Rashi of the tenth and eleventh centuries, prolonged by the commentaries of those who are called the Tosephites, prolonged further by commentaries from all sides and from all times. Typographically these pages hold something prodigious—a mixture of characters, references, referrals, reminders of all kinds" (*IRB*, 74).

Levinas refers to the "four compass points" of Jewish revelation: the Written and Oral Torah, and the *Halakhah* and *Aggadah*.¹¹ Each of these compass points guides the reader; each offers its own particular heading in the "sea of the Talmud."

The Written and Oral Torah

The earliest rabbis saw themselves as heirs to the Pharisees. The Pharisees were a lay movement of scholars or sages. They were keen interpreters of the Written Torah (the Scriptures), and these interpretations formed the

---

9. Edgerton, *Passion of Interpretation*, 45.
10. *Pirkei Avos* (*Ethics of the Fathers*), 3:3.
11. Levinas, "Revelation in the Jewish Tradition," in *LR*, 200. Note: *Torah* is a very rich word. It can refer to the first five books of Scripture (the Pentateuch); in wider usage, it includes the books of the Prophets (*Nevi'im*) and the books of the Writings (*Kethuvim*). The Jewish Scriptures (*Tanakh*) are arranged according to these three parts (Torah, Prophets, Writings). In a still wider sense, it includes the Written and Oral Torah, the whole body of sacred texts and its evolving tradition. It can also refer to the scroll from which Scripture is read in public worship. See Neusner, *Torah*.

The Talmudic Ocean

basis of the Oral Torah. After the destruction of the Temple in 70 CE, the Pharisees gathered at Javneh on the Mediterranean coast and began compiling the oral traditions. They shifted the focus of holiness from the temple to "houses of study" and ongoing interpretation in the events of daily life. Completed around 200 CE, the Mishnah records the details of the oral tradition under six major headings or "Orders," which are in turn divided into smaller topical sections called "tractates" (of which there are 63). The authors are referred to as *tannaim* ("teachers"), the most famous of whom is Rabbi Akiva. The Mishnah, in turn, generated additional commentaries—Gemara. The Mishnah and Gemara together constitute the essential elements of Talmud ("study," "learning").[12]

In the Jewish tradition, the book is always twofold. It is indeed God's original word, but it is also the people's response to God's word. The book is indeed written and given to be read. There is always a normative quality or an original "deep story" that marks every religious tradition. The rabbis refer to this as the Written Torah. In the Written Torah, God has given and intended all, such that everything is filled with divine intention and meaning. However, because the Written Torah is the word of God—filled with infinite and original meaning—it necessarily calls forth interpretation and commentary. The rabbis refer to this interpretive responsibility as Oral Torah. The following parable attempts to reveal the relationship between the Written and the Oral Torah:

> What is the difference between the Written and the Oral Law? To what can it be compared? To a king of flesh and blood who had two servants and loved them both with a perfect love. He gave each of them a measure of wheat and each a bundle of flax. What did the wise servant do? He took the flax and spun a cloth. He took the wheat and made flour. He cleaned the flour and ground, kneaded and baked it, and set it on top of the table. Then he spread the cloth over it until the king would come.
>
> The foolish servant, however, did nothing at all. After some time, the king returned from a journey and came into his house.

---

12. Goldenberg, "Talmud," in Holtz, *Back to the Sources*; Bosker and Bosker, "Introduction," in *The Talmud*, 7–14. See also ch. 3 in Lee, *The Galilean Jewishness of Jesus*. There are two versions of the Talmud. The earlier version dates from the fourth to fifth centuries and is known as the Palestinian or Jerusalem Talmud. The other is known as the Babylonian Talmud; twice the size of the Jerusalem Talmud (over two million words), it was edited a century or two later, with additions continuing for the next several centuries. The Babylonian Talmud is the great classic of Jewish Revelation. Adin Steinsaltz is gradually working at providing an English translation: *Talmud: The Steinsaltz Edition*.

Part Two—The Talmudic Ocean

> He said to his servants: my sons bring me what I gave you. One servant showed the wheat still in the box with the bundle of flax upon it. Alas for his shame, alas for his disgrace!
>
> When the Holy One, blessed be He, gave the Torah to Israel, he gave it only in the form of wheat—for us to make flour from it, and flax—to make a garment from it.[13]

The parable suggests that interpretation is a productive and creative craft that shapes "garments from flax" and creates "bread from wheat." The rabbis are suggesting that interpretation actively weaves, shapes, and "makes" the text—the text is experienced only in the activity of interpretation and commentary. As Paul Ricoeur reminds us, interpretation does not unveil established meanings "behind the text"; rather, it produces new meanings "in front of the text."[14]

The rabbis believed that ultimate authority could not be found in fixed texts alone but in a living interpretation of those texts. There is no question that the texts are sacred; however, given the finitude of the human condition and the pressures of new historical situations, these sacred texts must also be carefully interpreted as deep sources of wisdom for encountering daily dilemmas.[15] Much of this teaching, which was mostly oral, was eventually recorded and redacted, and ultimately what resulted was the Talmud—a vast encyclopedia of teachings and dialogical commentaries. The Talmud seeks "to preserve the record of earlier generations studying their own tradition and provide materials for later generations wishing to do the same."[16]

Jewish poet Edmond Jabès offers us an image of a people who, over centuries and centuries, live with such a deep attachment and attentiveness to their religious tradition that they return to it over and over again, as one returns to a fountain or to a well. "Turn it and turn it," the Mishnah says, "in it all things can be found."[17] Page after page, day after day, through long nights and difficult questions, across the centuries, the Jewish people bring their lives to these ancient and original sources, weaving their own voices into the texts they are reading. Jabès offers this beautiful image:

> To be in the book. To figure in the book of questions, to be part of it. To be responsible for a word or a sentence, a stanza or a chapter.

13. *Seder Eliyahu Zuta*, ch. 2, cited in Holtz, *Back to the Sources*, 28.
14. Ricoeur, *Hermeneutics and the Human Sciences*, 142.
15. Bosker and Bosker, "Introduction," in *The Talmud*, 11.
16. Goldenberg, "Talmud," in Holtz, *Back to the Sources*, 156.
17. *Pirkei Avos (Ethics of the Fathers)*, 5:26.

> To be able to say: "I am in the book. The book is my world, my country, my roof, and my riddle. The book is my breath and my rest."
>
> I get up with the page that is turned. I lie down with the page put down. To be able to reply: "I belong to the race of words, which homes are built with"—when I know full well that this answer is still another question, that this home is constantly threatened.
>
> I will evoke the book and provoke the questions.[18]

In speaking of "the book," Jabès is evoking a deeply felt sense of belonging to a tradition to which his own life is inexorably bound. He realizes that he is part of the Jewish story and the Jewish experience, that he lives within its pages, that he is "in the book." It is a place of belonging—"my roof" and "my rest"—yet it is also a place of questioning and being questioned.

The metaphor of the book is particularly interesting when we consider that a book can actually mean two things to us—it can mean *something that we read* and it can mean *something that we write*. Indeed, Jabès suggests that the book is always both:

> "What book do you mean?"
> "I mean the book within the book."
> "Is there another book hidden in what I read?"
> "The book you are writing."[19]

Though seemingly enigmatic, Jabès is referring to the unique ability of the Jewish tradition to speak of the book as both something that we *read* and something that we *write*, and that these two approaches are intimately related. Both approaches to the book are essential to the life and vitality of tradition—to "take it and read it," and "to write it and prolong it." Indeed, it is impossible for the rabbis to read the pages of tradition without at the same time writing their own commentary. Hidden within the story they are reading is the story they are writing. It is the very reading of the book that generates the creativity of interpretation and commentary, such that we can say, paradoxically, that the book is indeed both something that we read *and* something that we write. "Revelation is this continual process of hermeneutics," Levinas says, "discovering new landscapes in the written or oral word, uncovering problems and truths locked within each other" (*LR*, 199).

In *The People of the Book*, Samuel Heilman provides a rich account of the time-honored Jewish practice of *lernen*, "the eternal review and

---

18. Jabès, *Book of Questions*, 1:31.
19. Ibid., 291. Jabès attributes this to Reb Haod.

Part Two—The Talmudic Ocean

ritualized study of sacred Jewish texts."[20] Heilman describes the Talmudic study circle (*shiur*) as a place of communal, interactional drama through which *lerners* play the game of interpretation, taking their cue from the Talmud, which itself is a book of interacting, circling commentaries in the ever-expanding margins of the book:

> Both literally and in effect, the page is framed by commentaries: Rashi on the inside margin, his successors the Tosafists on the outside . . . They in turn may be reframed by later commentaries which have been added to the outer margins of the page . . . With each new edition of the Talmud, the publishers may add more commentaries or new appendices—new keys.
>
> . . . As the folio of Talmud is characterized by commentary, replies, responsa, questioning, debate, information exchange, digression, narrative, and repeated recountings, so the *shiur* is marked by keys of all of these . . . The conversations during *lernen* are always something different from the written page, patterned by it but not exactly the same . . .
>
> So complicated does the process—the *lernen* game—become that without a tape recording by means of which a transcript of the proceedings could be put together, one would have trouble determining where the written page leaves off and oral commentary and reframing begins.[21]

Commentaries are juxtaposed with commentaries, weaving together the very life of the work. "We have, therefore, alongside the written Torah, an oral Torah whose authority is at least as equal," Levinas says (*NTR*, 197). "Commentary is the life of a text. If a text is alive today, it is because we comment on it" (*IRB*, 163).

I sense that something in my own Catholic tradition shares the spirit of this vibrant interpretive activity. I recently came across this rather lively image of St. Thomas Aquinas:

> One imagines his study filled with books. As Thomas writes (or dictates) each article of the *Summa* one can see Scripture at his right hand, Augustine's great corpus at his left, Aristotle's philosophy on a table nearby, the works of the Fathers piled up on the floor, and the questions and perplexities of the monks he taught and lived with written on scraps of parchment and arranged in the order of topics as he would tackle them. One sees secretaries

---

20. Heilman, *People of the Book*, 1.
21. Ibid., 124–25.

scurrying to find the precise wording of the citations he has requested, and copyists awaiting the finished manuscript. And one can hear the clucking of those who criticized the new synthesis of truth and knowledge as it appeared.[22]

In some ways, there is a kinship between this interpretive activity of Aquinas and the interpretive activity of the rabbis. Aquinas has the Scriptures "at his right hand." They represent his primary text, the normative story. Yet he is also relying on past commentary, and so he has Augustine's work at his left hand. Augustine's "great corpus" has now become part of the story, and so too have all the commentaries of the Fathers, "piled up on the floor" beneath him. In other words, like the Talmudic page described above, Aquinas' work is "framed by commentaries" that have become authoritative texts themselves, incorporated into the very heart of the tradition.

However, Aquinas isn't simply "rehashing" these texts. Rather, he himself is offering a new commentary. "On a table nearby" is the philosophy of Aristotle. "On a table nearby" suggests perhaps that while Aristotle's work is proximate to Aquinas' new interpretive venture, the works of Aristotle are nevertheless a "strange" or "new" voice that have not yet gained the same credibility or authority as Aquinas' other sources. Aquinas is crafting his commentary by creatively playing with "the old" and "the new"—with the Scriptures, Augustine, and the Fathers all around him, but also with Aristotle, that "pagan philosopher," daringly positioned "on a table nearby."

Lastly, we should notice that all of this is taking place amidst "scraps of parchment" that represent the urgent questions and concerns of the monks Aquinas is teaching and living with. All these pressing and unanswered questions are crucial to his interpretive work. They are central in forming and shaping the new commentary he is crafting—a commentary that will, as we now know, outlive him and become itself a new and enduring voice in the pages of tradition.

Aquinas, who is now considered one of the great doctors of the church, was initially engaged, much like the rabbis, in the practice of commentary and interpretation "in the margins of tradition." It is in the margins of commentary and interpretation that the book either spills its borders to enlarge and expand itself or shrinks into virtual nonexistence through lack of provocation, questioning, commentary. It is in the margins that the book will become either a book of great size or a book of little measure. The success of the book depends largely on whether its margins

---

22. Charry, *By the Renewing of Your Minds*, 185–86.

are filled with commentary, question, and response—in other words, how much it provokes interpretive reading and writing among communities of interpretation.[23]

Halakhah and Aggadah

Halakhah (which can be translated as "law" or, even better, "the path" or "the way") is concerned with ethical living that requires study and practice. Central to Judaism's way of life are the *mitzvot*—the commandments of God and people's response to the divine call by way of action. As Levinas notes, Jewish revelation is based on "prescription" or "commandment" which binds the Jewish people—not as a doctrinal unity, but rather as the requirement to study and to practice God's ways. "The unity of Judaism depends on the Law, which is never experienced as some kind of stigma or mark of enslavement" (*LR*, 200). Levinas notes that the pages of the Talmud represent "intellectual struggle and courageous opening unto even the most irritating questions . . . It is important to bring them back to their life of dialogue or polemic in which multiple, though not arbitrary, meanings arise and buzz in each saying . . . These Talmudic pages seek contradiction and expect of a reader freedom, invention, and boldness" (*NTR*, 4–5).

Commenting on Levinas' Talmudic readings, Jacques Rolland writes, "There is no difference between the magnitude of the problems posed by the Talmud and the magnitude of the problems posed by philosophy. And the intellectual rigor in each field is exactly the same."[24]

In the Christian tradition, the Nicene and Apostles' Creeds begin with "We believe" or "I believe." The Jewish tradition, however, begins with "we will do." Levinas notes that Jewish revelation lacks the doctrinal authority of a Credo and cites the famous verse from Exodus 24:7: "All that the Lord has spoken we will do and we will be obedient (listen to it)" (*LR*, 206). Jewish tradition is shaped by commandment and response, rather than belief and assent. It gives priority to the question, "What must I do?" or "What is required of me?" rather than "What should I believe?" or "What should I know?"

The priority of the performed deed, of response, of giving an answer with my life, lies at the core of Judaism. Abraham Heschel refers to Judaism

---

23. Veling, *Living in the Margins*.
24. Malka, *Emmanuel Levinas*, 160 (citing Jacques Rolland).

as a "science of deeds."[25] He writes, "Here is a basic difference between the Greek and the biblical conception of man. To the Greek mind, man is above all a rational being; rationality makes him compatible with the cosmos. To the biblical mind, man is above all a commanded being, a being of whom demands are made. The central problem is not: What is being? But rather: What is required of me?"[26]

If theology is anything, it is first and foremost the word of God addressing our lives. It is first and foremost a *teaching*, a *commandment*, a *revelation*, a *deep well*, an *infinite* word, a *provocation*, an *announcement*, a *saying*, a speaking *to us* and *for us*—for our sake and for our salvation. It is a recognition that we exist within a vast discourse that is prompted by God's attention to humanity, that finds its origin in the first word of the Shema—"Hear!" (Deut 6:4).

Along with the teachings of *halahkah*, the Talmud consists of homiletic teachings, parables, sayings, legends, and biblical exegesis, which are grouped together under the concept of *aggadah*. These passages are often more accessible, yet as Levinas notes, they are by no means undemanding and display "an extreme attention to the Real" (*NTR*, 5).

Many of the rabbinic and gospel parables suggest that the Torah or God's word is more concerned with what we do and how we live than with what we know or what we believe. The following two parables (the first from the rabbinic tradition, the second from the gospels) serve as examples:

> A person who knows a great deal but does not do very much—what is this person like? To a tree with many branches but only a few roots: the wind will come and pluck it up and turn it over onto its face. But the person who does many good deeds, even without knowing a great deal—what is this person like? To a tree with few branches but many roots: all the winds in the world cannot move it from its place. (*Pirkei Avos, Ethics of the Fathers*, 3:22)

> Everyone who listens to these words of mine and acts on them will be like a sensible man who built his house on rock. Rain came down, floods rose, gales blew and hurled themselves against that house, and it did not fall: it was founded on rock. But everyone who listens to these words of mine and does not act on them will be like a stupid man who built his house on sand. Rain came down, floods rose, gales blew and struck that house, and it fell; and what a fall it had! (Matt 7:24–27)

25. Heschel, *God in Search of Man*, 281.
26. Heschel, *Who Is Man?*, 107

These two parables suggest that simply "hearing" or "knowing" is not enough. It is not our knowledge or our beliefs on their own that anchor our lives, which can all too easily be swept away and collapse if they are not rooted or founded in commitment and action. It is our deeds that offer the deepest roots, our actions that provide the true foundation—not simply our knowing.

The Talmud represents the creative interplay that results when a community reads-prays-studies-interprets their faith tradition in dialogue with an equally attentive reading of the events-needs-questions-concerns of their own current reality. The Jewish tradition preserves the link between the "house of study" (*bet ha-midrash*) and the "house of prayer" (*bet ha-tefillah*). According to the rabbis, the essential marks of the house of prayer and study are devotion to Scripture and its Talmudic interpretation, devotion to prayer and to God's Name, and devotion to our fellow human beings. "You need these all year," suggests one of the sages, "but never more than now." And again, "You are not required to complete the task, yet neither are you free to withdraw from it."[27]

2. Beyond History: The "Harmonics" of Talmud

Salomon Malka notes that Levinas learned from Chouchani the refusal to ever see in the Talmudic or biblical text an archaism or anachronism.[28] Levinas "was not preoccupied with the viewpoint of historians or philologists, or with the age in which these texts were written. It was enough for him to have found an intelligence, a subtlety, a spirituality."[29] In Levinas' view, there is a "miracle of confluence" in the Bible and the Talmud that creates an interpretive resonance across seemingly disparate texts. "Ideas worthy of their name rise above their own history, royally indifferent even to their historians" (*TN*, 3–4). Whereas the philological or historical reader tends to see the Bible as a collection of disparate books, such that each book is set within its own historical period, Levinas argues that the Talmudic tradition confers a unity on the texts in which all the sources can work together. They are not necessarily limited or reduced to their historical context. "The history of each piece of writing is less important than the lessons it contains," Levinas says, "and its inspiration is measured

27. *Pirkei Avos* (*Ethics of the Fathers*), 2:21.
28. Malka, *Emmanuel Levinas*, 126.
29. Ibid., 130.

in terms of what it has inspired" (*LR*, 198). He continues: "Tradition is the expression, perhaps, of a way of life thousands of years old, which conferred unity upon a collection of texts, however disparate historians say they were in their origins. The miracle of this confluence is as great as the miracle of the common origin attributed to the texts—and it is the miracle of that life" (*LR*, 197–98).

Levinas gives little credence to the rise of modern historical-critical methods of exegesis. He refers to himself as "post-critical" (*OS*, 131). "No one can refuse the insights of history. But we do not think they are sufficient for everything" (*NTR*, 5). In a rhetorical flush, he asks, "Did audiences in Shakespeare's theatre spend their time showing off their critical sense by pointing out that there were only wooden boards where the stage sign indicated a palace or a forest?" (*NTR*, 5). The historical-critical method impoverishes the rich, symbolic resonance of a text by reducing it to a bland, historical circumstance of a certain period or era. "We are in less of a hurry than the historians and philologists to deconstruct the traditional landscape of the text, which for more than a millennium sheltered the soul of Judaism," says Levinas (*NTR*, 92).

The human heart is always deeply involved and engaged in the art of interpretation, such that anyone who truly encounters a sacred or poetic text—especially one that involves a teaching—knows that little of its beauty or truth can be discovered by detached, methodological or historical analysis alone. Truth's beauty and goodness is essentially creative in its expression and therefore needs an equally creative reception. Method offers us only a sense of "controlled" meaning, whereas the poetic or revelatory word knows nothing of this cool and detached approach. Rather, what is required is a deeply felt movement of the heart—a *resonance* that responds rather than a method that controls. The art of interpretation is intimately tied to the art of creativity, and this is as it should be, for the creativity of a work necessarily calls forth the creativity of the interpreter.

Levinas notes that the meanings taught by Talmudic texts are drawn from the deeply symbolic well of Scripture, filled with signs, stories, and teachings. "Despite the variations of sense that the elements of this signifying inventory might have undergone throughout the ages, despite the contingency of the circumstances in which these signs are inscribed and from which they received their power of suggestion, we do not think that a purely historical approach suffices to clarify this symbolism" (*NTR*, 6).

Part Two—The Talmudic Ocean

We moderns often favor an interpretive stance of historical-critical distance, rather than an interpretive approach of personal-communal engagement. What is lost to us is an appreciation of tradition as a deep font of *interpretive resonance*. If resonance (or "harmonics") with a work is crucial to the art of interpretation, then surely much is to be gained from the wisdom of past generations who have learned, over the years, to *attune* their hearts to the essential contours of a work.[30] Levinas refers to tradition as "ancient newness" and asks, "Must not tradition be seen in this case, not as guaranteeing the purity of the sources and fidelity of transmission, but as a 'place' wherein all the harmonics of the *said* resonate, wherein an entire life is breathed into the letters of the text, inspiring it?" (*OS*, 127).

The nineteenth and twentieth centuries were filled with the spirit and the fervor of historical consciousness. Samuel Moyn notes that Levinas was never entirely comfortable with this heightened sense of historical consciousness: "As the foe and former student of Heidegger, in whose work the historicism of the nineteenth century climaxed, Levinas insisted on the viability of counter-historicism."[31] "Ism" is probably the correct suffix. Levinas was not against time and temporality and the conditions of living "on earth," yet he was against the "ism" of history, historicism—an "ism" that marked the age of enlightened intellectualism, namely, that all things can be reduced to the circumstances and conditioning factors of history. In exasperation he writes, "Must one not admit that the presence of the Bible within the pluri-dimensional space opened up by its verses, interpreted in keeping with the pluralism claimed for the Word of God, distances it from the Old Testament as torn to pieces by historians who, in the process, have torn one another to pieces? The vessel of Scripture, afloat in the immense ocean of rabbinical dialectic, can hardly be endangered by the squalls of a few philologists who do not even know the vessel's draught" (*OS*, 130).

Levinas bemoans the fact that the nineteenth century "wore itself out with the philology of Judaism." For over a hundred years, historical-critical methods were preoccupied with efforts to shine a light on the text, whereas all the time it was the text that sought to shine its light on us, the readers. "The philologist who subjects texts to a critical apparatus . . . becomes more intelligent than his object." All this historical-critical work—"What a graveyard!" Levinas exclaims (*DF*, 268).

---

30. This is a key theme in Gadamer's masterwork on hermeneutics, *Truth and Method*.
31. Moyn, "Emmanuel Levinas' Talmudic Readings," 25.

The Talmudic Ocean

In his Talmudic reading titled "Model of the West," Levinas chides the idea of history as simply a succession of relativized "moments" or historical events: "The West professes the historical relativity of values and their questioning, but perhaps it takes every moment too seriously, calls them all historical too quickly, and leaves this history the right both to judge the values and to sink into relativity. Hence the incessant re-evaluation of values, an incessant collapse of values, an incessant genealogy of morals. A history without permanence and without holiness" (*BV*, 21).

If it were only history that determined the place and relevance of Jewish thought, Levinas suggests, then Judaism would simply be reduced to "folklore" or "anecdotes" or "little local histories" and, as such, "would not be worth continuing" (*DF*, 68). Moyn comments, "A conventional image of Judaism casts it as a deeply historical faith. But Levinas explained, in introducing his Talmudic methodology, that Judaism is important only insofar as it is separable from the irrelevancies of history."[32] The tradition is worth continuing only because the words of the Jewish sages "fix categories and intellectual structures that are absolute in thought, even if these truths were determined by circumstances, conflicts, and polemics long since forgotten" (*DF*, 68). Rather than let history be the great judge and determiner of Jewish texts, it is rather the opposite. Judaism is the refusal to allow the authority of history to be the all-powerful determinant of truth and value. It is the deep well of tradition, rather than the shallow pools of historical-critical method, that allows access to the meaning of a revelatory text and that preserves the text over time. "Herein, no doubt, lies the originality of Judaism," Levinas says, "the existence of a tradition, uninterrupted through the very transmission and commentary of the Talmudic texts, commentaries overlapping commentaries" (*NTR*, 6–7).

In her introduction to Levinas' Talmudic readings, Annette Aronowicz notes that Levinas is not suggesting that the Talmud somehow floats above history, unaffected. Rather, the eternity and universality of the Talmudic text means "it can time and again illuminate varying historical contexts." In this sense, "to be timeless is thus an infinite capacity to enter history" (*NTR*, xxiv). Nevertheless, the text does not simply accommodate itself to present historical conditions. Aronowicz highlights this significant point, namely, the Talmudic sources judge history, rather than history judging the sources: "Levinas insists that it is this very willingness to be judged by these sources that has maintained the Jews as the eternal people. It is eternal in that it has

---

32. Ibid., 32.

not allowed the judgment of history, the judgment of the powers-that-be, to determine the truth or reality of a situation" (*NTR*, xxvi).

3. Memory and Association

Each of us lives in the world of memory and association much more than we think. Memory is the thread that weaves our life into a "whole," such that we are more than passing and transient moments of instantaneous time.

Think, for example, of all those times when a piece of music evokes deep associations with earlier events in your life, or a particular perfume or scent takes you back to another time and another place. Or the way that, when you are lost in thought, unexpected associations suddenly occur—such that the line of a verse comes to mind, or the fragment of a dream reappears, or something you once learned suddenly comes back to you.

Our past functions in human discourse much as it functions in our personal lives—it is our living memory. Imagine, for example, what your life would be like without memory. You would have no sense of who you are because you would have no sense of the important events, people, and connections that have shaped your life. Deprived of memory, you would simply exist in the present, but you would have no way of understanding that present, because it would be divorced from the rich fabric of connection and meaning that memory provides you.

Even a casual reflection upon our lives will reveal how much of our "past" accompanies and shapes our present. Our past is not simply that which has been and is now gone; rather, it is present to us in shaping our current responses to life. Similarly, our future is not simply a vacant "not yet" that is always deferred; rather, it too shapes our present reality by drawing us to pursue innovative and fresh possibilities of life inherent in any given situation. Our lives are both "memory-laden" and "future-expectant."

Similarly, religious tradition serves as a reminder that there is more to my life than can be construed from the present alone. It hints or points to a memory that exceeds the simple renderings of present reality. This memory "stretches back" to a time that is not purely contemporaneous with the "current time." Rather, it holds the current time answerable to a longer view, a deeper trajectory, a wider frame of reference.

We sometimes think of tradition as tired and worn, old and dusty, but it is first and foremost a *gift*. Among other things, it is the gift of memory—a memory that is older and larger than my life. Tradition is not of my own

The Talmudic Ocean

making. It is not generated by my own resources alone. Rather, it is *given* to me. In this sense, it exists prior to my arrival on the scene. It is already "written" or inscribed, and it is given to me to read, to respond, to interpret, to listen to its voice. Tradition calls out from a deep memory, not to celebrate nostalgia or comforting doctrines, nor to enshrine some truth in a timeless vault. It is no quaint or comforting reminiscence; rather, it is the memory of a passionate people with deeply spiritual longings and burning hearts.

"The proximity of God is experienced in Judaism through memory," Levinas says. "It is a sensibility in which the past plays a central role in the Jewish psyche, to the point of resonating with, and telling itself in, the actuality of every lived present. A consciousness that is immediately narration, an interiority in which some story stirs, giving the present its meaning" (*TN*, 65–66).

Such is the way the rabbis view Talmudic tradition. It is full of memory and rich in allusions and associations—like a symbolic well, deeply drawn. The text is full of meaning such that one word—or even one letter—can evoke intimate associations with other words and other letters. "There is not one verse, not one word, of the Old Testament," Levinas writes, "that does not open up an entire world, unsuspected at first, in which the text to be read is embedded." He goes on to note that "Rabbi Akiba used to interpret even the decorations on the letters of the Holy text . . . as if the letters were the folded wings of the Holy Spirit" (*LR*, 194). A word, a verse, a letter—all these are potential recollections, pointing to other times and other places in the textual tradition, in the vast "Talmudic ocean."

According to Levinas, Talmudic interpretation seeks "to make the harmonics of a particular verse resound with other verses" (*LR*, 197). He writes, "When the biblical text refers to another biblical text—even if the reference is arbitrary—one must read carefully the quoted passage . . . At issue here is the association of one biblical 'landscape' with another, in order to extract, through this pairing, the secret of the first" (*NTR*, 55).

For example, in one of his Talmudic readings, Levinas discusses a text about the law and justice and notes that one of the images the rabbis draw upon is a "hedge of roses." The Torah is like a "hedge of roses"—the thinnest of barriers—yet it separates us from evil: "Judaism conceives the humanity of man as capable of a culture which preserves him from evil by separating him from it by a simple barrier of roses" (*NTR*, 81). Where does the image of a "hedge of roses" come from? It comes from the rabbinic memory of the

Song of Songs, which speaks of "a hedge of lilies" (7:2). And so the rabbis create the wonderful association of the Law, not as a stricture or constraint, but as a beautiful hedge of lilies. It is not, Levinas notes, "the unbearable yoke of the Law, which frightened St. Paul, but a hedge of roses. The obligation to follow the commandments—the *mitzvot*—is not a curse for us. It brings us the first scents of paradise" (*NTR*, 82). The boundaries of God's Law are not harsh or strict; rather, they are as soft as lilies. The Law's ethical teachings are "a hedge of flowers bordering a garden path—cultivated for the beauty they impart to a way of life cherished for its lovely blossoms and sweet fruit."[33] The Torah is a law of life that is rich in the sweet fruits of kindness, love, and mercy. "God's law *is* mercy," Abraham Heschel says, and "God's mercy *is* law."[34]

Levinas maintains that the Scriptures and the Talmudic commentaries are a "whole" and, as such, the text is "full of meaning." "Everything is in it," the rabbis say. And like memory, it continually evokes new significances and rich associations, such that we can "turn it and turn it" and never exhaust its depths of resonance. "Just as the strings of the violin are stretched across its wood, so is the text stretched across all the amplifications brought by tradition" (*LR*, 198).

Tradition preserves the vital work of Scripture. Its task consists in finding the resonance or reverberation of God's original word, such that this word can resound with new voice and fresh meanings. Tradition searches for the ways of the original, the contours of the original, so that something of the original is revealed and claims our attention. Martin Buber, for example, writes, "It is characteristic of the great imperishable sayings of religious teaching that they are bound to situations . . . But once this original word has entered into the memory and tradition of other generations, each generation fashions out of that word the counsel and encouragement, the exhortation and comfort, it has need of in the new conditions of its existence. The original saying proves to be able to bestow manifold gifts far beyond its initial intention, gifts for manifold situations in historical and personal life."[35]

Rather than a mere reproduction, tradition is engaged in the unique and revelatory claims of God's original word. It is never a pure reflection or

---

33. *Song of Songs Rabbah* 7:3.2, cited in Goodman, *Love Thy Neighbor as Thyself*, 65–66.

34. Heschel, *Man Is Not Alone*, 118.

35. Buber, *Pointing the Way*, 208.

The Talmudic Ocean

mirror image of the original. It knows that its relationship with the original is never one of pure correspondence, as though "being the same" were the only or ultimate goal; rather, tradition shines a new light on the original word, revealing its diamondlike qualities.

The "given" text (Written Torah) is at the same time an infinitely open text (Oral Torah). The renowned commentator Gershom Scholem writes of the Jewish interpretive experience, "It is precisely the wealth of contradictions, of differing views, which is encompassed and unqualifiedly affirmed by tradition... In other words, not *system* but *commentary* is the legitimate form through which truth is approached."[36]

According to David Stern, the rabbinic tradition displays an almost total lack of interest in developing a systematic account of its various beliefs. This absence of a systematic theology is not a failure of rabbinic Judaism, however, but one of its greatest virtues. It preserves tradition against the fixing of meaning and replaces mastery and control over tradition with openness to new meanings and insight.[37] The rabbis celebrate and take pleasure in interpreting Torah's multiple meanings because they connect "the infinity of God's being with the infinity of meanings to be found in Torah."[38] This is especially true in the Jewish mystical tradition of Kabbalah, where multiple, paradoxical and pluralistic interpretations are seen as an essential consequence of unravelling Revelation's infinite meanings. Since the source of Revelation is a Name unbound by any one meaning, each word of the Torah can be interpreted in an infinite number of ways. Indeed, the Talmud speaks of the great delight God takes in the interpretive dialogue of the rabbis. At the conclusion of a famous debate among the sages, we are told,

> You have leave to interpret according to your will, and by your will all the worlds will be conducted. Do not think that God feels woe at this sense of being "defeated"; on the contrary, it is a source of pleasure and joy to God. Thus the Rabbis said: "What was God doing? Smiling and saying, 'My children have defeated me.'"[39]

While acknowledging the interpretive genius of the rabbis, Stern nevertheless makes the important point that their unique ability to generate

---

36. Scholem, "Tradition and Commentary as Religious Categories in Judaism," 27.
37. Stern, "Midrash and Indeterminacy," 146.
38. Ibid., 151.
39. Rabbi Levi Yizhak, *Kedushat Levi* (citing *Bava Metzia* 59b), in Holtz, *Back to the Sources*, 384. Levinas comments on this famous apologue in "Revelation in the Jewish Tradition," *LR*, 204–5.

and live with a multiplicity of interpretations actually represents a claim to stability rather than its opposite, namely, an indeterminate state of endlessly deferred meanings. Talmudic commentary represents a world in which divergence, difference, and dispute can be held together in the larger context of harmony and textual stability; all these interpretations can actually stand together and exist side by side as guaranteed by the divine authorship of Torah.[40]

"Without any need for a magisterium," Levinas writes, "or an authority in doctrinal matters, the 'subjective' interpretations of the Jewish Revelation have managed to maintain, in this people, the consciousness of the unity, despite their geographical dispersion" (*LR*, 196). What guards against merely subjective or relativistic meanings? "This is provided by the necessity of referring subjective findings to the continuity of readings through the tradition of commentaries" (*LR*, 196). While each person and each generation must necessarily undertake their own reading and their own appropriation of the Scriptures, they are nevertheless subjected to "the lessons of everyone else." For Levinas, the prism of tradition is indispensable: "Hence the way that readings continually refer to origins across history going from pupil to master; hence the discussion in gatherings between colleagues questioning one another from century to century, the whole thing integrating itself as tradition . . . that is both erudite and modern. Hence the commentaries of commentaries, the very structure of the Torah, reflected even in the typographical feature of the Tractates overladen on all sides and all margins" (*BV*, xiii).

4. Spirit-Letter

Prior to the rise of historical-critical approaches, early theologies of Scripture assumed that Scripture "speaks as a whole," such that any "seeming inconsistencies between the different books may be due to our lack of understanding, or they may even be intended to stimulate our minds to greater effort. But scripture agrees with itself."[41] There was no "biblical studies" distinct and separate from "systematic theology," as is sadly the case in Christian approaches today.

---

40. Stern, "Midrash and Indeterminacy," 153–56.
41. Ayres, "Patristic and Medieval Theologies of Scripture," in Holcomb, *Christian Theologies of Scripture*, 16.

The Talmudic Ocean

In the Middle Ages, Jews and Christians elaborated a fourfold method for interpreting Scripture.[42] The Jewish tradition referred to PaRDeS—an acronym for *Peshat*, the literal or "plain-sense" meaning; *Remez*, the symbolic or allegorical meaning; *Derash*, the metaphorical or moral meaning; and *Sod*, the mystical or transcendent meaning. The word *pardes* itself means "orchard" or "paradise," and the four interpretive approaches were seen as a way of tilling the "garden of Torah" (*BV*, 101).

In some ways, our modern historical-critical approaches are similar to the quest for the plain-sense meaning of scriptural texts—that is, before we engage in any interpretive flights of fancy, let's first seek the original or historical or plain-sense meaning of the text. However, as Abraham Heschel has masterfully shown in his *Heavenly Torah*, the rabbinic tradition never rested easily on adopting a plain-sense approach to scriptural interpretation alone. Of the four hermeneutical approaches, the primary dilemma and debate generally came down to a tussle between those who advocated the plain-sense approach (*peshat*) and those who advocated the metaphorical or figurative approach (*derash*).[43] Heschel explains the dilemma this way: "The life of man is embodied in earthly concerns, but his soul opens somewhat to heavenly matters. He is therefore obliged to speak in two tongues, one entirely earthly, the other entirely heavenly. He must, perforce, use two types of idiom. Moreover, he must search for the place where heaven and earth embrace. Language is a ladder set on earth whose head reaches heaven—it is both all earthly and all heavenly" (234).

The two "idioms" to which Heschel refers are the plain sense ("earthly") and the figurative or mystical sense ("heavenly"). The advocates of the plain-sense approach appeal to the verse "It is not in heaven" (Deut 30:12). Secret meanings are not our preserve; they belong to heaven. Our concern should be only that which has been revealed in the text, and dabbling in hidden or secret meanings is vanity. The advocates of the figurative sense counter with: "Woe to them that have made the Torah such a parched land because they have banned the study of wisdom and mystical sense, causing

---

42. Fishbane, *Garments of Torah*, 112–20; Greenstein, "Medieval Bible Commentaries," in Holtz, *Back to the Sources*, 213–61; Ouaknin, *Burnt Book*, 65–69; Scholem, *Kabbalah*, 172ff.; de Lubac, *Medieval Exegesis*.

43. The two key proponents of this debate are Rabbi Akiva and Rabbi Ishmael, who were contemporaries in the second century CE. Ishmael argued for the plain-sense approach and Akiva for the figurative approach. On the ever-present tension between these two approaches, see Heschel, *Heavenly Torah*. Subsequent references to this text are provided in parentheses.

Part Two—The Talmudic Ocean

the flow of wisdom to cease" (257). In other words, a Torah without interpretation, without *derash* and the seeking of new meanings, is simply a parched and shrivelled text.

It is important to note that, as Heschel reminds us, the plain-sense approach to interpreting Scripture is not identical with a "literalist" approach. For example, the plain meaning may indeed be a metaphorical or symbolic meaning and not literal at all. "Do not think that the task of the plain-sense interpreters was simple!" Heschel exclaims. Rather, "we must ponder the nuance of language in each text. Some texts speak precisely, others poetically. The rule that a verse may not depart from its plain-sense meaning applies to both types!" (254). In other words, no symbolic meaning can be found except through the "plain" or literal text—the letters, the words, the signs—and yet, no text ever simply points to itself; it always escapes its plain meaning in a surprising "surplus of meaning" (*BV*, 109).

The plain sense (*peshat*) anchors the text like the roots of a tree. The metaphorical sense (*derash*) opens the text like the branches, spreading into multifarious meanings. Thus, these two approaches need not be in opposition. The letters are given. The text is written. Here it is, in front of you now—"It is not in heaven." Rather, "the Torah speaks in human language" (49). It is "a work of human hands," one might say. And yet, this plain-sense letter of the text requires us to "search out" and "to inquire"—*derash*, from which the Hebrew word for *midrash* is derived. Heschel notes the Talmudic rule that states, "A scriptural text may not lose its literal meaning. However, it does not say that the text has *only* one meaning" (253). Or again: "The entire Torah may be compared to a living human being: its body is nourished by words that are explicit, but its soul is nourished by ideas that are embedded in the words, invisible to the naked eye" (256). Even the great mystical interpreters of the text, the kabbalists, "did not quarrel with those who insisted on the plain meaning of a text; their quarrel was with those who maintained that the Torah teaches nothing beyond the plain meaning" (256). The primary text of Kabbalah, the *Zohar*, puts it this way: "The Torah [is] dressed with human narratives. These narratives are the garments of the Torah . . . Foolish people pay attention only to the externals and disregard what is behind it. Those who are more perceptive do not look at the clothes, but at the substance within the garment" (256).

In his volume of Talmudic lectures, *Beyond the Verse*, Levinas begins by asking the obvious question, "Why beyond the verse?" Levinas' answer: "Because the strict contours of the verses outlined in the Holy Scriptures have a plain meaning which is also enigmatic" (*BV*, x). He goes on to say

The Talmudic Ocean

that it is *in* and *beyond* the "plain meaning" that the inexhaustible "surplus of meaning" arises, that while the "Torah speaks in the language of men" (that is, in the letter, in the verse, in the finite), it also speaks "the more" or the "beyond" of God's infinite word: "The great thought behind this principle consists in admitting that the Word of God can be maintained in the spoken language used by created beings amongst themselves. The marvellous contraction of the Infinite, the 'more' inhabiting the 'less,' the Infinite in the Finite . . ." (*BV*, x).

What is given in the "plain sense"—as "the plain language of men"—is given "on earth," that is, concretely, in human relations, here among us; and yet, what is given "on earth" also contains the seeds of heaven. "Signifying beyond their plain meaning, they invite the exegesis—be it straightforward or torturous, but by no means frivolous—that is spiritual life" (*BV*, xi). The literal, the plain, the letter—these also contain the mystical, the spiritual, the symbolic. In Christian language, one might be tempted to say that the incarnate word also expresses or reveals the transcendent word. The finite, "the less," also contains the infinite, "the more." Thus the finite is to be treasured as the honored place where the infinite comes to pass. According to Heschel, "Whatever exists on high exists on earth" (259). Indeed, the "heavenly realm" arose at the "earthly time" of creation, such that the heavenly realm is inextricably linked with the creation of the world. "The boundary of heaven and earth is permeable," Heschel says (260).

According to Levinas, this is the way that symbol works, or the way that symbol is efficacious: "Sacred signs, sacred letters, sacred scriptures. Never does the meaning of these symbols fully dismiss the materiality of the symbols which suggest it. They always preserve some unexpected capacity for renewing this meaning. Never does the spirit dismiss the letter which revealed it. Quite the contrary, the spirit awakens new possibilities of suggestion in the letter" (*NTR*, 8).

Heschel notes that against the "plain sense," Rabbi Akiva says, "what is secreted within the Torah far outweighs what is there on the surface." And yet, Akiva was not against the given letters of the text. Rather, Akiva extracted meaning from "every jot and tittle in the text" because he believed it is "impossible that there be in the Torah a single superfluous word or letter" (47). "Rabbi Simeon ben Eleazar compared Rabbi Akiva's work to that of a stonecutter who was chipping away in a mountain range" (52). Or, to extend the analogy, and citing one of Levinas' favorite verses (attributed to Rabbi Ishmael): "Behold, My word is like a fire—declares the Lord—like a hammer that shatters rock (Jeremiah 23:29)—even as a hammer sends out many sparks, so a text lends itself to many interpretations" (252, citing BT Sanhedrin, 34a).

Heschel notes that there is an infinite quality to the Talmud that is like the ocean. The sages wrote, "There is the sea, vast and wide (Psalm 104:25)—this is the Torah." He suggests that Rabbi Akiva extends the metaphor: "Just as in the case of the sea, the depths greatly exceed the surface, so in the Torah, the latent and the hidden greatly exceed what is apparent on the surface" (52). The Talmud takes on the vastness of a deep ocean. "Its content, as it is perceived only in the narrow confines of the text's plain meaning, is but a drop in the ocean" (55). Similarly, Levinas is fond of noting that the dialectic of the Talmud takes on an "oceanic rhythm" and that rabbinic commentary "causes the waves of the Talmudic sea" (*NTR*, 8; *LR*, 200).

5. The Universal in the Particular

In her introduction to *Nine Talmudic Readings,* Aronowicz notes that each of Levinas' Talmudic readings addresses the following question: "What teachings about the human being do the rabbis convey that cannot be found anywhere else but here, but which apply to the entire world?" (*NTR*, xv).

Levinas does not see an opposition between the universal and the particular. He speaks of finding "the Universal in the unique" (*TN*, xx). "The chief goal of our exegesis," he says, "is to extricate the universal intentions from the apparent particularism" (*NTR*, 5).

Only through entering and engaging "the particular" can we gain a sense of "the whole." As David Tracy suggests, this involves "a journey of intensification into the concreteness of each particular reality—*this* body, *this* people, *this* community, *this* tradition, *this* tree, *this* place, this *moment*, *this* neighbor—until the very concreteness in any particularity releases us to sense the concreteness of the whole as internally related through and through."[44]

In a similar fashion, Levinas writes, "The universal dimension is inaccessible to us unless it passes through a concrete, particular people, for only through the way of life of such concrete particulars does what is true for all human beings shine through. Without this embodiment, the universal dimension runs the risk of evaporating or becoming mere idea" (*NTR*, xxix). The danger with intellectual systems is their tendency to confuse thought

---

44. Tracy, *Analogical Imagination*, 382.

with existence. The speculative thinker forgets that knowledge involves passion, struggle, decision, and personal appropriation—that we must live and act out of our knowing. Former Archbishop of Canterbury Rowan Williams puts it well: "A religious discourse with some chance of being honest will not move too far from the particular, with all its irresolution and resistance to systematizing: it will be trying to give shape to that response to the particular that is least evasive of its solid historical otherness *and* that is also rooted in the conviction that God is to be sought and listened for in all occasions."[45]

Levinas always looks for interpretation of the text in universal ethical terms. The particulars of Jewish tradition are ultimately an intense expression of what is a universal human experience. For example, Levinas notes that "the traumatism of my enslavement in Egypt constitutes my very humanity, that which draws me closer to the problems of the wretched of the earth, to all persecuted people" (*LR*, 202). Or again, when Levinas uses the word *Israel*, he asks us to interpret this as meaning "all of humanity" (*NTR*, 191). Each of us, in our own way, is called and chosen to respond to the suffering of our fellow brothers and sisters, to seek the welfare of each other.

It is not the "humanism" of Western culture that Levinas appeals to. Rather, it is the "humanism of the other person" (*NTR*, 98). As Malka notes, "Levinas devoted all of his spiritual energy, all of his philosophical genius, to providing an entirely universal form to biblical ethics . . . He transcribed in 'Greek' terms (which is to say, scientific and moral, understood by *all* thinking humanity) the altogether particular message of biblical ethics."[46]

The sanctification or hallowing of God's name takes place through the sanctification or hallowing of our own humanity and the relations between us. To hallow God's name is to hallow each other. This mode of thought is central to Levinas' understanding of Judaism. "All that is said of God in Judaism *signifies* through human *praxis*" (*NTR*, 14). Everything *of God* is ultimately concerned with everything *of humanity*. In his book *The Dignity of Difference,* Rabbi Jonathan Sacks offers this reflection on the universal value of religious traditions:

> Economic superpowers, seemingly invincible in their time, have a relatively short life-span . . . The great religions, by contrast, survive . . . The world faiths embody truths unavailable to economics and politics, and they remain salient even when everything else

---

45. Williams, *On Christian Theology,* 6–7.
46. Malka, *Emmanuel Levinas,* xi.

changes. They remind us that civilizations survive not by strength but by how they respond to the weak; not by wealth but by the care they show for the poor; not by power but by their concern for the powerless. The ironic and yet utterly humane lesson of history is that what renders a culture invulnerable is the compassion it shows to the vulnerable. The ultimate value we should be concerned to maximize is human dignity—the dignity of all human beings, equally, as children . . . of God.[47]

6. Obedience and Instruction: Texts that Teach

In his biography of Levinas, Malka includes a chapter where he recalls various accounts of the Saturday morning classes Levinas gave at the school where he taught in the postwar years. The last account begins thus:

> The lesson was very brief. From the beginning, the attendees could sense that he was not feeling well. He remained sitting in front of his open books while coffee was being served nearby in the school cafeteria.
>
> A young girl read out loud clearly, articulating each word, just as he liked. In other circumstances, he would have complimented her warmly. But now, he seemed absent, enfeebled. The class lasted fifteen minutes, then he asked to be excused.

The brief lesson that Levinas gave was a reflection on Rashi's Talmudic commentary. Rashi wonders why a list of descendants from the book of Numbers mentions those of Aaron and not those of Moses:

> Rashi comments: "For what reason are the descendants of Moses not mentioned (and only those of Aaron)? When one teaches the Torah to the sons of one's fellow man, it is as if one had engendered them oneself. The true descendants are students, those whom one has taught."
>
> "You see," says Levinas, "this is why I stayed, to tell you this. That the true filiation in Judaism is giving instruction."[48]

This brief lesson nevertheless seemed important to Levinas. The Jewish tradition survives—or better, is generative—through its teachings and the practices of living and learning together. One of the oldest and most concentrated statements in the Jewish tradition is the Shema, "Hear, O Israel"

---

47. Sacks, *Dignity of Difference*, 195.
48. Malka, *Emmanuel Levinas*, 124.

(*Shema Yisra'el* [Deut 6:4]). It carries no immediate message, except that we listen. Somewhere, way back when, an ancient people realized that their lives were not simply caught in a chain of events, nor less that their lives were simply autonomous and of their own making. Rather, they experienced a prior condition that required of them "to listen"—a condition of *being addressed*.

This condition of being addressed is crucial to Talmudic hermeneutics and, indeed, to hermeneutics generally. The interpretive question—"What is this word saying to me?"—can only be asked if I first acknowledge that I am being addressed. The first act of hermeneutics, therefore, is to listen, to hear the word. Whether it be my encounter with a sacred text, a poem, an artwork, or another person—I sense that something is claiming my attention, and I am drawn to interpret what is being said to me. Whatever meaning I may subsequently discover, its origin is not first *in myself*, but comes originally from *the speaking of another*.

One of the central questions of hermeneutics is, what does it mean to hear a word? To willingly hear a word requires a certain passivity and openness, a willingness to be spoken to, to be addressed. Otherwise, we may as well not listen at all. Moreover, nothing will be heard if it has to fight its way across the clamor of our cluttered minds, filled with so many ready-made opinions and prejudgments. Nothing will be heard if our hearts are hardened and unreceptive.

When we truly listen to a word, we realize that something is being asked of us. Hans-Georg Gadamer calls this "the priority of the question."[49] We hear the word as a question put to our lives. We realize that we didn't know something as well as we thought. We feel something of the limits of our own horizons. There is yet more depth to be discovered, a deeper insight to be lived.

The question, however, is not one that we raise purely out of our own self-reflection. Rather, the question comes to us, is put to us, addresses our lives. Questions are rarely of our own making. Rather, they come to us as provocations that address our lives and invite our response. They are, if you like, out of our control, and that is precisely why a question is a question and not an answer that I already possess, or a certainty that I am already sure of. "The most exciting part" of Talmudic interpretation, Levinas says, "is the explication of a text which poses its questions to you, and where the effort consists in reanimating dissimulated questions" (*IRB*, 80).

---

49. Gadamer, *Truth and Method*, 362–79.

I am all the time put in question, though I typically live out of my already well-formed answers. I know what it means to be a good spouse, a good parent, a good teacher, a good friend, a good neighbor, a good citizen, a good human being. And yet, in all of these contexts, there is a question constantly put to me: Do you really know? Are you that sure? What are you missing or not attending to?

According to Gadamer, the "word" that speaks to me is like a "thou"—it is like another person in my life. It is an awareness that I do not stand alone in the world, that my existence is not solitary; rather, I am all the time exposed to what is other than my own life. To hear a word means listening to another who speaks to me. It means "heeding" a voice that is not my own. It means paying attention to that which addresses my life as a "Thou": "In human relations, the important thing is to experience the 'Thou' truly as 'Thou,' i.e., not to overlook his claim and listen to what he has to say to us. To this end, openness is necessary . . . Without this kind of openness to one another there is no genuine human relationship. Belonging together always also means being able to listen to one another."[50]

According to Levinas, Jewish Revelation is rooted in a "spirituality of obedience" (*LR*, 209). Obedience is listening. The act of listening is crucial. Although it evokes a certain passivity, it is a passivity that seeks to open one's mind and heart to the word of God. It is an attempt to create a clearing for God's word to be heard. It is receptivity and openness—an effort to expose oneself to a word that is *revelatory*, a word that speaks to our lives. Indeed, Levinas notes that "the uniqueness of each act of listening carries the secret of the text" (*LR*, 195). It is perhaps not surprising that many Jewish sages (including Jesus himself) often framed their parables and teachings with a Shema-like phrase, "for those who are listening," for those "who have ears to hear."

Levinas assumes the superiority of the texts before the act of reading. They are "teaching texts" (*DF*, 268). Humility before the text is a prerequisite. "One accepts the Torah before one knows it" (*NTR*, 42). In other words, Levinas gives himself over to the superiority or "height" of the text, trusting in its teaching power, as the very precondition for encountering the text. He does not yield to the text *after* the act of reading, but *before* the act of reading.

We do not stand as masters over the text, or masters over each other, or masters over God, or masters over our own lives. Yet this does not mean

---

50. Ibid., 361.

humiliation. Rather, it is a "heteronomy which does not involve servitude, a receptive ear which still retains its reason, an obedience which does not alienate the person listening" (*LR*, 206).

The Talmud is organized according to the "order of the heart" (*NTR*, xviii). There is a fundamental work at the heart of the biblical and Talmudic tradition that is concerned with "turning our hearts" (*teshuva*) toward the love of God and neighbor. This work is central to Levinas' hermeneutics: "The Torah, a rigorous, divine charter, educates and elevates the *care-for-self* of living beings to the *care-for-the-other* in man" (*TN*, xv). This work is not easily achieved in the human heart. Neither is it easily achieved in human society.

According to Levinas, there is a "mistrust" in the Talmud of "everything that could pass for a piece of information about God's life." God's name, "the most familiar to men," is also "the most obscure and subject to every abuse," especially if God is treated as an object of information. Rather, God's name is best revealed "to the degree that it speaks of the moral experience of human beings." Levinas continues: "God—whatever his ultimate and, in some sense, naked meaning—appears to human consciousness 'clothed' in values, and this clothing is not foreign to his nature or to his supra-nature . . . Religious experience, at least for the Talmud, can only be primarily a moral experience—the values through which the Divine shines forth" (*NTR*, 14–15).

If Levinas is in search of "meanings" or "truths," these are first and foremost ethical meanings—as such, they are more like teachings or commandments or "orders." The Torah "extracts *ethical meaning as the ultimate intelligibility of the human* and even of the cosmic" (*NTR*, 93). To know God's attributes is to know what we are called to do: "'God is merciful', which means: 'Be merciful like Him.' The attributes of God are given not in the indicative, but in the imperative. The knowledge of God comes to us like a commandment, like a *Mitzvah*. To know God is to know what must be done" (*DF*, 17).

Paul Ricoeur suggests that the sacred texts and classic testimonies of a faith tradition are primarily concerned with offering us a "proposed world which I could inhabit," not simply a mirror of the world as it is.[51] He reminds us that the work of interpretation is primarily led by the "proposal of the text." The text is offering a message or a meaning—a proposal—for us to consider. This is what matters to a text. This is its "subject matter." This is

---

51. Ricoeur, *Hermeneutics and the Human Sciences*, 142.

what it is "about"—a "proposed world which I could inhabit"—and this is what interpretation seeks to understand.

In other words, what matters to a text matters little unless it also matters to me. For interpretation to happen at all, the concern of the text must also become my concern. It is only at this point that interpretation comes into play, when I am led to consider what the text is saying as a teaching or a possibility for my own life. All good interpretation is oriented by this futurity—the "proposed world which I could inhabit." Everything of creative interpretation happens *in front of the text* as each new generation—right up to our own generation and our own times—feels that something here matters, and is able to make the matter and concern of the text the matter and concern of their own lives.

If we ask, "Where does interpretation lead?" or "What is its goal?" or "To what end and for what purpose?"—Ricoeur suggests that it is finally concerned with opening the horizons of our hearts and minds toward a new understanding, a new possibility, a new way of living in the world. Revelation is a *saying* to us today, and not simply an already "said." "It is necessary to consider these texts from different epochs *as if they were contemporary*," Levinas says, that is, as if they spoke to us today, and not simply from a bygone era (*LR*, 201, 203).

To interpret or understand a text is not just to understand something back there and back then. Rather, the path of interpretation always stretches out in front of us, such that we are led to consider how our ways in the world could be made different, made new, transformed by a possibility that exceeds the way things are. Interpretation happens when the subject matter of the text (what it is about) becomes the subject matter of our own lives (and what we could also be "about"). Ricoeur writes, "The 'matter of the text' and what I call the world of the work ... is not *behind* the text ... but *in front of* it, as that which the work unfolds, discovers, reveals. Henceforth, to understand is *to understand oneself in front of the text*. It is not a question of imposing upon the text our finite capacity of understanding, but of exposing ourselves to the text and receiving from it an enlarged self..."[52]

Ricoeur goes on to say that in seeking to understand a text, we are not the sole possessors of the "key" to meaning. Rather, it is often the text that possesses the key that unlocks our own narrow worlds and opens our horizons to newer and wider understandings and possibilities. It is the text that is revelatory and inspired and that stirs our imaginations.

---

52. Ibid., 143.

When the text asks us to interpret what it is saying, it is at the same time interpreting our own lives—placing our own lives in question—as if the text were raising interpretive questions of us. This is where the true "rub" of hermeneutics happens. As David Tracy suggests, if "the text is a genuinely classic one, my present horizon of understanding should always be provoked, challenged, transformed. In encountering a classic we are compelled to believe . . . *that something else might be the case than is the case.*"[53]

Levinas recalls a story that Hannah Arendt told just prior to her death. As a child, she said to the rabbi who was teaching her, "You know, I have lost my faith." The rabbi responded, "Who's asking you for it?" Levinas suggests that what matters is not faith alone, but also doing. "What is faith made of? Words, ideas? Convictions? . . . What the rabbi meant was: 'Doing good is the act of belief itself.' That is my conclusion" (*TN*, 148).

7. Application: "I Am Required"

"The Talmud, according to the great masters of this science, can be understood only from the basis of life itself" (*NTR*, 8). Levinas' Talmudic readings were always delivered as a response to some question or concern that the colloquia thought urgent to address. As Aronowicz notes, "Levinas' Talmudic commentaries are themselves soaked in the present historical context . . . But this immersion in the times is the very way to testify to the *etrernity* of the Jewish sources, for it clothes them in actuality, in the present. The Talmudic commentaries are, Levinas tells us, this generation's testimony to the way it has understood its own tradition when it sought from it 'food for thought and a teaching concerning what is fundamental' and, as such, a link to the eternity of the texts" (*NTR*, xxiv).

Malka lists the various themes that were addressed at the Talmudic colloquia between 1957 and 1989: "Timidity and audacity. Morals and politics. Messianism and the end of history. Pardon. Temptation. Israel. Does the world need Jews? Judaism and revolution. Youth of Israel. The Jews and desacralized society. *Shabbat*. War. Muslim community. Religion and politics. Community. The Bible today. Israel, Judaism and Europe. Idolatry. *Zekhor,* memory and history. The seventy nations. Money. The question of the State. Aloofness."[54]

53. Tracy, *Analogical Imagination*, 102.
54. Malka, *Emmanuel Levinas*, 131.

Part Two—The Talmudic Ocean

The Talmud shuns the theoretical and the conceptual "in order to turn fully to everyday life, to matters of human commerce, family relations, birth and death. 'Back to the things themselves!' said the phenomenologists. 'Sublime materialism!' Levinas would say."[55]

Levinas' hermeneutic method is similar to Gadamer's comments on the place of "application" as integral to the hermeneutical process. Application is not an afterthought or postscript that exploits some previously determined meaning for some contemporary purpose. As Levinas notes, the human person is not a mere "receiver of sublime messages" but an active site of revelation, "the one through whom there *is* Revelation" (*LR*, 205).

Hermeneutics is concerned with the event of understanding. For understanding to *happen* at all, it must necessarily have this *eventlike* quality—otherwise, it is not really understanding, but simply something I have *already* known, *already* understood, *already* assimilated. Understanding is an *event*—a *happening*—more than it is something that I already possess. Who among us can say that they have no need for further understanding? Those who say that they "have it" or are "in possession of it" are those who are furthest from it. Yet those who recognize that faith is not *possessing* but *seeking* understanding are those who grow in grace and wisdom. The wise person is "full of understanding" because they continually seek it, unlike those who smugly proclaim their possession of it.

Understanding—if it truly warrants this name—is always a present event, a happening, an occurrence, something that comes to us and suddenly impacts us. In traditional theological language, this event is *revelatory*. I begin to understand something differently, with new eyes, with a changed perspective, with a renewed heart. Or, as Gadamer says, "it is enough to say that we understand in a *different* way, *if we understand at all.*"[56] Moreover, for understanding to truly warrant its name, it must be something that *affects* the way I live. No real understanding takes place unless it touches life in all its concreteness and particularity. The event of understanding can never be separated from the event of *applicacio* ("application") in our current situation. The text, "if it is to be understood properly—i.e., according to the claim it makes—must be understood at every moment, in every concrete situation, in a new and different way. Understanding is always application."[57] A text's meaning is never simply

55. Ibid., 125.
56. Gadamer, *Truth and Method*, 297.
57. Ibid., 309.

given "back then" but only becomes meaningful when its message can be re-stated or re-presented for us today. "Is this not true of every text," writes Gadamer, "that it must be understood in terms of what it says? Does this not mean that it always needs to be restated? And does not this restatement always take place through its being related to the present?"[58] Only when the meaning of a text becomes a concern for us today—affecting our values, our behaviors, our actions, our relationships—only then can we say that the event of understanding is actually underway.

In the Christian tradition, theology is often spoken of as "faith seeking understanding." In the Jewish tradition, this seeking is referred to as *midrash*—to search, to inquire into the meaning of a text. Levinas notes Rashi's expression: "The verses cry out *darshenu*—interpret us!" It is as if each verse of Scripture were saying over and over, "Interpret me!" (*IRB*, 240). Or, if you like, "read me, listen to my words, tell me what I am saying to you." This is a crucial interpretive moment as an imperative given in the present. "What am I saying to you today?" It is this question that lends to the Scriptures (or any classic text) their wonderful open quality. For there are no readers of the Scriptures who can exempt themselves from this question, as though they already knew the meaning, as though they already understood, as though the Scriptures had nothing more to say. A midrashic text states, "The Torah should be so dear to you that each day should be, for you, the very day of the Revelation."[59]

As soon as we hear this demand, "interpret me," our own lives are instantly "brought into play."[60] They come into play because they are put in question by the text, which asks of us, "What am I saying *to you*?" The hermeneutical demand—"interpret me"—clearly places the practice of interpretation in our hands. It is up to us to interpret the meaning of the text. As Levinas says, "The Torah is no longer in heaven; it is given to men; henceforth it is at their disposal" (*LR*, 204, referring to *Baba Mezia* 59b). He also notes that when the text ceases to call for interpretation, or when its call is unheeded, it loses its status: "When the voice of the exegete no longer sounds . . . the texts return to their immobility, becoming once again silent and enigmatic" (*NTR*, 13–14).

In one of Levinas' favorite images, rabbinic commentary is compared to "glowing coals"—"the words of the sages are like glowing embers." Why

---

58. Ibid., 328.
59. Ouaknin, *Burnt Book*, 89 (citing *Tanhuma Midrash*).
60. Gadamer, *Truth and Method*, 299.

embers? Why not a flame? "Because it only becomes a flame when one learns to blow on it." One must blow on the embers so that the flame arises. "The coals light up by being blown on, the glow of the flame that thus comes alive depends on the interpreter's length of breath" (*IRB*, 77; *BV*, 210).

The text does not mean "by itself" but requires the act of the interpreter to bring its meaning to light. "The invitation to seek, to decipher, to the *Midrash*, already marks the reader's participation in the Revelation, in the Scriptures. The reader is, in his own fashion, a scribe" (*LR*, 194). Levinas continues: "This contribution of the readers, listeners and pupils to the open-ended work of the Revelation is essential." Even the "slightest question" put by a novice "constitutes an ineluctable articulation of the Revelation which was heard at Sinai" (*LR*, 195). "The Revelation has a particular way of producing meaning, which lies in its calling upon the unique within me. It is as if a multiplicity of persons . . . were the condition for the plenitude of 'absolute truth,' as if each person, by virtue of his own uniqueness, were able to guarantee the revelation of one unique aspect of the truth, so that some of its facets would never have been revealed if certain people had been absent from mankind" (*LR*, 195).

You who read, you who interpret—you are required: "This constitutes the foundation of the inestimable or absolute value of every self and all receptivity, in this revelation which is non-transferable, like a responsibility, and is incumbent afresh upon every person and every epoch" (*BV*, xiii).

"The Final Overture"

> "Learn to regard words as the sea, for it is their first vocable, just as Adam is our first man," wrote Reb Siami.

". . . it all began by the sea while, from one of the overhanging rocks,
I watched her relax in the sun, play with the rays as with swords, set the dark—
her secrets—against the light—her intoxication.

"It began while I was all eyes and ears for her expressive, heavy silence, her glistening speech, her sporadic onslaught, her outbursts as well as her barely audible confidences.

"On her calm surface, at first a few wrinkles, then suddenly huge holes from which she reared up metamorphosed, hostile to the world and herself, rending herself, spitting out her soul, her liquid body, she seemed to howl: this is what I carry, salt-burned ocean, untamed, mad, these unsuspected, countless words of a different alphabet, too cumbersome, too crowded, and this silence of swallowed skies to whom I owe my infinite variety of color.

"I bent over the sea as over the last page of an unfinished story whose vastness froze my hand in a void and—had I not often done so in love?—
I closed my eyes to melt into her," he had written.

"This is how we learned," said the disciple, "that the universe had entered into the book."

—Edmond Jabès[61]

---

61. Jabès, *Book of Resemblances*, 3:16.

7

"We Will Do and We Will Hear"

During the festival of *Shavuot*, the Jewish people celebrate "the giving of the Torah," calling to mind the dramatic events of Mount Sinai:

> On the morning of the third day there was thunder and lightning, as well as a thick cloud on the mountain, and a blast of a trumpet so loud that all the people who were in the camp trembled. Moses brought the people out of the camp to meet God. They took their stand at the foot of the mountain. Now Mount Sinai was wrapped in smoke, because the Lord had descended upon it in fire; the smoke went up like the smoke of a kiln, while the whole mountain shook violently. (Exod 19:16–18)

The people panic and beg Moses to ascend the mountain and accept the teachings on their behalf. When Moses comes down from the mountain, the people respond, "we will do, and we will obey" (Exod 24:7).

This is a celebrated verse in Jewish tradition, especially because of its strange inversion. "We will do" (*na'aseh*) is followed by "we will obey" (*nishma*), where *nishma* means both "obey" and "hear." Similarly, in Latin, *obedience* comes from the root *audire*, which means "to listen." What could it mean to say "we will do" before saying "we will hear"?

The question of the relationship between hearing and doing can be considered a question concerning the relationship between "theory" and "practice." Normally, we give priority to theory over practice, placing "hearing" before "doing." In the following chart, for example, all the words associated with "to hear" are given primacy over all the words associated

"We Will Do and We Will Hear"

with "to do." We work out our theory before we put it into practice. We think before we act. We engage in reflection and discernment before we respond or make a commitment. The normal ordering is that "we hear" before "we do," and not the other way around.

To hear:	To do:
Theory	Practice
Reflection	Action
Knowing	Doing
Thinking	Applying
Discernment	Commitment
Listening	Responding
Hearing	Answering

The verse "we will do and we will hear" is puzzling because it reverses our normal ordering of the relationship between theory and practice. Placing doing before hearing creates a dissonance within us. How can doing come before hearing? Surely we must first hear or know what we are to do before we can do it? Surely we must first "work it out" (theorize) before we can put it into practice (application)? Surely we must first understand something before we can act on it?

"We will do and will we hear" overturns the primacy we typically give to theory over practice. Levinas cites a well-known passage from the Talmud in which the Israelites are rewarded for doing *before* hearing, for acting even before they have understood, and each Israelite receives two crowns—one for *doing*, the other for *hearing*:

> Rav Simai taught: When the Israelites committed themselves to doing [*na'aseh*—"we will do"] *before* hearing (*nishma*—"we will hear"), 600,000 angels came down and attached two crowns to each Israelite, one for the *doing*, and the other for the *hearing*. (*NTR*, 30; Tractate *Shabbath*, 88a)

"We will do and we will hear" is a strange teaching, especially for a tradition that is founded upon the Shema—"Hear, O Israel," which is directly followed by the words "You shall love the Lord your God" (Deut 6:4–5). The first word is *hear*, which is then followed by what we must do: "you shall love."

Part Two—The Talmudic Ocean

"We will do and we will hear" is a puzzling verse because of its strange reversal and, as Levinas says, the rabbis "keep being astonished by it" (*NTR*, 45). They are astonished by this "error in logic" that is nevertheless full of the "merit which consists in acting before understanding" (*NTR*, 42). This chapter explores this strange "error" that places doing before hearing, practice before theory, acting before knowing, to see what merit it may hold for us.

The Security of Knowing

"Every philosophy seeks truth," Levinas says in a wonderfully plain statement (PI, 88). It begins in a search that takes us out of our familiar world, toward a truth that is unknown. If we already knew the truth, we would not seek it. So our search takes us outside of ourselves, toward a truth that is other than what I know, other-than-me, toward "another region, toward a beyond" (PI, 89). We are "turned toward the 'elsewhere' and the 'otherwise' and the 'other'" (*TI*, 33). We are led by a desire to seek truth, even if truth is something we can never fully attain and, thereby, always "infinite," "beyond," "more-than-me."

Every philosophy seeks truth, yet Levinas suggests that its search is also motivated by another factor—it also wants to *know* the truth. Our *search* for truth can all too easily be tempted by the need to *possess* truth, to make it *my own*, something I can now claim that *I know* as a truth *belonging to me*. In other words, the search for truth is often tamed or domesticated—no longer infinite in its horizon, but reduced to my own horizon of knowing. Truth is scaled down to coincide with myself, such that anything strange or different or other is now secured, safely incorporated into my own world of knowing, brought home to me and made comfortably "the same." Knowledge becomes *self-knowledge*, rather than a response to the call of the other, and it is this movement of philosophy that worries Levinas—the movement toward knowledge that assimilates and appropriates truth to our own familiar designs and frameworks.

Knowing, in other words, becomes a way of securing ourselves in the world. We treasure our ability to know and give it pride of place—it grants us our *reason for being*—or, in that now popular phrase of Descartes, "I think, therefore I am."

However, I am more than a self who simply thinks. I also act. Life is something that is lived, not just something we think about. We *do* life. We engage life through our actions. So, in some respects, that puzzling verse that begins with "we will do" seems right in the priority it gives to acting *before* knowing.

However, in his commentary on this verse, Levinas suggests that our actions nevertheless remain "tempted" by knowledge, by the need to know *before* we act. There is a certain security in knowing that safeguards the risk of acting. Before we act, we subject our actions to knowledge: "We want to know before we do" (*NTR*, 34). Our priority lies with the temptation of knowledge that offers us a reasonable base from which to secure our actions and to lessen the risk—to first "work it out" before we put it into practice, to first understand something before we act on it, to know before we do.

Our actions "arise only after calculation, after a careful weighing of the pros and cons" (*NTR*, 35). We want to take the risk of acting, but only if we can be sure! Thinking comes first. Knowing takes precedence. Only when we can act within a certain security of knowing *beforehand* will we finally commit to the task of doing. To suggest otherwise, to place doing before hearing, is often considered imprudent and unreasonable. "Any act not preceded by knowledge," Levinas says, "is considered in an unfavorable light" (*NTR*, 36); it is considered either naïve or foolish, or even crazy.

"Think before you act," goes the popular saying. Maybe Descartes is right—we are thinkers first and foremost, before we are doers.

The Risk of Acting

I recall my younger days as a graduate student when I took a class in "the sociology of knowledge" at Harvard University, and I still remember the professor's opening words. "The search for truth," he said, "is a privilege of leisure that most people in the world do not enjoy." Knowledge is often a luxury that affords us a time of leisure. Action, however, is a point of urgency.

This reminds me of a line from Søren Kierkegaard: "The instant of decision is a madness."[1] Kierkegaard suggests that action typically requires an "instant of decision," a moment of acting that carries no prior guarantees.

Before we decide, we typically engage in a "careful weighing of the pros and cons." We subject our action to the counsel of knowledge, to what we can reasonably discern beforehand. However, we cannot stay forever in this realm of knowledge that is always a prelude, always a *before* "we will do." At some point we have to decide and to act. No amount of prior

---

1. Cited in Derrida, "Force of the Law," 26. See also Caputo, *Against Ethics,* 103–6.

Part Two—The Talmudic Ocean

deliberation (knowing *before* we act) will save us from finally stepping into the realm of action that is fraught with uncertainty, and without the guarantees of knowing in advance, *beforehand*. Eventually we must forego the temptation to knowledge and succumb to a certain madness of acting without knowing.

Think of Abraham, for example, whom Paul calls "the ancestor of all who believe" (Rom 4:11). He is perhaps the exemplary figure of doing before hearing. Even before he "believed" (Gen 15:6), we are told, he "went forth" (Gen 12:4). God said to Abraham, "Go from your country and your kindred and your father's house to the land I will show you" (Gen 12:1). So Abraham departed, going "toward another region, toward a beyond" (recalling Levinas' words). He left, "not knowing where he was going" (Heb 11:8). He had no clear indication of where the journey would lead. There was not even the suggestion that he might eventually return to his familiar home. There was no certainty, no knowing. Just this: "Go, leave, do it!" *Vayomer hashem el-Avram lech-lecha* (The Lord said to Abram, "Get thee out, go forth . . ."). As Rabbi Barry Leff says, "Everyone, at some time or another in their life, has had to pick up and leave, if not physically, as in to go off to college, at least metaphorically, as in deciding to jump into the uncharted territory of getting married. Everyone sees their life in some way as a journey, and at some point something or someone comes along which gets them to move in a different direction."[2]

We do not always act purely or solely on the basis of what we know. Perhaps this is our first clue to the strange verse that says "we will do" *before* "we will hear." Often in the course of life, we take decisive steps or actions *before* we know, sometimes even without knowing, without any guarantees or certainties. If we had to wait until we knew everything *before* we acted, we probably wouldn't act at all; we would be paralyzed by uncertainty.

When Kierkegaard speaks of a "madness" that accompanies every decision to act, he is probably alluding to his famous "leap of faith." Whereas knowledge tempts us into thinking that we can act securely and on a firm basis, faith asks us to act without knowing all the ins and outs or reasons why, without having any prior certitude. Faith asks us to trust—go, leave, take the step, do it.

Saying "we will do" before "we will hear" is perhaps telling us that we often have to act on faith before we know all the reasons why. And even though St. Anselm says that theology is faith seeking understanding, he also

2. Leff, "Lech Lecha," unpublished sermon.

says that we must first have faith *before* we can understand: "I do not seek to understand so that I may believe, but I believe so that I may understand."[3] Or as Augustine says, "Unless you believe, you will not understand."[4]

The Test of Faith

We can approach the verse "we will do and we will hear" from yet another angle. It is, after all, a diamond-like phrase that can be turned this way or that to catch its various rays of light. Indeed, the rabbis recommend this "turning" of a verse, because we are dealing with the Torah, with God's infinite word: "Turn it and turn it; in it all things can be found" (*Pirkei Avos* 5:26).

What happens if we turn this verse such that its light angles toward me? Such that it might read, "I do, therefore I hear," which carries a different tone than does Descartes' "I think, therefore I am." Put another way, what happens if we take this verse and read it as a verse referring to my own life: *Look at the way I live, and you will see what I therefore hear and understand. Look at what I do, and you will see what I truly know and believe; you will see my faith.*

Put this way, referring to me, this verse takes on a fearful tone—as though it were a judgment that is suddenly measuring me, rather than a judgment of my own knowledge by which I measure everything and everybody else. The "plank" is now squarely in my own eye (see Matt 7:1–5). Indeed, St. Augustine suggests that often the truth is not only that which enlightens me; it can also be that which accuses me (*veritas redarguens*).[5] It can often arrive as a truth that strikes me with a great blow, rather than with a flash of enlightenment. We rarely choose this type of truth; rather, it befalls us.

"You will know them by their fruits" (Matt 7:20). Isn't this the true test of faith? In other words, our lives are meant to bear witness, as if saying, "Look at my life, at the way I live, and you will see a testimony to faith. Look at my life, at the integrity of my words and actions, and you will see a witness to truth. Look at my life, at what I do, and you will see a mirror of divine goodness. Look at my life, at the way it is patterned, and you will see an exemplar of God."

3. Anselm, *Proslogion*, 115.
4. Augustine, *On the Trinity*, 15:2.2.
5. Augustine, *Confessions*, 23.

This is the severest of criteria, pointing directly at me—a scrutiny from which I am never released. My life is constantly put in question, as though someone said to me, "Well, you may believe it, you may know it, but do you really live it?" Or: "That is fine in theory, but how are you applying that in your life; show me where you are doing it?" In other words, *action* is a very daunting and severe criterion—I will always fall short of living a completely responsive and responsible life—and also quite inescapable—I can never put up my feet and say, "no more is required of me."

According to Abraham Heschel, the realm of faith asks us to "take a *leap of action* rather than a *leap of thought*."[6] A person of faith is asked "to do more than he understands in order to understand more than he does." "We will do" claims priority because our *doing* leads to *knowing*, rather than the other way around. "Right living is a way to right thinking," writes Heschel.[7] Doing leads to faith. Again, Heschel: "We do not have faith because of deeds; we may attain faith through sacred deeds."[8] In the Christian tradition, it is the letter of St. James that offers us the classic example:

> Take the case, my brothers, of someone who has never done a single good act but claims that he has faith. Will that faith save him? If one of the brothers or one of the sisters is in need of clothes and has not enough food to live on, and one of you says to them, "I wish you well; keep yourself warm and eat plenty," without giving them these bare necessities of life, then what good is that? Faith is like that: if good works do not go with it, it is quite dead. (2:14–18)

The Answerable Life

In his posthumous work *Toward a Philosophy of the Act* (found in a damp, rat-infested attic), Russian writer Mikhail Bakhtin says that each and every human life is an "answerable life" without any "alibi."[9] I cannot ask someone else to answer for my life. I have no "alibi" that can come to my defense. I cannot evade "the answerable act or deed" of my own life—no one can answer for me or take my place. Only I can respond to another, and this is

---

6. Heschel, *God in Search of Man*, 283.
7. Ibid.
8. Ibid., 282.
9. Bakhtin, *Toward a Philosophy of the Act*, 40–42.

what constitutes the singularity of my unique place in existence, and the unique vocation or answerability of my life. In other words, I am required.

The biblical phrase that Levinas evokes to call to mind this answerability is the prophetic response to the call of God, "Here I am" (*hineni*). Here I am, for you. "To *be* is to *stand for*," Heschel says.[10] The meaning of my life, what it signifies or stands for, is to-be-for-you. The self ("I am") is positioned as a responsive, answering self ("Here I am"). "The word *I* means here I am," writes Levinas (*OB*, 114). The priority is not with the *I* constituting itself, but with the call of the other who asks after me. It is this call that comes first, that is always prior, that is always before me, and constitutes my identity as a response-ability and answer-ability. This is the election of the *I* as chosen and responsible before the face of God and neighbor. "I am," says Levinas, "as if I had been chosen" (*OS*, 35).

"We will do" is not the doing of an autonomous and self-sufficient subject; rather, it is the doing of an answering and responding subject. It is not a doing based on my own self-choosing; rather, it is my being chosen to respond to the call of the other. It is not a doing based in power and control; rather, it is a doing based in service and hospitality. It is not a self-made doing in which I accomplish the project of my life; rather, it is a responsive doing in which I answer with my life.

Karol Wojtyla (Pope John Paul II) suggests, in ways similar to Levinas and Bakhtin, that the answerable life is what constitutes our very personhood. The key thesis of his book *The Acting Person* is that "action *reveals* the person." The way a person lives, the commitments they make, the actions they take, the way they answer with their life, "gives us the best insight into the inherent essence of the person and allows us to understand the person most fully." Action "constitutes the specific moment whereby the person is revealed."[11] Or, as Heschel says, "The deed is the distillation of the self."[12]

"We will do" *before* "we will hear"—why does "doing" come first? Perhaps this verse is trying to remind us that life is encountered first and foremost in action, rather than in thought. Bernard Lee, for example, suggests that classical theology typically gives pride of place to reason. It "presupposes that reason is what is most definingly human about us, the finest exercise of which constitutes human fulfillment." By contrast, practical theology is an attempt to give priority to "we will do"—to human

---

10. Heschel, *God in Search of Man*, 413.
11. Wojtyla, *Acting Person*, 11.
12. Heschel, *Who Is Man?*, 94.

action—and "presupposes that historical agency is what is most definingly human about us, the finest exercise of which constitutes human fulfillment." Our relationship with God is more than a contemplated act; it is a performed deed. "Human action (living) that cleaves with God's action (living) is the end of human life."[13]

In the last chapter of his slim yet beautifully written volume *Who Is Man?*, Heschel recasts and transforms the language of modernity and autonomy into the language of biblical commandment and prophetic response. Following are some brief but exemplary selections that speak to us about the "answerable life"[14]:

How to live

> Modern thinking has often lost its way by separating the problem of truth from the problem of living . . . Reflection alone will not procure self-understanding. The human situation is disclosed in the thick of living. The deed is the distillation of the self . . .
>
> Where does man come upon himself most directly? Is it in abstract self-consciousness, in the generality of "knowing that I am," of "knowing that I think"? Man encounters himself, he is surprised to know himself, in the words he utters, in the deeds he does, and above all in living as an answer. (94)

Being-challenged-in-the-world

> Human living is not simply being here and now, being around, a matter of fact; it is being in dilemma, being cross-examined, called upon to answer. Man is not left alone. . . .
>
> Human living is being-challenged-in-the-world, not simply being-in-the-world. The world forces itself upon me, and there is no escape from it. Man is continuously exposed to it . . . He cannot evade the world. It is as if the world were involved in man, had a stake in man. (104–5)

---

13. Lee, "Classical and Practical Theology," unpublished paper.
14. Heschel, *Who Is Man?* Subsequent page references are provided in parentheses.

"We Will Do and We Will Hear"

Requiredness

Significant living is an attempt to adjust to what is expected and required of being human. This sense of requiredness is as essential to being human as the capacity for reasoning . . . The sense of requiredness is not an afterthought; it is given with being human; not added to it but rooted in it. (106)

Indebtedness

Here is a basic difference between the Greek and the biblical conception of man. To the Greek mind, man is above all a rational being; rationality makes him compatible with the cosmos. To the biblical mind, man is above all a commanded being, a being of whom demands are made. The central problem is not: What is being? But rather: What is required of me? (107)

This is the most important experience in the life of every human being: something is asked of me . . . there is a calling, a demanding, a waiting, an expectation. There is a question that follows me wherever I turn: What is expected of me? What is demanded of me? . . . We know ourselves as exposed, challenged, judged, encountered. (108)

Indebetdness is given with our very being. It is not derived from conceptions; it lives in us as an awareness before it is conceptualized or clarified in content. It means having a task, being called. It experiences living as receiving, not only as taking. Its content is gratitude for a gift received. (108)

I am commanded—therefore I am

Do I exist as a human being? My answer is: *I am commanded—therefore I am.*

There is a built-in *sense of indebtedness in the consciousness of man,* an awareness of *owing gratitude,* of being *called upon* at certain moments to reciprocate, to answer, to live in a way which is compatible with the grandeur and mystery of living. (111)

"Thou art" precedes "I am." (98)

Part Two—The Talmudic Ocean

"I Do"

In most wedding ceremonies, two people dedicate their lives to each other in an exchange of vows and reply, "I do." This *I do* is also used in swearing-in ceremonies of various kinds, including those of public office. "Do you promise to love, to uphold, to serve . . . ?" "Yes. I do." Such are fundamental acts of answerability.

"I do" is perhaps another clue to the verse that says "we will do" before "we will hear." Perhaps saying "I do" *at the very beginning* is a way of saying "I promise" or "I will," even before I know. Perhaps covenantal relationships all require this *I do* as their very foundation. *Before* anything can get underway, "I do" must be said from the very beginning.

I do. I promise in advance. I give my word. This is my answer. Before I hear or understand, before I know what lies ahead, I say "I do"—to you, to the future, to what is coming, none of which I can ever know in advance. According to Jacques Derrida, the act of promising is the original act that begins everything, that gets everything underway: "When I say 'yes' to the other, in the form of a promise or an oath, the 'yes' must be absolutely inaugural . . . I say 'yes' as a starting point. Nothing precedes the 'yes.' The 'yes' is the moment of institution, of the origin: it is absolutely originary."[15]

Everything *begins* with this "yes, I will"—this answering promise. It is the very basis of faith and hope, of love and fidelity. "Yes, I will" is always first and foremost, before all else. Nothing would move or live or have its being without this orginary "yes." Indeed, John Caputo calls this *yes* an "amen," which is like the infinite and ever-renewing affirmation of the world by God, whose "let there be" is a perennially creative event that affirms and sustains all creation. The best way to think of *yes* is "to think of a great and sweeping *amen!*"[16] To say *yes* is to "choose life" and to say "I do," to say *amen* to life, to you, to the future.

Hannah Arendt sees this ability to say "I do" as one of the most creative and sustaining acts of human life. Human action that is life-giving shares in the creative action of God, who is continually "bringing forth" and sustaining life and existence. Every act that serves life is an act of "bringing forth," of pledging oneself to the coming of something new, to the promise of new life:

---

15. Derrida, *Deconstruction in a Nutshell*, 27.
16. Caputo, *Prayers and Tears of Jacques Derrida*, 256.

> Without action, without the capacity to start something new and thus articulate the new beginning that comes into the world with the birth of each human being, the life of man, spent between birth and death, would indeed be doomed beyond salvation ... Action, with all its uncertainties, is like an ever-present reminder that men, though they must die, are not born in order to die but in order to begin something new. *Initium ut esset homo creatus est*—"that there be a beginning man was created," said Augustine. With the creation of man, the principle of beginning came into the world ...[17]

To say "I promise, I am here *for you*" is one of our most fundamental human acts. "Binding ourselves through promises," says Arendt, is the only way we can sustain our life together. "Without being bound to the fulfillment of promises, each of us would be condemned helplessly and without direction in the darkness of his own lonely heart."[18] The act of promising invests the future with hope. Promising looks forward as a commitment to the future and to each other.

Arendt knows, however, that we live in a world of broken promises, that our social and interpersonal relationships are wounded and frail and in need of healing and repair. For this reason, she suggests that acts of promising must also be accompanied by acts of forgiveness.

Promising and forgiving belong together, go hand in hand, because we often fail in our promises, and forgiveness allows us to begin again, to renew the covenantal relations between us. "Without being forgiven," writes Arendt, without being "released from the consequences of what we have done, our capacity to act would, as it were, be confined to one single deed from which we could never recover; we would remain the victims of its consequences forever ..."[19]

To promise and to forgive are the threads that keep us woven and bound to each other. We need to keep saying "I do." We need to keep promising, over and over again. And because we know our human frailty, we also need to keep forgiving, over and over again. "How often should I forgive?" Peter asks Jesus. "As many as seven times?" "Not seven times," Jesus replies, "but seventy-seven times" (Matt 18:21–22). In other words, all the time, because we are continually failing each other.

---

17. Arendt, *Portable Hannah Arendt*, 181.
18. Ibid.
19. Ibid.

Trespassing is a daily occurrence in life and needs acts of forgiveness in order to make it possible for the promise of life to go on. Rather than clinging tight to past hurts and injuries, forgiveness offers us the promise of a new future, a new beginning. Forgiveness sets us free from the burden of sin and catalyzes a new chain of events. "Go, and sin no more" (John 8:11). By constantly releasing us from the burden of what we have done to one another, acts of forgiveness break the cycles of violence and vengeance, of death and destruction. Only in this way can we "choose life" rather than always "keeping score."[20]

Doing the Word

When I was a Golda Meir Fellow at the Hebrew University of Jerusalem I had the great privilege of studying Torah with Professor Michael Rosenak.[21] One of the things I learned from the rabbinic tradition was that as the rabbis searched for the meaning of a text, they were always drawn to finding its *ethical* message. Even when the ethical message was not immediately apparent to them, they would stay with the text, "turning it and turning it," until its ethical import twisted free. The meaning of a text was primarily about *the way one should live*. God's word, the Torah, is something *to live, to do*, and such was the purpose of study and prayer, to bring our lives into alignment with the teachings and commandments of Torah.

In his book *The Word in the Desert*, Douglas Burton-Christie shows how this concern for living or *doing* the word was central to the ancient asceticism of early Christian monasticism. This tradition took shape in the fourth century among the "desert fathers" of Egypt. Interestingly, he notes that the roots of this monastic tradition were deeply influenced by "the life of the early Church, particularly in areas with a strong Jewish influence."[22] Many of the collected sayings of these holy men and women make frequent allusion to "keeping the commandments" or "fulfilling the commandments" or "doing what is written" as the essential key to spiritual growth (151).

---

20. Caputo, *Against Ethics*, 111–12.

21. Readers may wish to consult Rosenak's *Commandments and Concerns; Roads to the Palace;* and *Tree of Life, Tree of Knowledge*. At the time of writing I learned of Michael Rosenak's death. May his soul be kept in the bundle of life.

22. Burton-Christie, *Word in the Desert*, 39. Subsequent references in parentheses.

"We Will Do and We Will Hear"

The sayings are typically framed in the context of a dialogue between a monk and an elder: "Abba, give me a *word*." The meaning of the *word*, however, is never left to pure speculation, but is always tied to the question of how one should live: "Abba, what should I do?" (134). "The questioners wanted to know," writes Burton-Christie, "what they were to *do*, how they were to *act*." He continues: "Their questions took various forms: 'What should I do?' 'How should a person behave?' 'How should we conduct ourselves?' 'What good work should I do that I might live in it?' These practical questions reveal the kinds of concerns the monks brought to the elders. They sought not so much ideas about the spiritual life narrowly conceived, but rather a new way to live" (150).

This concern for the *speaking word* carried an *eventlike* quality that closely resembles the Hebrew word *dabar*, as "a deed or an 'event' which is announced by a word, expressing the close correlation between life and action" (77). Those who came to the elders seeking a *word* were not seeking an "extended spiritual discourse" or "general, universal prescriptions." Rather, they were seeking "concrete and precise keys" to help them unlock the very real difficulties and practical concerns of their lives. For these desert-dwelling monks, the best way to "unleash the power of the word" was not to focus on its theoretical meaning, but to focus attention on the "earthly" and "practical demands of their life" (157). Burton-Christie writes, "Because the desert fathers held integrity of words and life to be so important, the question of how to bring one's life into conformity with Scripture became a burning question. They were convinced that only through *doing* what the text enjoined could one hope to gain any understanding of its meaning"(135).

The performed deed superseded the contemplated act. "The elders made it abundantly clear," says Burton-Christie, "that their words were spoken only for the sake of being taken up and integrated into the hearts, minds, and actions of those who received them" (134). Of the numerous and telling stories that fill the pages of Burton-Christie's book, the following is but one striking example:

> We can gain further insight into this practical orientation by examining the attitude of Abba Pambo toward Scripture: Pambo was . . . reticent to speak about Scripture: "If he was asked to interpret part of the Scriptures he would not reply immediately, but he would say *he did not know* that saying. If he was asked again, he would say no more." We hear elsewhere that the reason for Pambo's silence before Scripture had to do with his strong conviction that words

without practice were useless. Early in his monastic career, he went to one of his elders to learn a psalm. Having heard the first verse of Psalm 38 ("I said I will take heed to thy way, that I offend not with my tongue"), he departed without staying to hear the second verse. He said to himself: "This one will suffice, if I can practically acquire it." More than six months passed before he returned to consult the elder again. When he did so, the old man reproved Pambo for staying away for so long. But Pambo told him that the reason for his long absence was that he had been fully occupied with the verse he had been given. Even now, he said, "he had not yet learnt to practice the verse of the Psalm." Many years later, Pambo was asked by one of his companions whether he had finally mastered the verse. He responded, "I have scarcely succeeded in accomplishing it during nineteen years." Such honesty and humility served as an example for anyone who wished to unlock the mysteries of Scripture: no amount of speculation and conversation about the text was as valuable as a silent and earnest effort to realize in one's life the meaning of even a single verse. (156)

We Will Do and We Will Hear

According to Levinas, "we will do and we will hear" means that "one accepts the Torah before one knows it" (*NTR*, 42). In a similar way, the story of Abba Pambo tells us that he accepts the verse given him, not because he knows it; rather, he says, "I do not know that saying." He accepts the verse by trying to live it in his life, by "doing the word," so that he might one day come to know it and understand it.

Rabbi Leff suggests that it is only by keeping God's commandments, by accepting them and doing them, that we are able to better hear and understand their meaning and their wisdom for life. He offers the example of observing Shabbat:

> We will do and we will understand. This is a very profound teaching. I could give a dozen brilliant sermons about why it is a wonderful thing to observe Shabbat, and someone who has never tried it would still not get what Shabbat is about. To understand Shabbat, you simply have to do it . . . Taking 25 hours out of a busy life, and spending it doing nothing but being with friends and family, eating good meals, drinking wine, singing, hanging out, is incredibly restorative. Not to run around from here to there, not to watch TV, not to run errands, not to do the laundry, but to simply *be*, and be with each other, is an incredible experience. But

"We Will Do and We Will Hear"

to appreciate it requires a "leap of action"—a willingness to try it and experience it, and understand what it's about later.[23]

To do before we understand means that it is through our doing that we are led to deeper understanding. As we do, we hear or we learn. As I teach, for example, I learn more and more what it means to be a good teacher. As I parent, I learn more and more what it means to be a good parent. As I practice forgiveness, I begin to understand more deeply what forgiveness is. As we follow the ways of God, we become more and more like the people of God.

The Israelites were rewarded for doing before understanding, yet they nevertheless received *two crowns*—"one for the doing *and one for the hearing*." Doing without hearing is just thoughtless "activity." In the Jewish tradition, right action is always accompanied by *kavanah*.[24] Kavanah is attentiveness, acting purposefully, being aware of what we are doing, reflecting upon and learning from our doing. Any good artisan or practitioner knows what kavanah means. It is no mere external performance or blind obedience. It is not a "mechanical act" but an "artistic act." Who could imagine a poet or a musician who does not write or compose with their heart, or a teacher who does not care for their students, or a parent who lacks attentiveness to their children, or a ministering person who does not discern or pray?

Along with our deeds, "God asks for the heart," Heschel says, "for insight, not only for obedience; for understanding and knowledge of God, not only for acceptance."[25] "You shall love the Lord your God with all your heart, and with all your soul, and with all your strength, and with all your mind . . ." (Luke 10:27; cf. Deut 6:5). Jesus often supplemented his teachings with references to the person's "heart," to kavanah:

> The good person out of the good treasure of the heart produces good, and the evil person out of evil treasure produces evil; for it is out of the abundance of the heart that the mouth speaks. (Luke 6:45)

> This people honors me with their lips, but their hearts are far from me. (Matt 15:8; cf. Isa 29:13)

Kavanah means that while we are living and acting on earth, we should keep our hearts turned toward heaven and attentive to the ways of God.

23. Leff, "Lech Lecha," unpublished sermon.
24. Heschel, *God in Search of Man*, 314–19.
25. Ibid., 309.

Part Two—The Talmudic Ocean

"But strive first for the kingdom of heaven," Jesus says (Matt 6:33). "For where your treasure is, there your heart will also be" (Luke 12:34). "We have learnt," the rabbis say, that "it matters not whether one does much or little, if only he directs his heart to heaven."[26] Action is not action without love, action is not action without faith and concern, action is not action without thoughtfulness and understanding, without reflection and contemplation, without the involvement of the heart.

Binding Heaven and Earth

> Truly I tell you, whatever you bind on earth will be bound in heaven, and whatever you loose on earth will be loosed in heaven. (Matt 18:18)

Commentary

According to Abraham Heschel (1907–1972):

> It is in *deeds* that man becomes aware of what life really is, of his power to harm and to hurt, to wreck and to ruin; of his ability to derive joy and to bestow it upon others; to relieve or to increase his own and other people's tensions. . . .
>
> The deed is the test, the trial, and the risk. What we perform may seem slight, but the aftermath is immense. An individual's misdeed can be the beginning of a nation's disaster. The sun goes down, but the deed goes on. Darkness is over all we have done. If man were to survey at a glance all he has done in the course of his life, what would he feel? He would be terrified at the extent of his own power . . . Even a single deed generates an endless set of effects . . . Gazing soberly at the world man is often overcome with a fear of action, a fear that, without knowledge of God's ways, turns to despair.[27]

According to the Trappist monk Thomas Merton (1915–1968):

> Here was [my] will . . . ready to generate tremendous immanent powers of light or darkness, peace or conflict, order or confusion, love or sin. The bias which my will was to acquire from the circumstance of its acts would eventually be the direction of my

26. Ibid. (citing *Berachot* 17a).
27. Ibid., 284.

"We Will Do and We Will Hear"

whole being towards happiness or misery, life or death, heaven or hell.

More than that: since no man ever can, or could, live by himself and for himself alone, the destinies of thousands of other people were bound to be affected, some remotely, but some very directly and near-at-hand, by my own choices and decisions and desires, as my own life would also be formed and modified according to theirs. I was entering into a moral universe in which I would be related to every other living being, and in which whole masses of us, as thick as swarming bees, would drag one another along towards some common end of good or evil, peace or war.[28]

According to Rabbi Hayyim Volozhiner (1759–1821):

Let nobody in Israel—God forbid!—ask himself: "What am I, and what can my humble acts achieve in the world?" Let him rather understand this, that he may know it and fix it in his thoughts: not one detail of his acts, of his words and of his thoughts is ever lost. Each one leads back to its origin, where it takes effect in the height of heights ... The man of intelligence who understands this in its truth will be fearful of heart and will tremble as he thinks how far his bad acts reach and what corruption and destruction even a small misdeed can cause. (*Nefesh ha'Hayyim*, or "The Soul of Life," cited in *LR*, 230)

Our actions and words are not performed or spoken into a vacuum or a void. They can do good or harm; they bear responsibility; they carry the weight of life and death, good and evil. We can serve or hinder the association of God with the world. The rabbis offer a commentary on Isaiah 43:12, "You are my witnesses, says the Lord, and I am God." According to the rabbis this means, "When you are my witnesses I am God, but when you are not my witnesses I am not God" (*Sifre Deut.*, 346).[29] It is the answering and promising life that testifies to God's living presence in our midst, that binds heaven and earth.

---

28. Merton, *Seven Storey Mountain*, 12.
29. Heschel, *Man Is Not Alone*, 243–44.

8

"Love Your Neighbor as Yourself"

The Talmud relates a famous story about the beloved Hillel:

> It happened that a certain Gentile came before Shammai and said to him, "Convert me on the condition that you teach me the entire Torah while I am standing on one foot." Shammai drove him away with the builder's measuring stick that was in his hand. He then came before Hillel who converted him. Hillel said to him, "That which is hateful to you, do not do to your neighbor. This is the entire Torah; all the rest is commentary—now go and study." (*Shabbat* 31a)[1]

Hillel teaches the entire Torah in a single verse. He makes it sound quite simple: "That which is hateful to you, do not do to your neighbor." However, Hillel reminds us that maybe it isn't as simple as it seems, for there is much commentary on this verse that requires our attention. To practice the entire Torah requires much study. Notice that although Hillel says "all the rest is commentary," he does not exempt the student from studying that commentary. We should not be lulled into thinking that the practice of the Torah is easy. Practice also requires reflection. Practice also requires learning. Practice also requires that we "go and study." "What is Torah's substance?" Abraham Heschel asks. "The answer seems simple, but it is not.

---

1. Cited by Holtz, *Back to the Sources*, 11. The command "to love your neighbor as yourself" is often related to the Golden Rule: "Do to others as you would have them do to you" (cf. Luke 6:31). This is typically referred to as the "positive" version of the rule, and Hillel's "that which is hateful to you, do not do to your neighbor" as the "negative" version.

"Love Your Neighbor as Yourself"

The sages who were involved in it day and night found it difficult to grasp its essence."[2]

There is a story in the gospels that is very similar to the story of Hillel, but first let me offer a brief aside. Scholars have noted that two schools of rabbinic thought were circulating during Jesus' time—the "house of Shammai" and the "house of Hillel."[3] Hillel and Shammai were older contemporaries of Jesus. Shammai was a leader of the Sanhedrin, known for the strictness of his opinions. Hillel was known for his humility and the leniency of his opinions, along with his social reforms and his warm love of humanity.[4] Now to the story:

> A lawyer stood up to test Jesus. "Teacher," he said, "what must I do to inherit eternal life?" He said to him, "What is written in the law? What do you read there?" He answered, "You shall love the Lord your God with all your heart, and with all your soul, and with all your strength, and with all your mind; and your neighbor as yourself." And he said to him, "You have given the right answer; do this, and you will live." (Luke 10:25–28)

Whereas in the story of Hillel it is a Gentile who comes to test the rabbis, in Luke's story it is a scholar of the law (the Torah) who comes to test the teacher, Jesus. Jesus takes the scholar's question and, in typical rabbinic fashion, bounces it straight back: "What do you read in Torah? What has your study taught you?" The scholar is obviously well versed in Torah and has studied it well, for he creatively brings together two seemingly disparate verses—the first from the book of Deuteronomy (6:5) and the second from the book of Leviticus (19:18). By combining these two verses he manages to encapsulate the very essence of the Torah, to which Jesus replies, "You have given the right answer; do this, and you will live."

Such is Luke's version, which differs from Matthew's account, in which it is Jesus himself who comes up with the brilliant reply (much like Hillel): "On these two commandments hang the whole Law, and the Prophets also" (22:40). Mark's version is different too, for he sets the scene in a more cordial environment of rabbinic discussion, without much hint of an acrimonious or testing exchange. The interlocutor in Mark's Gospel seems to appreciate Jesus' response, and says, "Well spoken, teacher," to which Jesus replies, "You are not far from the kingdom of heaven" (12:34).

2. Heschel, *Heavenly Torah*, 322.
3. Shanks, *Christianity and Rabbinic Judaism*, 11, 132–33.
4. Hilton and Marshall, *Gospels and Rabbinic Judaism*, 18.

Luke's account, however, is interesting because, like the story of Hillel, it ends with a twist. The scholar in Luke's story offers the correct response, but when Jesus says, "do this, and you will live," he feels a need to justify himself and so challenges Jesus further: "And who is my neighbor?" (10:29). Jesus responds by telling the parable of the Good Samaritan. We need to consider, Jesus suggests, not only who my neighbor is, but also whether I can be a neighbor to another. We need to go and study, to look more closely at the practices of our lives, to consider those we pass by too readily, or those we condemn too quickly, or those we judge too hastily.

The scholar's question, "who is my neighbor?" is one of those questions that defy ready-made answers. It is a perennial question that cannot be answered definitively or once and for all time. Rather, it is a question that resonates anew in the lives of human beings who are forever learning to live together in the contours of their own personal lives and in the changing social contexts of human history.

There is another question hidden in the commandment "love your neighbor as yourself." Rather than ask "who is my neighbor?" this question asks, what does "as yourself" mean?

In this chapter, I offer seven responses to this question. In my own novice fashion, I adopt a type of Talmudic style—citing various viewpoints in the vein of "Rabbi X" says. One of the things rabbinic commentary has taught me is that nothing is extraneous. Even the most unlikely reference is pertinent. I am interested in capturing a certain "oral" quality to the commentary, with various voices entering the dialogue in a somewhat random or unstructured manner. The voices include a range of sources—ancient and contemporary, rabbinic and Christian, philosophers and theologians. I am not attempting an exhaustive or systematic account. Rather, I am interested in the dialectical approach of Talmudic thought: "on the one hand" and "on the other hand." The following responses represent commentary on a verse that, as Hillel says, "is the entire Torah" and, as Jesus says, "sums up the entire law and the prophets."

1. Your neighbor, like yourself, is created in the "image of God."

The Talmud relates a dialogue between Rabbi Akiva and his student Ben Azzai. According to Akiva, the commandment "to love your neighbor as yourself" is the greatest principle of the Torah. Ben Azzai, however, argues that the greatest principle is the creation of humanity in God's own image and likeness.[5]

According to Ben Azzai, the formal principle "to love your neighbor as yourself" is susceptible to a facile reciprocity or a "tit-for-tat" measure, whereby my love for others is measured by the way I want others to love me. The creation of humankind in God's image, however, means that the "love of one's fellow human being is not measured by love of oneself."[6] Rather, a person "is your neighbor on the basis of equality with you before God—every person has this equality and has it unconditionally."[7]

Catholic theologian Edward Schillebeeckx stresses this point: "The great symbol of the human as *imago Dei* is the one permissible image of God that is not an idolatry."[8] While there are many things that can lead to idolatry—that is, falsity or illusion—the one image of God that never leads to idolatry is the human person. The *humanum* represents the *foundational* symbol of the Holy. To quote the U.S. Conference of Catholic Bishops, "We believe the person is sacred—the clearest reflection of God among us . . . Human personhood must be respected with a reverence that is religious. When we deal with each other, we should do so with the sense of awe that arises in the presence of something holy and sacred."[9]

Levinas notes that every human person is an "absolute identity—non-interchangeable, incomparable and unique" (*OS*, 117). He cites a Talmudic passage that plays on the image of minting coins: "Behold man, who strikes coins with the same die and gets coins all alike; but behold the Holy-Blessed-Be-He, who strikes all men with the die of Adam and not one is the same as another. That is why each is obliged to say: The world was created for me!" (*OS*, 118).

Human beings are not like minted coins, interchangeable and alike; rather, human beings are incomparable and unique. This incomparableness reveals "the trace of God" in humanity. Each person's existence is holy and irreplaceable because each person is made in the image of God, who is holy and like no other.

---

5. *Sifra on Leviticus* 19.18; *Genesis Rabba* 24.7; cited in Hilton and Marshall, *Gospels and Rabbinic Judaism*, 14–15. See also Goodman, *Love Thy Neighor as Thyself,* 31.
6. Leibowitz, *New Studies in Vayikra (Leviticus),* 371.
7. Kierkegaard, *Works of Love,* 60.
8. Schillebeeckx, *Schillebeeckx Reader,* 174.
9. United States Conference of Catholic Bishops, *Economic Justice for All,* nos. 13, 28.

Part Two—The Talmudic Ocean

In the Jewish tradition, the act of service and response to another human being is an act of *imatatio dei*: it reproduces or represents (testifies to) God's mercy and compassion. Offenses against a fellow human being are seen as a denial of God's own self who created men and women in God's image. "It was for this that *adam* was created singly," the Talmud says, "to teach you that the one who destroys a single soul is, in the eyes of Torah, as one who destroyed a whole world. And the one who saves a single soul is as one who saved an entire world" (*Sanhedrin* 37a). Similarly, in the Christian tradition, the judgment of God takes place under the following condition: "I tell you solemnly, in so far as you did this to one of the least . . . you did it to me" (Matt 25:40).

Liberation theologian Gustavo Gutiérrez maintains that human beings are most prone to inflicting violence upon others precisely when the other person is considered anything but human—indeed, considered a "nonperson." History abounds with examples, and the times have not changed very much. We continue to depersonalize and dehumanize our fellow human beings. "The majority of peoples today are still nonpersons," Gutiérrez says, "they are not even considered as human persons."[10] I am often reminded of a striking example from a civil rights march of the 1960s, an image of African-American men walking down the streets with placards declaring, "I am a man."[11]

"The idea of 'neighbor' ought to be no less absolutely conceived than the idea of 'God.'"[12] To disparage the human person or any living creature is to make a mockery of God, rather than to respect the image of God. The Hebrew prophets constantly rallied against idolatry and false worship. They always spoke in the name of the living God who is concerned for creation and the welfare and *shalom* of human persons.

"To sense the sacred," Abraham Heschel says, "is to sense what is dear to God."[13] God's concerns are personal. The personal and the relational have everything to do with the holiness of life. Personality draws us continually into the realm of real human living, where there is both joy and sorrow and where we find that our thoughts and our actions are most real when we are

---

10. Gutiérrez, "Bartolome de Las Casas," 272.

11. It was while attending this march that Dr. Martin Luther King was assassinated outside his hotel room. The "I am a man" photograph was taken by the civil rights photojournalist Ernest C. Withers.

12. Furnish, *Love Command in the New Testament*, 210.

13. Heschel, *Who Is Man?*, 49.

"Love Your Neighbor as Yourself"

engaged with another, rather than aloof and indifferent or arrogant and blind. The concerns of God are personal. If not, then I don't know how we can speak of God's relationality, or God's communication, or God's justice and mercy. These concerns are either matters of personal concern or empty "matter-less" theories.[14]

2. Your neighbor is a "subject" or a person like yourself.

Every religious tradition worth its salt teaches fundamental respect for the dignity of the human person. However, religious traditions themselves are always in danger of forgetting this fundamental precept. One of the greatest temptations of religion is idolatry, as the Hebrew prophets knew so well. Idolatry forgets that the human person, not religion, is made in the image of God.

According to Martin Buber, I can relate to you as an object, as an "it," or I can relate to you as a subject, as a "thou."[15] Our first obligation to one another is to respect each person's "subjecthood" or "personhood." To love your neighbor "as yourself" means to love another human subject, to love a person, because each human person is a subject like me.

In Hebrew, the phrase "as yourself" can also mean "as though he were yourself." According to rabbinic commentary, the commandment then reads: "Love your neighbor for he is like yourself."[16] Rabbi Hanina (who lived approximately one generation after Jesus) taught that "if you hate your neighbor whose deeds are wicked like your own, I, the Lord, will punish you as your judge; and if you love your neighbor whose deeds are good like your own, I, the Lord, will be faithful to you and have mercy on you."[17] To love your neighbor "as yourself" means that we are one with our neighbor both in our good inclinations and our evil inclinations.

Franz Rosenzweig notes that in Hebrew and also in Greek, the neighbor is always the nearest one, the one who is nighest to me.[18] It is difficult to avoid the neighbor, the "near-dweller": "Out of the endless chaos of

---

14. Veling, "Personal and Spiritual Life."
15. Buber, *I and Thou*.
16. Leibowitz, *New Studies in Vayikra (Leviticus)*, 368–69.
17. *Aboth de R. Nathan* 53, cited in Flusser, *Sage from Galilee*, 60. See also Flusser, "Jesus, His Ancestry, and the Commandment of Love," in Charlesworth, *Jesus' Jewishness*, 169.
18. Rosenzweig, *Star of Redemption*, 218.

the world, one nighest thing, his neighbor, is placed before his soul, and concerning this one and well-nigh only concerning this one he is told: he is like you. 'Like you', and thus not 'you'. You remain You and you are to remain just that. But he is not to remain a He for you, and thus a mere It for your You. Rather he is like You, like your You, a You like You, an I—a soul."[19]

"Love your neighbor as yourself." According to the rabbis, the text should read, "Love thy neighbor as your own soul."[20] Each human person is a subject like you, "another you," a person like yourself. Perhaps this is the meaning behind Paul Celan's mysterious verse, "I am you, when I am I."[21]

Russian religious philosopher Nikolai Berdyaev suggests that if we want to call to mind what is essential to humanity, we cannot speak of humanity "in general," because the essence of the human person is no generality but rather the unrepeatable and irreplaceable—this one, this human person like no other. He writes, "In human personality there is much that is generic, belonging to the human race, much which belongs to history, tradition, society, class, family, much that is hereditary and imitative, much that is 'common.' But it is precisely this which is not 'personal' in personality. That which is 'personal' is original . . . Personality is the exception, not the rule. The secret of personality lies in its absolute irreplaceability, its happening but once, its uniqueness, its incomparableness."[22]

"That which is personal is original." This originality means that human personality is not interchangeable, but rather incomparable and unique. Berdyaev calls this the "secret of existence" that belongs to each and every person. It is a secret because no human personality can ever be fully known by systems of thought, or subsumed by social processes, or reduced to any other form of contingency or conditioning.

According to Berdyaev, "personality is like nothing else in the world." When speaking of the person, Berdyaev stresses this "like nothing else." He writes, "When a person enters the world, a unique and unrepeatable personality, then the world process is broken into and compelled to change its course . . . Personality finds no place in the continuous complex process of world life, it cannot be a moment or an element in the evolution of the world. Personality presupposes interruption; it is inexplicable by any sort of

19. Ibid., 240.
20. Leibowitz, *New Studies in Vayikra (Leviticus)*, 369.
21. Celan, "Praise of Distance," in *Selected Poems and Prose of Paul Celan*, 85.
22. Berdyaev, *Slavery and Freedom*, 23–24.

uninterrupted continuity . . . Personality is a break through, a breaking in upon this world; it is the introduction of something new."[23]

It is worth noting Berdyaev's words: *unique, unrepeatable, like nothing else, interruption, a breaking in, something new*. These are difficult and yet beautiful words. There is nothing quite like encountering the beauty of uniqueness, yet the difficulty is that this experience is not repeatable or programmable; it is one-off, happening only once, and cannot be replayed or revisited in quite the same manner again. It really is like nothing else. And yet, this means that newness is always possible, interrupting the otherwise routine and repetitive chain of events. Personality persuades me that history need not repeat itself. Rather, there is always the possibility of newness and interruption—novelty and creativity—something unrepeatable, something that thereby does not repeat what went before, but instigates a brand new future, a change of course in the otherwise unrelenting drone of history.

While each of us is caught in the flow of historical time, situated within the world and shaped by society and culture, Berdyaev insists that human personality can never be reduced to its conditioning environs, to "the continuous complex process of world life." Rather, human personality also opens onto the unconditional, "breaking in upon the world," such that in the life of the human person "the form of unconditioned being is reflected."[24]

Personality is incomparable and unprecedented. This sense of being without precedent conveys a sense of the "newbornness" of the world. As Hannah Arendt notes, with the creation of humanity, the principle of beginning came into the world. She cites St. Augustine: "That there be a beginning, man was created."[25] The birth of a new human being is always unprecedented: "The miracle that saves the world, the realm of human affairs, from its normal, 'natural' ruin is ultimately the fact of natality."[26] The world is not doomed to the inexorable forces of history. Rather, with the birth of each person, a new world is made possible: "It is this faith in and hope for the world that found perhaps its most glorious and most succinct

---

23. Ibid., 21.
24. Ibid.
25. Arendt, *Human Condition*, 157.
26. Ibid., 222.

expression in the few words with which the Gospels announced their 'glad tidings': 'A child has been born to us.'"[27]

If the task of religious faith is to try to "humanize" our world, or as Berdyaev says, to "personalize" our world, or as Buber says, "to overcome the world of "It" and welcome the presence of "Thou," then surely this is also what it means to "divinize" our world. There should be no separation between the love of God and the love of neighbor. As St. John says, "Those who say, 'I love God,' and hate their brothers or sisters, are liars; for those who do not love a brother or a sister whom they have seen, cannot love God whom they have not seen" (1 John 4:20). To hallow God's name is to hallow each other. Everything *of God* is ultimately concerned with everything *of humanity*. *Divinitas* can never be disassociated from *humanitas*. "I consider the human person," Buber says, "to be the irremovable central place of the struggle between the world's movement away from God and its movement towards God."[28]

3. I know my neighbor's quest for love.

"You shall love the stranger as yourself, because you were once strangers in the land of Egypt" (Lev 19:34). Commenting on this verse, the rabbis note that the phrase "as yourself" does not qualify the degree of love; rather, it denotes "one who is like yourself, who needs your love."[29]

"You know how a stranger feels, for you lived as strangers in the land of Egypt" (Exod 23:9). "You know how it feels." We all carry a burden, and we all seek to be supported and loved. "As yourself" signifies our shared humanity. You shall love the one who is weighed down, because you yourself know how it feels to be weighed down. You shall love the one who is in need of another, because you yourself know this need. You shall love the one who has sinned or who bears a fault, because you yourself know what it is to sin and to bear a fault.

"The love of our neighbor in all its fullness," writes Simone Weil, "simply means being able to say: 'What are you going through?'"[30] We can ask this question because we too know what it is to "suffer" or "undergo" the conditions of life. That which brings me close to my neighbor and binds

---

27. Ibid., 223.
28. Buber, *Between Man and Man*, 70.
29. Leibowitz, *New Studies in Vayikra (Leviticus)*, 369.
30. Weil, *Waiting on God*, 60.

me to their existence is the knowledge that I have passed through similar difficulties in life, that I know what it is to be in need of another's love and support, that I know my neighbor's "quest for love."[31]

In his book *Works of Love*, Søren Kierkegaard says, "The neighbor is an affirmation of the kinship of all human beings... The neighbor is understood as every person—the whole human race, all people, even the enemy, and we are not to make exceptions, neither of preference nor of aversion."[32]

"As yourself" signifies our shared humanity, our fraternity, our awareness that we share a common bond. What affects one affects the other. "For we are members of one another" (Eph 4:25), St. Paul says, and the well-being of one is tied to the well-being of all: "If one member suffers, all suffer together with it" (1 Cor 12:26). We need our neighbor in all things; we can't survive by ourselves alone. St. Bernard of Clairvaux writes, "The merciful quickly grasp the truth in their neighbors when their heart goes out to them with a love that unites them so closely that they feel their neighbor's good and ill as if it were their own. 'They rejoice with those who rejoice and weep with those who weep' (Rom 12:15). Their hearts are made more clear-sighted by love. It is fellow sufferers that readily feel compassion for the sick and the hungry."[33]

To "feel with" our neighbor—both our joys and our ills—expresses the conviction that we are bound together as human beings. Our hearts are made more "clear-sighted" by this shared love. The rabbis refer to the commandments of God as "duties of the heart." Heschel writes, "'You shall love your neighbor as yourself' refers not to any action but to the love we must nurture in our heart."[34]

According to Levinas, when we are addressed by the gaze of our neighbor there is a sense in which we are addressed by all of humanity. "My relation with the other as my neighbor gives meaning to my relations with all others" (*OB*, 159). In the face of our neighbor we see the face of every other, such that our neighbor attests to "the whole of humanity, in the eyes that look at me" (*TI*, 213).

Levinas often speaks of "responsibility" for the neighbor rather than "love." We are bound to our neighbor, tied up, like a hostage. The neighbor will always be there. "One is never quits with regard to the other" (*EI*, 105). Can we ever say, "I have loved enough and no more is required of me?"

31. Leibowitz, *New Studies in Vayikra (Leviticus)*, 369.
32. Kierkegaard, *Works of Love*, 36.
33. Bernard of Clairvaux, *Steps of Humility and Pride*, 34.
34. Heschel, *Heavenly Torah*, 204.

Part Two—The Talmudic Ocean

Kierkegaard speaks of "our duty to be in the debt of love to each other."[35] Dorothy Day refers to the "duty of delight."[36] Ricoeur speaks of a mutual indebtedness: "being-enjoined" to each other, or beholden to each other.[37]

To "love your neighbor as yourself" is to recognize that we are bound together. The meaning of existence is never the meaning of my life alone. You are always there. There is always "I and Thou," and whatever happens in life happens *between* us. There is no love, unless it happens between us. There is no forgiveness, unless it happens between us. There is no justice, unless it happens between us. Nothing moves between heaven and earth, unless it moves between us. Humanity "is the knot in which heaven and earth are interlaced," Heschel says.[38]

4. Self-esteem and respect: "Let your fellow's honor be as dear as your own."

In his study of the "love command," Victor Paul Furnish notes that the reference to self-love is not intended as a *third* command. There are not three commandments: to love God, to love neighbor, to love oneself. The biblical tradition assumes, rather than commands, that we love ourselves.[39]

Nevertheless, part of our duty to others is to care for ourselves. Kierkegaard notes that there is a "proper" place for self-love or self-esteem. "Whoever has any knowledge of men will certainly admit that whenever he has desired the capacity of moving others to relinquish self-love, he has also frequently been constrained to wish that it were possible to teach them to love themselves."[40]

Self-care need not be a selfish act; rather, "it is simply good stewardship of the only gift I have, the gift I was put on earth to offer to others. Anytime we can listen to our true self and give it the care it requires, we do so not only for ourselves but for the many others whose lives we touch."[41] Each of us is required to appreciate our uniqueness in the world and to fulfill our particular task or vocation. Just prior to his death, Rabbi Zusya

35. Kierkegaard, *Works of Love*, 171.
36. Day, *The Duty of Delight*.
37. Ricoeur, *Oneself as Another*, 354.
38. Heschel, *Who Is Man?*, 103.
39. Furnish, *Love Command in the New Testament*, 199.
40. Kierkegaard, *Works of Love*, 39.
41. Palmer, *Let Your Life Speak*, 31.

"Love Your Neighbor as Yourself"

said to his disciples, "In the coming world, they will not ask me: 'Why were you not Moses?' They will ask me: 'Why were you not Zusya?'"[42]

Self-respect is intimately connected with respect for others. "Let your fellow's honor be as dear to you as your own," Rabbi Eliezer says.[43] In his 2005 Gifford Lectures, devoted to the verse we are considering, Lenn Goodman writes, "The respect one shows others reflects self-respect, just as disrespect for others betrays insecurity... A healthy self-respect, neither bloated with self-conceit nor quivering between abjectness and abasement, has the strength to honor and respect others without a sense of loss or diminution."[44]

"I cannot myself have self-esteem unless I esteem others *as* myself," writes Ricoeur.[45] One is respected who shows respect, and one is esteemed who shows esteem. "Our human dignity calls on us to see in every human being sparks of divinity. It is in recognizing that dignity that we attain the very dignity we impart."[46] "As your self" means that a healthy self-respect creates a healthy community. When we live with respect and care for ourselves, we are better able to extend this respect and care to the lives of others. "Who has dignity in God's eyes?" a Jewish sage asks. "One who treats others with the respect they deserve as God's precious creatures."[47]

Self-esteem, social esteem, and mutual recognition are important expressions of love and friendship.[48] Each human being seeks an affirmation or confirmation of their existence as esteemed and dignified—as loved, as worthwhile, as good. To affirm another's existence in this way is one of our most precious acts. It means building one another up, rather than tearing each other down. Or, as St. Paul says, "Let no evil come out of your mouths, but only what is useful for building up... so that your words may give grace to those who hear you" (Eph 4:29).

Kierkegaard suggests that proper self-love is often an index or a standard for our love of others. "How shall I love my neighbor?" Kierkegaard

---

42. Ouaknin, *Burnt Book*, 59.
43. *Pirkei Avos* (*Ethics of the Fathers*), 2:15.
44. Goodman, *Love Thy Neighbour as Thyself*, 59.
45. Ricoeur, *Oneself as Another*, 193.
46. Goodman, *Love Thy Neighbour as Thyself*, 60.
47. Ibid., 10 (citing Bahya Ibn Paquda, *Book of Guidance to the Duties of the Heart* 5.5).
48. Ricoeur, *Course of Recognition*, ch. 3, "Mutual Recognition."

asks. The commandment keeps replying: "as yourself."[49] We know what it means to be treated with respect; we don't want to be put down or humiliated. We know what it means to be forgiven our faults and weaknesses; we don't want to be condemned or treated harshly. We know what it means to be loved; we don't want to be hated by others. As Kierkegaard suggests, "All of these provide a pattern or model, so that we are never at a loss as to 'how' to love our neighbor."[50]

According to Ricoeur, "love your neighbor" represents an active form of doing, and "as yourself" represents a passive form of undergoing. Doing to others is an agency, whereas undergoing the actions of others is a passivity. As we undergo the actions of others upon ourselves (the good done to us or, conversely, the evil done to us), we are able to use this experience of "undergoing" to guide us in our "doing."[51]

"As yourself" is the manner in which we are the "patients" of other's actions upon us. "As yourself" is the manner in which we "undergo" the love or the fault of others. This very undergoing or passivity is perhaps the best guide we have for our agency or our actions toward loving our neighbor. Thus, the classic formulation of the golden rule reflects the active form of doing in the light of the passive form of undergoing—"as yourself" means doing to others as you want them to "do to you," or not doing to others as you do not want them to "do to you."[52]

Karen Armstrong offers three suggested practices. First, resolve to act at least once each day according to the positive version of the golden rule: "Treat others as you would wish to be treated yourself." Small and simple acts are sufficient, such as listening to a friend, opening a door, or helping a neighbor. Second, resolve each day to act according to the negative rule: "Do not do to others what you would not like them to do to you." For example, try to catch yourself before you make that "brilliantly wounding remark," asking yourself how you would like to be "on the receiving end of such sarcasm." Or try to imagine another person's situation before you too quickly judge their circumstance. Third, make an effort each day to change your thought patterns: "If you find yourself indulging in a bout of anger or self-pity, try to channel all that negative energy into a more kindly direction." Or, if you are "in a rut of resentment, make an effort to think of

49. Kierkegaard, *Works of Love*, 37.
50. Ferreira, "Kierkegaard and Levinas," 89.
51. Ricouer, *Oneself as Another*, 219.
52. Ibid., 330.

something for which you should be grateful." Finally, "at the end of the day, check yourself to see if you have performed your three actions."[53]

5. I am commanded—"Someone's asking for you."

The early forebears of Western monasticism, the desert fathers, knew how difficult it was to practice even the smallest acts of love. Their *Sayings* "are full of questions of how to overcome the legion of dark impulses within oneself that prevented one from loving."[54] They spoke in direct and realistic language about the Rule to offer hospitality, a practice that surmounted all other spiritual practices:

> A brother came up to a hermit: and as he was taking his leave, he said, "Forgive me, abba, for preventing you from keeping your rule." The hermit answered, "My rule is to welcome you with hospitality, and to send you on your way in peace."
>
> A hermit who was very holy lived near to a community of monks. Some visitors to the community happened to go to see him and eat, though it was not the proper time. Later the monks of the community said to him, "Weren't you upset, abba?" He answered, "I am upset when I do my own will... When visitors come we should welcome them and celebrate with them. It is when we are by ourselves that we ought to be sorrowful."[55]

"You *shall* love." Kierkegaard writes, "When you open the door which you have shut in order to pray to God, the first person you meet as you go out is your neighbor whom you *shall* love."[56]

Rosenzweig asks, "What does it mean to be *commanded* to love?"[57] What is the difference between "love as obedience" and "love as compassion"?

Levinas has little doubt that love can be commanded: "I am *ordered* toward the face of the other who *commands* me," he says (*OB*, 11). The face calls for me and "ordains me," as if I were being asked after: "Someone's asking for you" (*EI*, 97–98).

If love is a "sovereign command," then it is without restriction or limitation—it is infinite, immeasurable, unconditional. The love command

---

53. Armstrong, *Twelve Steps to a Compassionate Life*, 114–15.
54. Burton-Christie, *Word in the Desert*, 266.
55. Ward, *Desert Fathers*, 134–36.
56. Kierkegaard, *Works of Love*, 64.
57. Rosenzweig, *Star of Redemption*, 176.

always remains a *command* and, as such, stands watch over every ethical or administrative system that may be tempted to think it is no longer under love's requirement. According to Kierkegaard, "There where the merely human would lose courage, the command strengthens; there where the merely human would become tired and clever, the command flames up and gives wisdom. The command consumes and burns out what is unsound in your love, but through the command you shall be able to kindle it again when humanly considered it would cease."[58]

Love is not always something "spontaneous" but something that must be "repeatedly called forth and repeatedly obeyed."[59] It is not an "abstract effort" (based on some generalized morality or ethical reason), but a particular love exercised in concretely given situations. Kierkegaard writes, "To be sure, *neighbor* in itself is manifold, for *neighbor* means *all men*; and yet in another sense one person is enough in order that you may practice the law."[60]

The commandment to love is not seen as the impossible task of caring for everyone, but the possible task of caring for each one who comes our way, requiring our love and attention. Commanded love is "practical love"—not generalized love. It is love that issues forth in the actuality of caring for and upholding one's neighbor. According to Heschel, "It is always one [person] at a time whom we keep in mind . . . when trying to fulfill: 'Love thy neighbor as thyself.'" A human being is not valuable because he or she is a member of the human race; "it is rather the opposite: the human race is valuable because it is composed of human beings."[61] The neighbor is the next person encountered, the "nighest one," the "highest one." As Furnish notes, "The love command does not demand general love of man based on an abstract or ideal view of man, but love of the real man with whom I am bound."[62]

The command to love is not self-fulfilling; there is always one more person to love. Love will be demanded again and again; it is an infinite demand. "Love of neighbor always erupts anew. It is a matter of always starting over from the beginning."[63] The commandment to love reminds

58. Kierkegaard, *Works of Love*, 57.
59. Furnish, *Love Command in the New Testament*, 201.
60. Kierkegaard, *Works of Love*, 37.
61. Heschel, *Between God and Man*, 133.
62. Furnish, *Love Command in the New Testament*, 202–3.
63. Rosenzweig, *Star of Redemption*, 215.

"Love Your Neighbor as Yourself"

us that "loving" is no settled state, but "a vocation, a being called, a being claimed."[64]

Paul Ricoeur offers a commentary[65] on the following teaching of Jesus in Luke's Gospel (6:27–35):

> But I say to you that listen, Love your enemies, do good to those who hate you, bless those who curse you, pray for those who abuse you. If anyone strikes you on the cheek, offer the other also; and from anyone who takes away your coat do not withhold even your shirt. Give to everyone who begs from you; and if anyone takes away your goods, do not ask for them again. (vv. 27–30)

Strangely, at this point in Luke's text, Jesus offers the classic formulation of the golden rule: "Do to others as you would have them do to you" (v. 31). It is strange the way this typical "standard of love" suddenly appears in the middle of this text. It seems out of place, because the previous verses, and the ones that follow, seem to be questioning even this standard of love, calling into question this sense of love's equivalence, whereby we simply love others as we want them to love us. Luke's text places in question this notion that love is a reciprocal measure, rather than a love that is *immeasurable*—loving even those who do not return love, loving even those who are our "enemies."

> If you love those who love you, what credit is that to you? For even sinners love those who love them. If you do good to those who do good to you, what credit is that to you? For even sinners do the same. If you lend to those from whom you hope to receive, what credit is that to you? Even sinners lend to sinners, to receive as much again. But love your enemies, do good, and lend, expecting nothing in return. Your reward will be great, and you will be children of the Most High; for he is kind to the ungrateful and the wicked. (vv. 32–35)

"Is not the golden rule retracted by these harsh words?" asks Ricoeur.[66] Harsh, maybe, and yet, if we cannot love our enemies, or if we cannot give to another without expecting something in return, then in what sense can we say that we are loving? Aren't we rather caught up in games of calculation and exchange, whereby love is measured and meted out to those who

---

64. Furnish, *Love Command in the New Testament*, 201.

65. Ricoeur, "Ethical and Theological Considerations on the Golden Rule" (ch. 19) and "Love and Justice" (ch. 21) in *Figuring the Sacred*.

66. Ibid., 326.

will love us in return? And if this is the way we love, is it really love? Can love be negotiated? "A carefully checked and measured love," Karl Rahner says, "always ceases to be love."[67]

Maybe there is a role for equivalence and measurement in the realm of justice ("to give to each his or her due"), but in the realm of love this "logic of equivalence" gives way to a "poetics of love," or what Ricoeur calls the "logic of superabundance."[68] Superabundant love is excessive and immeasurable. It is "crazy love" that gives without worrying whether it will "work" or not, whether it will attain a return or achieve a balanced outcome. Ricoeur writes, "Without the corrective of the commandment to love, the golden rule would be constantly drawn in the direction of a utilitarian maxim whose formula is: 'I give *in order that* you will give.'"[69] Similarly, Levinas continually insists that love and responsibility can never be based on reciprocity: "I am responsible for the Other without waiting for reciprocity," he says. The other's obligation to me is "*his* affair," not mine (*EI*, 98).

However, Ricoeur maintains that reciprocity need not always be a "vicious" circle ("measure for measure") but can also be a "virtuous" circle ("gift for gift"). Love can be nurtured, rather than negated, "in the practice of a gift in return."[70] To give love in return is an act of appreciation. It is thankfulness, and returning love for love. "The gift in return," Ricoeur says, "comes in the wake of the generosity of the first gift."

Returning love need not always be seen as "owing" love, or "paying love" back. Rather, "to recognize the generosity of the first giver through a corresponding gesture of reciprocity" is an expression of mutual recognition and mutual love.[71] It is an expression of gratitude: give as you have been given; love as you have been loved. Give and receive, receive and return.[72]

6. The love of your neighbor is the work of yourself.

In a strange and maybe mystical statement, Kierkegaard says that the other is not *"the other I"* but rather *"the first Thou."*[73] Our neighbor is preeminent.

67. Rahner, "'Commandment' of Love," 453.
68. Ricoeur, *Figuring the Sacred*, 329.
69. Ibid., 328.
70. Ricoeur, *Course of Recognition*, 228.
71. Ibid., 232–33.
72. Ibid., 243.
73. Kierkegaard, *Works of Love*, 69.

"Love Your Neighbor as Yourself"

The "neighbor is what philosophers would call the *other*, that by which the selfishness in self-love is to be tested."[74] Kierkegaard asks, "Should it not be possible to love a person *more than oneself?*"[75]

In a similar vein, Levinas asks the following question: "Does not 'as yourself' mean that one loves oneself most?" Moreover, can we trust ourselves as the measure of love? "The phrase 'love your neighbor as yourself' still presupposes self-love as the prototype of love" (*BV*, 84). In contrast, Levinas offers an alternative translation: "Love your neighbor; all that is yourself; this work is yourself; this love is yourself" (*GCM*, 90).

Buber notes that "as yourself" does not refer to "self-love" (a notion that nowhere appears in the Scriptures). Rather, it means "to conduct thyself in such a way as if it concerned thyself."[76] Only I—"as myself"—can love my neighbor. I am required. No one else can do it for me. "I am commanded, that is, recognized as capable of a work" (*EN*, 35).

"Love calls you by your name," sings the poet Leonard Cohen.[77] I am irreplaceable in this work of love. "Responsibility is what is incumbent on me exclusively, and what, *humanly*, I cannot refuse," Levinas says (*EI*, 101). I cannot shift my responsibility onto someone else. "The uniqueness of the *I* consists in the fact that no one can answer in his or her place" (*PN*, 73).

"Here I am" is not the negation of the other, but the very sign of "the-one-for-the-other" (*OB*, 151). Here-I-am-for-you, as though "I am" meant (is a sign of) "for you." As though my name meant "in the name of." As though I stood for you, took my stance for you, lived for you. "To become what I am, I only have to accept this 'to you' which co-constitutes myself."[78] You are the one who calls me into existence, and you are also the one who cannot survive without me, without my response. "The I is a privilege and an election," Levinas says, "whereby no one can replace me and from which no one can release me. To be unable to shirk: this is the I" (*TI*, 245).

In an essay devoted to the verse we are considering, Catholic theologian Karl Rahner writes, "Love may already be present and yet may still have the task of realizing itself." Love may indeed be present, and yet the love of God (with all one's heart and soul) and the love of neighbor "may still be a task not yet completed by this man."[79]

74. Ibid., 37.
75. Ibid., 35.
76. Buber, *Two Types of Faith*, 69.
77. Cohen, "Love Calls You by Your Name."
78. Peperzak, *Beyond*, 186.
79. Rahner, "'Commandment' of Love," 443–44.

"Be perfect, therefore, as your heavenly Father is perfect" (Matt 5:48). According to Rahner, "What else is this obligation to strive for perfection but the duty of a greater love than one actually possesses . . . Love today is, therefore, what it should be today only if it acknowledges today that it is something of which more will be demanded tomorrow."[80]

The task is not complete-able, yet this does not mean it is impossible. The command to love our neighbor is not a realm of knowledge beyond our reach, but a teaching that teaches what is possible for us. Rabbi Tarfon says, "You are not required to complete the task, yet neither are you free to withdraw from it."[81]

7. "As you yourself are loved."

At the beginning of *Works of Love*, Kierkegaard offers this prayer: "How could love be rightly discussed if You were forgotten, O God of Love, source of all love in heaven and on earth, You who spared nothing but gave all in love, You who are love, so that one who loves is what he is only by being in You!"[82]

In John's Gospel, Jesus says, "A new commandment I give you, that you love one another as I have loved you" (13:34). Instead of saying "love your neighbor as yourself," this verse says we should love our neighbor as we have been loved.

St. John's hymn to God's love is one of the most beautiful and tender passages of the New Testament: "My dear people," he says, "let us love one another, since love comes from God, and everyone who loves is begotten of God and knows God" (1 John 4:7). The high point of St. John's hymn is when he asks us to consider the love of which he speaks. "This is the love I mean," he says, "not our love for God, but God's love for us" (4:10). Or as Leonard Cohen sings,

> I swept the marble chambers,
> But you sent me down below.
> You kept me from believing
> Until you let me know:
> That I am not the one who loves—
> It's love that seizes me . . .

---

80. Ibid., 452.
81. *Pirkei Avos* (*Ethics of the Fathers*), 2:21.
82. Kierkegaard, *Works of Love*, 20.

"Love Your Neighbor as Yourself"

You whisper, "You have loved enough,
Now let me be the Lover."[83]

In his reflection on the death of his wife, *A Grief Observed*, C. S. Lewis recalls how his wife underwent a "mystical experience" in the course of a very ordinary day: "Long ago, before we were married, H. was haunted all one morning as she went about her work with the obscure sense of God (so to speak) 'at her elbow,' demanding her attention. And of course, not being a perfected saint, she had the feeling that it would be a question, as it usually is, of some unrepented sin or tedious duty. At last she gave in—I know how one puts it off—and faced Him. But the message was, 'I want to *give* you something' and instantly she entered into joy."[84]

As though God were saying, "I've got such a lot of love; I want to give it to you."[85] According to Karl Rahner, we need a desire or a willingness to allow ourselves to be loved. "Every sin is ultimately merely the refusal to trust in love's boundlessness; sin is the lesser love which, because it refuses to wish to become greater love, is no longer love at all."[86] It is far better to be loved than to be mired in competitiveness or driven by fear and anxiety.

"Love your neighbor as yourself." Perhaps the best translation of this verse is "Love your neighbor as you are loved by God." Or as Rosenzweig writes, "Man can express himself in the act of love only after he has first become a soul awakened by God. It is only in being loved by God that the soul can make of its act of love more than a mere act, can make of it, that is, the fulfillment of a—commandment to love. Only the soul beloved of God can receive the commandment to love their neighbor and fulfill it. Ere man can turn himself over to God's will, God must first have turned to man."[87]

Levinas speaks approvingly of chapter 25 in Matthew's Gospel, where the one who loves an other, knowingly or unknowingly, finds themselves in relation to God. "The relation to God is presented there as a relation to another person . . . In his or her face I hear the word of God" (*IRB*, 171). Similarly, the Talmud expounds,

> What is the meaning of the verse, "ye shall walk after the Lord your God" (Dt 14:4)? It is to follow the attributes of the Holy One,

---

83. Cohen, "You Have Loved Enough," in *Book of Longing*, 55.
84. Lewis, *Grief Observed*, 38.
85. Morrison, "Hungry for Your Love."
86 Rahner, "'Commandment' of Love," 456.
87. Rosenzweig, *Star of Redemption*, 214–15.

> blessed be He: As He clothed the naked (Gn 3:21), so do you clothe the naked; as He visited the sick (Gn 18:1), so do you visit the sick; as He comforted mourners (Gn 25:11), so do you comfort those who mourn; as He buried the dead (Dt 34:6), so do you bury the dead. (*Sotah* 14a)

The same thought is expressed in the following midrash:

> As the All-present is called compassionate and gracious, so be you compassionate and gracious and offer thy gifts freely to all. As the Holy One, blessed be He, is called righteous (Ps 145:17), be you also righteous; and as He is called loving (ibid.), be you also loving. (*Sifre Deut* 49)[88]

"As God is merciful and compassionate, so too you be merciful and compassionate" (*Shabbat* 133b; cf. Matt 5:48). Love as you have been loved, give as you have been given, forgive as you have been forgiven. As it is with God, so too with us. As it is in heaven, so too on earth.

---

88. The passages are cited in "Introduction: The Spirituality of the Talmud," in Bosker and Bosker, *The Talmud*, 43–44.

9

Suffering for Nothing or Suffering for You

> I thought of God and sighed,
> I pondered and my spirit failed me.
>
> You stopped me closing my eyes,
> I was too distraught to speak;
> I thought of the olden days,
> years long past came back to me,
> I spent all night meditating in my heart,
> I pondered and my spirit asked this question:
>
> "If the Lord has rejected you, is this final?
> If he withholds his favour, is this for ever?
> Is his love over for good
> and the promise void for all time?
> Has God forgotten to show mercy,
> or has his anger overcome his tenderness?
>
> "This" I said then "is what distresses me:
> that the power of the Most High is no longer what it was."
>
> —Psalm 77:3–7, Jerusalem Bible

> Even God needs a witness.
>
> —Maurice Blanchot

Part Two—The Talmudic Ocean

"Useless Suffering" and "Non-Useless Love"

The twentieth century began as a very self-assured century, yet it ended as a very wounded century. It began with a surge of confidence in the ideals of human progress, yet its high hopes were dashed by a litany of suffering and shattered dreams. "This is the century," Levinas writes, "that has known two world wars, the totalitarianisms of right and left, Hitlerism and Stalinism, Hiroshima, the Gulag, and the genocides of Auschwitz and Cambodia" (*EN*, 97).

Today, we are less likely to speak as confidently about an enlightened age of progress, scientific advancement, and human achievement. Robert Schreiter notes that the twentieth century was one of "the most violent of all centuries known to humankind." He cites the numbing statistic that "more than 100 million people have perished so far in wars and civil conflict."[1] The early years of the twenty-first century are not faring much better.

It is understandable that people of moral and religious sensitivity struggle to discern a meaning to the disasters of history, to the acts of cruelty that have rent the fabric of human life. We do not want to consign this vast loss of life to a voidlike meaninglessness. However, to find a meaning to these horrific deaths runs the risk of suggesting that somehow these deaths were meant to be, that they are explainable (and hence understandable) within the realms of history or other explainable causes. According to Levinas, we should not too readily situate these horrific events within a totality (an overarching theory or framework) that lends them "meaning." In a sense, violence and acts of terror should remain what they are—meaningless acts performed within a void, without any light of truth or any trace of goodness. This is precisely why we call them acts of "terror" or "disaster."

In *The Writing of the Disaster*, Maurice Blanchot says that disaster ruins writing and wrecks language. How do we write in the aftermath of disaster? What words suffice? Is writing possible? What type of writing? There are no words. But do we just remain silent? Are blank pages adequate? Is silence the only testimony—or must we speak? And, if silence is not enough, how do we begin to speak with words that need to be spoken even as they cannot be spoken, or struggle to be spoken?

Blanchot (who rescued Levinas' wife and daughter in the war) urges us to "keep watch over absent meaning."[2] Absence is a difficult "text" to

---

1. Schreiter, *Ministry of Reconciliation*, 3.
2. Blanchot, *Writing of the Disaster*, 42.

read. When we keep watch over absence, we are keeping watch over an incalculable text full of questions, cries, and meaningless suffering. "The question concerning disaster," Blanchot says, " is a part of the disaster: it is not an interrogation, but a prayer, an entreaty, a call for help."[3]

It is perhaps not surprising that Levinas, as a survivor of the Nazi regime, addressed the question of suffering. Why? What purpose? What reason? A philosopher, so-called, could hardly avoid these questions.

In an essay titled "Useless Suffering," Levinas suggests that rather than try to find a meaning or reason for suffering, we may do better to admit that suffering is "useless." It amounts to nothing. It serves no purpose. It has no reason. "The least one can say about suffering is that . . . it is useless: 'for nothing'" (*EN*, 93).

There is a danger in trying to justify suffering, to make it meaningful, to encapsulate it, or to make it count for something. Levinas sees a strategy like this evident in the question of theodicy, the attempt to justify God in the face of suffering. He calls theodicy a great "temptation." If God is justified, then suffering is justified. "The evil that fills the earth would be explained by a 'grand design' . . . necessary to the inner peace of souls in our distressed world" (*EN*, 96). In our efforts to "make God innocent," we perhaps forget, all too conveniently, our own guilt and responsibility. Moreover, in attempting to justify suffering before God, do we not also attempt to "justify my neighbor's suffering?" (*EN*, 98). Suffering is "useless" in the sense that it is unjustifiable, and the attempt to make it justifiable or useful is "the source of all immorality" (*EN*, 99).

A question nevertheless arises. Is all suffering useless? Or can we speak, for example, of "redemptive suffering"? Not so much as "useful" suffering, but as non-useless suffering that evokes human compassion, healing, and solidarity?

Levinas suggests that there is a "Job-like" question or prayer hidden within suffering: "Why do *you* make *me* suffer, why do you not reserve for me an eternal beatitude instead?" (TE, 175). The afflicted ask this question when they are hurting and in pain: "a first question or lamentation, or a first prayer." To undergo suffering is not only to undergo Evil, it is also to appeal to the Good—"a calling out to You and a glimpse of the Good behind Evil." In the experience of suffering, "the I is awakened to the condition of the soul that calls out to God" (TE, 175).

In this sense, there may be times when suffering is not totally useless. Sometimes the travail of suffering awakens us to God and to the suffering of

---

3. Ibid., 13.

our fellow human beings. Here it may be possible to speak of a "meaning" to suffering that "begins in the soul's relation to God and from its being awakened by evil" (TE, 176). We are awakened to God in the suffering of evil that calls out for love: "The experience of evil therefore would be also our waiting for the good—the love of God" (TE, 178). Encountering suffering and evil, I am not taken away from God. Rather, "evil hits me within my horror at evil and thus reveals—or already is—my association with the Good" (TE, 178).

We cannot abandon existence to useless suffering. Indeed, Levinas urges us to adopt a "compassion which is a non-useless suffering (or love), which is no longer suffering 'for nothing'" (EN, 100). In other words, it is important that we do no succumb to a useless suffering "for nothing" but turn our hearts instead toward a non-useless suffering "for the other," for God and for our fellow human beings.

The evil of suffering is "extreme passivity, helplessness, abandonment and solitude . . . the half opening that a moan, a cry, a groan or a sigh slips through—the original call for aid, for curative help, for help from the other . . ." (EN, 93).

According to Levinas, those who suffer and cry out are appealing to "a beyond"—to something or someone who might take them out of their suffering or "beyond" their suffering. This "beyond" may indeed be an appeal to God, but it is equally an appeal to human response and responsibility. "A beyond appears in the form of the inter-human" (EN, 94). Suffering calls upon human compassion and solidarity—the "inter-human." While suffering is "useless" to the other person, it can be "meaningful" to me as the one who is called to reach out to the suffering other (EN, 100). The horror of evil becomes "the horror at the evil besetting the other person" (TE, 181). Suffering "for nothing" is transformed into suffering "for you."

Suffering attains a "meaning" when it is "a suffering for the suffering of someone else" (EN, 94). This is the inter-human, when we suffer for "the useless suffering of others." This is what binds us together as human beings: "The just suffering for the unjustifiable suffering of the other" (EN, 94). Levinas writes,

> It is this attention to the suffering of the other that, through the cruelties of our century (despite these cruelties, because of these cruelties) can be affirmed as the very nexus of human subjectivity, to the point of being raised to a supreme ethical principle—the only one it is impossible to question—shaping the hopes and commanding the practical discipline of vast human groups. This

attention and this action are so imperiously and directly incumbent on human beings (on their *I*'s) that it makes awaiting them from an all-powerful God impossible without lowering ourselves. The consciousness of this inescapable obligation brings us close to God in a more difficult, but also more spiritual, way than does confidence in any kind of theodicy. (*EN*, 94)

If theodicy is an attempt to give reasons for evil and suffering before God, then this is something God never asks us to do. Rather, God protests the suffering enacted in the world and asks us to exercise compassion and love, which, unlike suffering, is never useless.

Abraham Heschel notes that the question of suffering can drive you mad. He tells the story of four learned rabbis who struggled with the problem of theodicy: "One died, one went mad, one lost his faith; and only one—Rabbi Akiva—entered and exited in peace." Why did Rabbi Akiva survive? He survived because he didn't accuse or question God in the face of human suffering. Rather, he believed in God's compassionate identification with human suffering. "Perhaps only a passionate belief in the divine identification with our travails can enable one to struggle and emerge in peace."[4] Why we suffer is a problem that can drive you mad, but why we love is a problem that becomes, in the end, the least problematic or the least useless.

"You gotta help me, I can't do it all by myself"

In his essay "Judaism and Kenosis," Levinas notes that while the Christian understanding of divine incarnation is foreign to Jewish spirituality, the idea of God's humility is not. "Terms evoking Divine Majesty and loftiness are often followed or preceded by those describing God bending down to look at human misery or *inhabiting* human misery" (*TN*, 101). God's height is often paired with God's lowliness. Thus, in Psalm 147, "He who heals the broken in heart, and binds up their wounds" is also the one "who counts the number of the stars and gives them all their names." Jewish liturgy evokes the height and exaltation of God in the equally humbling acts of God's identification with human suffering. "There is an inseparable bond between God's descent and his elevation" (*TN*, 102).

Levinas refers to a posthumously published text by Lithuanian rabbi Haim of Volozhin (1759–1821). The text, *Nefesh Hahaim* (*The Soul of Life*),

---

4. Tucker, "Translator's Introduction," in Heschel, *Heavenly Torah*, 105.

draws widely on rabbinic and kabbalistic sources. Two aspects of God are highlighted. On the one hand, God is the "unsayable," the infinite, the absolute (*Ein-Sof*) who remains disassociated from the world and the world's history. On the other hand, God stands in relation to the world through continuous creation and life-sustaining identification (*Elohim*). However, and this is Levinas' main point, "God is powerless to associate himself with the world he creates and recreates . . . without a certain behavior of man." The master of the world is subordinate, to a certain extent, to the human. The vocation of humanity is "to provide the necessary conditions for the association of God with the world" (*TN*, 108–9). Levinas writes, "Man, by acts in agreement with the Torah, *nourishes* the association of God with the world; or, by his transgressions, he exhausts the powers of that divine association . . . God associates with or withdraws from the world, depending upon human behavior . . . God's reign depends on me" (*TN*, 111–12).

It is as if God were saying, "You gotta help me, I can't do it all by myself," while all the time we are also directing this same prayer to God.[5] Abraham Heschel cites the following rabbinic maxim: "If my people do not enthrone Me on earth, then it is as if I have no Kingdom in heaven."[6] Similarly: "'So you are my witnesses—declares the Lord—and I am God' (Isaiah 43:12)—if you are My witnesses, then I am God, but if you are not My witnesses, then I am, as it were, not God."[7]

In the Jewish mystical tradition (Kabbalah), it is suggested that each person has the inherent capacity to affect the life of God. The dividing line between good and evil runs through each of us. Loving deeds contribute to the life of God's association with the world, while evil deeds reinforce disunity with divine life. The injury that humans inflict upon each other causes injury to God, such that God is broken and shattered, and only shards of divine light remain in the world. Prayer and compassionate deeds are vehicles for "repairing" (*tikkun*) divine life and enabling the divine association with the world. For the kabbalists, we not only enable God's association with the world, we help mend or heal God's brokenness in the world.[8]

When it comes to the tension between affirming, on the one hand, God's omnipotence, and affirming, on the other hand, God's goodness,

---

5. The verse is from Van Morrison's version of the Sonny Boy Williamson song "Help Me," from *It's Too Late to Stop Now*.

6. Heschel, *Heavenly Torah*, 117.

7. Ibid., 110 (citing *Sifre Deut* 346).

8. Fine, "Kabbalistic Texts," in Holtz, *Back to the Sources*, 327–29.

Heschel cites Rabbi Akiva: "It is better to limit belief in God's power than to dampen faith in God's mercy."⁹ Levinas also takes this Akivian view that God participates in human suffering, that the human condition is not foreign to God's heart, that God is merciful and suffers in the suffering of humanity: "The suffering self prays to alleviate the 'great suffering' of God who suffers, to relieve the suffering of God, who suffers both for man's sin and for the suffering of his atonement" (*TN*, 116). Can I pray for my own suffering? Levinas replies, "I do not have to pray for my suffering. God, prior to any demand, is already there with me . . . The suffering self prays on behalf of God's suffering, for the God who suffers both through man's transgression and through the suffering by which this transgression can be expiated" (*LR*, 234).

Abraham Heschel's classic two-volume work on the prophets begins by challenging the notion of an autonomous, omnipotent, self-sufficient God. According to Heschel, the prophets were concerned not with God's immovable essence or nature, but with God's concerns. The prophets were not philosophers but lovers of God who felt God's feelings and God's concern for humanity. To cite one of Heschel's favorite images, God is not the "unmoved mover" but the "most moved mover" who participates in the world's travails.¹⁰ The prophets were deeply moved by God's concerns, even to the point of feeling God's pain at our inhumanity. "The basic feature of this prophetic pathos," Heschel writes, "and the primary content of the prophet's consciousness is a *divine attentiveness and concern* for humanity." It is God's concern for humanity that is at the root of the prophet's work, such that the prophetic soul may be defined, according to Heschel, "not as what man does with his ultimate concern, but rather *what man does with God's concern.*" He goes on to say that "unless we share this concern, we know nothing about the living God."¹¹ In his Stanford University lectures, Heschel writes,

> Who is the human person? *A being in travail with God's dreams and designs*, with God's dream of a world redeemed, of reconciliation of heaven and earth, of a humanity which is living truly in God's image, reflecting God's wisdom, justice, and compassion. God's dream is not to be alone and self-sufficient, but to have humanity as a partner in the drama of continuous creation. By

---

9. Heschel, *Heavenly Torah*, 119.
10. Ibid., 128.
11. Heschel, *The Prophets*, 2:264.

Part Two—The Talmudic Ocean

whatever we do, by every act we carry out, we either advance or obstruct the drama of redemption; we either reduce or enhance the power of evil.[12]

It is up to God. It is up to us. This is an abiding tension that shows up in many theological debates. In the Christian tradition, not unlike the Jewish tradition, God and humanity are bound to each other. Their affairs are bound together. This is what Catholic theologian Edward Schillebeeckx says: "The essence of the Gospel is that humanity's affair is God's affair and God's affair must become humanity's affair."[13] God cannot be fully God unless we are fully human. And we cannot be fully human unless we allow God to be fully God.

God enables us, but also depends on us to respond. When we respond, then God's enabling ways take effect. If we do not respond, God's enabling ways are blocked or frustrated. In the gospels Jesus expresses this frustration when he says, on one occasion, that he could do no miracles because he could find no faith (Matt 13:58). On another occasion he says, "Truly I tell you, whatever you bind on earth will be bound in heaven, and whatever you loose on earth will be loosed in heaven" (Matt 18:18).

In his book *The Divine Milieu*, scientist-theologian Teilhard de Chardin speaks of two practices, both of which lend themselves to divine endorsement: "the divinisation of our activities" and "the divinisation of our passivities." Neither acting nor surrendering is better than the other. Rather, both are required and both are divine. To be active is just as divine as to be passive. To be an agent is just as divine as to be a "sufferer" or an "undergoer" or a "patient."

Humans are suffering and acting beings. We are "agents" in the sense that we have freedom and responsibility. Our capacity to act in the world is a crucial mark of our human creativity and responsibility. The divinization of our activity means that humans can share in the creative activity of God in naming and shaping our world. Artists and scientists both, in their respective disciplines, engender meaningful responses and deep discoveries into the "divine milieu."

However, we do not live in the realm of activity alone. We are also subject to various forms of passivity—to undergo, to suffer, to surrender, to lose control or power—none of which can ever be surmounted by activity. This too is a "divinization," a divinization of "passivity."

12. Heschel, *Who Is Man?*, 119 (adapted for inclusive language).
13. Schillebeeckx, *God Is New Each Moment*, 59.

Suffering is as divine as acting. This is perhaps less recognized in Western culture, a culture that generally celebrates activity more than it does passivity. In this sense, Western culture is only half-divine, missing the other half that Teilhard calls "the divinization of our passivity."

Aside from or along with action, why is passivity divine? The divine milieu is not made up of feverish and accomplished action only, it is also made up of listening and attentive response. It is not made up of my doing and choosing only, it is also made up of my being chosen and called. It is not made up of useful action only, it is also made up of non-useless suffering. The divinization of passivity is the surrendering and self-offering of my love for you.

Suffering for You

The experience of injustice is, among other things, the experience of a wound. It is an experience of alienation or disharmony, a rift or rupture of relationships—from God who creates and loves us, from our fellow human beings, from our selves. "The afflicted are overwhelmed with evil and starving for good," writes Simone Weil.[14] Injustice severs the vital law of life that seeks the peace and well-being of all of creation.

Both the Jewish and Christian traditions are intimately aware of the world's brokenness. Both know of God's suffering in the passion of suffering people—the "little ones" and the "forgotten ones," the "orphans, widows and strangers" (Isa 1:17). The Christian tradition knows of this brokenness in the *via dolorosa* or the "way of sorrows"—the *via crucis*. Drawing on the rich tradition of the Hebrew Scriptures, Christ is seen as the Suffering Servant, the "man of sorrows" (Isa 53:2–6). The events of Good Friday represent this mystery of "expiation" or "substitution." Christ dies *pro nobis*—*for us* and for the sake of our salvation. The mysticism of Christianity suggests that if we "live in Christ," then we too must bear the sins of others, we too must suffer the effects of human hatred, we too must take sin into our flesh—renouncing violence, renouncing hatred, renouncing all the ways in which humanity deals in death. When we love each other, we must necessarily suffer each other's fault and undergo each other's sin, in forgiveness and forbearance, upholding rather than condemning each other in our shared humanity.

---

14. Weil, *Simone Weil*, 86.

Christians know the "crown of thorns," yet as Heschel reminds us, the Jewish tradition is not unfamiliar with thorns:

> When the Holy and Blessed One revealed Himself to Moses at the thornbush, He said to him, "Do you not sense that I dwell in sorrow just as my people Israel dwells in sorrow. Know that in speaking to you here in the midst of thorns, I participate in their suffering." (*Exodus Rabbah* 2:5)[15]

One of Levinas' most difficult thoughts is that suffering-for-the-other extends even to accepting responsibility for the sin and persecution in the world that I did not commit. "I am responsible for the other even when he bothers me, even when he persecutes me . . . even when he or she commits crimes" (*EN*, 106–7). In his Talmudic commentary "As Old as the World," Levinas asks this question: "How to preserve oneself from evil?" He replies, "By each taking upon himself the responsibility of the others. Men are not only and in their ultimate essence 'for self' but 'for others,' and this 'for others' must be probed deeply" (*NTR*, 85).

If being-for-the-other, rather than violence, is embedded in life as its most ancient character, then this "for the other" cannot simply mean that we "love those who love us" (Matt 5:46). Rather, Levinas probes more deeply and asks us to consider the ways in which "I can be responsible for that which I did not do and take upon myself a distress which is not mine." Responsibility for the other extends even as far as bearing responsibility for the sins I did not commit. "For the other" becomes "for the fault of the other," taking on the sin of the other, "which wants absolutely and unto death to substitute itself for the other—for his sin and his distress"—as though it were my own. If we ask, is this love that offers itself, even in taking on the sin and fault of the other, "as old as the world"?—Levinas replies, "For the human world to be possible . . . at each moment there must be someone who can be responsible for the other" (*NTR*, 85–86).

It is a difficult thought that Levinas proposes. I have often struggled with it, though nevertheless sensing in this difficulty a deep truth of life—as old as the world. Could it really be true that suffering for the fault of another is redemptive—a type of non-useless suffering? I recall reading Nelson Mandela's book *Long Walk to Freedom* and wondering to myself, "How could it be that after a quarter of a century in prison, Mandela could still bring himself to meet around the table with his oppressors, in his

---

15. Heschel, *Heavenly Torah*, 119.

efforts to create a new government for South Africa?" Near the end of his book, Mandela answered my question: "It was during those long and lonely years in prison that my hunger for the freedom of my own people became a hunger for the freedom of all people, white and black. I knew as well as I knew anything that the oppressor must be liberated just as surely as the oppressed ... When I walked out of prison, that was my mission, to liberate the oppressed and oppressor both."[16]

Mandela's words remind me of Paulo Freire, the great Brazilian educator, who wrote, in *Pedagogy of the Oppressed*, "This is the great humanistic and historical task of the oppressed: to liberate themselves and their oppressors as well. Only the oppressed can initiate this task."[17] We are responsible for each other, even for those who offend us. As Levinas suggests in the title of one of his books, this is a "difficult freedom," a "difficult liberty."

And then this, from Mohandas Gandhi:

> It is a difficult truth to observe, to suffer in order to put an end to suffering. And yet, the more I think about it, the more I see that there is no other way to fight our ills and those of others. I even feel that the world has no other really effective remedy to offer ... Satyagrahis [those whose voices are true] bear no ill will, do not lay down their life in anger ... but will always try to overcome evil by good, anger by love, untruth by truth, violence by nonviolence. There is no other way of purging the world of evil.[18]

While suffering for another is a form of activity, it is more readily a form of passivity—a divine passivity that suffers or undergoes "evil and hatred" rather than a divine activity that is well within its rights to condemn the evildoer. The "power" of God's intervention, if you like, is in bearing evil rather than striking back at evil. "It is in God's suffering that the redemption of sin is realized," Levinas says (*TN*, 116).

---

16. Mandela, *Long Walk to Freedom*, xxx.

17. Freire, *Pedagogy of the Oppressed*, 21. Similarly, Levinas says in another Talmudic reading, "Only the persecuted must answer for everyone, even for his persecutor" (*NTR*, 114–15). "Only the persecuted" is similar to Freire's "only the oppressed"—only they have the "power" and the responsibility for the other, to free the other, oppressed and oppressor both.

18. Gandhi, *Essential Writings*, 89, 91.

Part Two—The Talmudic Ocean

"If It Be Your Will"

Jewish poet and songwriter Leonard Cohen describes a time in his life when he was "faced with some obstacles" and wrote a song—"well, it's more a prayer," he says. Here are the lyrics:

> If it be your will
> that I speak no more,
> and my voice be still
> as it was before;
> I will speak no more,
> I shall abide until
> I am spoken for,
> if it be your will.
>
> If it be your will
> that a voice be true,
> from this broken hill
> I will sing to you.
> From this broken hill
> all your praises they shall ring
> if it be your will
> to let me sing.
>
> If it be your will,
> if there is a choice,
> let the rivers fill,
> let the hills rejoice.
> Let your mercy spill
> on all these burning hearts in hell,
> if it be your will
> to make us well.
>
> And draw us near
> and bind us tight,
> all your children here
> in their rags of light;
> in our rags of light,
> all dressed to kill;
> and end this night,
> if it be your will.[19]

---

19. Cohen, "If It Be Your Will," in *Stranger Music*, 343–44. Cohen introduces this song in his own words at the *Leonard Cohen Live in London* concert, available on DVD (Sony, 2009).

This poem/song undoubtedly evokes several meanings and associations, as one might expect of any good poem.[20] With its phrases "if it be your will" and "from this broken hill," Cohen's lyrics have always reminded me of Jesus' prayer in the garden of Gethsemane, at the foot of the Mount of Olives: "Abba, Father, if you are willing, remove this cup from me; yet, not my will but yours be done" (Luke 22:42). Set in this context, I hear a very haunting thought in Cohen's song. It is better to suffer violence than to perpetrate it. It is better to bear the fault of another's sin than to be the cause of further sin. Only in this way can we "end this night."

What does it mean to speak of "another will"? Is there another "will" happening alongside my own? What does it mean to pray, "Thy will be done"? What other will is this? This is surely a nonsensical question. There is no other mysterious will. There is only my own life and the choices I make. To pray to (or acknowledge) another will is naïve, as though there might be some other purpose or cause aside from myself. Rather, each of us faces the very stark reality that everything boils down to me and to my own life and will, to my choices and actions and how I decide to live. Choice and freedom go hand in hand. In this sense, to speak of "another will" is somewhat bizarre or useless.

And yet, as a parent raising four children, I have often mused to myself, "One family, yet six wills." While our family is not devoid of love, the contestation of "wills" has nevertheless always struck me as very palpable. I am often impressed that a small family of some six "wills" can nevertheless find a measure of harmony and peace. I am often equally impressed that a society of some millions of "wills" can strive to achieve a similar goal.

"Not my will, but yours be done" is perhaps not as nonsensical as it first sounds. There is always another will, another life and energy that exists alongside my own. This could even be taken as a bare definition of society.

I could pray, for example, "Only my will, only mine be done." But that would bring instant collapse to any social or communal effort. The result would be a raw battle of contested wills.

"Not my will, but yours be done" might be a way of saying, "Be careful not to overpower people with your own will. Remember that they too have a will of their own." Recognizing or respecting the "will of another" strikes

---

20. In his biography of Cohen, *Various Positions*, Ira Nadel notes that "If It Be Your Will" was inspired by the Kol Nidre service on Yom Kippur eve when the petitioner cries out, "May it therefore be Your will, Lord our God, and God of our Fathers, to forgive us all our sins, to pardon all our iniquities, to grant atonement for all our transgressions" (239).

Part Two—The Talmudic Ocean

me as essential for any effort of living together—familial or social. Along with my own will, there is always the will of another.

Yet why then don't we pray something more reasonable—for example, "Not my will be done, nor yours. Rather, let's negotiate (or vote)"? Or, let's accord equality to both your will and to mine. Or, let's be democratic. Or, let's try to be as tolerant and as peaceful as we can. Is this what it means to "pray" that "another will be done"?

When I hear the prayer that Jesus prayed in the garden of Gethsemane, I hear a prayer that is devoted to the will of another rather than simply or only to the will of oneself. Giving or surrendering oneself to another "will" is perhaps an extreme passivity. Yet it is not totally robbed of all choice or decision. When Jesus prayed, "Not my will, but yours be done," he was not surrendering himself to the will of the Romans, or the will of the people, or the will of all believers, or the will of revolutionaries, or the will of sleep and death; he was surrendering himself to the will of God, whose will is indeed difficult at times, but whose will is ultimately one of love.

Very few of us trust love. That is why we have police, courts, parliaments, charities, policies, charters, ethics, and so on. We are all the time trying to "administer" or "regulate" our respective personal, cultural, national "wills" into some sort of harmony or peace. None of this happens without violence. No civilization is ever so civilized that it is without barbaric acts.[21]

When Jesus prayed, "Not my will, but yours be done," he sweated blood. He was in agony. He was alone. The disciples had all fallen asleep. He was alone with his Father, and about to be crucified by the wickedness of people. "Father, if this cup could pass . . ." But unfortunately it couldn't, and he cried out as one who felt totally abandoned. Even before the crown of thorns was placed on his head, the torture had already begun like thorns around his heart: "Not my will, but yours be done."

Whose will? Not the will of vengeful people, people who cry out for so-called justice; nor the will of ignorant people, people who don't know what they are doing; nor the will of scoffing people, people who offer vinegar and say, "He saved others, let him save himself." Whose will? "Father, into your hands I commend my spirit" (Luke 23:46). This "man of sorrows" ultimately gives his spirit into the hands of God, whom he perceives as love, rather than into the hands of spite and hatred and ignorance. "Not my will, but may your loving graciousness hold sway, somehow."

"And end this night."

21. Benjamin, *Illuminations*, 256.

Bibliography

Anselm. *Proslogion*. Translated by M. J. Charlesworth. Notre Dame: University of Notre Dame Press, 1979.
Arendt, Hannah. *The Human Condition*. Garden City, NY: Doubleday, 1959.
———. *The Portable Hannah Arendt*. Edited by Peter Baehr. New York: Penguin, 2000.
Armstrong, Karen. *Twelve Steps to a Compassionate Life*. New York: Knopf, 2011.
Atterton, Peter, Matthew Calarco, and Maurice Friedman, eds. *Levinas and Buber: Dialogue and Difference*. Pittsburgh: Duquesne University Press, 2004.
Augustine. *Confessions*. Translated by R. S. Pine-Coffin. London: Penguin, 1961.
Bakhtin, M. M. *Toward a Philosophy of the Act*. Translated by Vadim Liapunov. Austin: University of Texas Press, 1993.
Beeck, Frans Jozef van. *Loving the Torah More than God? Toward a Catholic Appreciation of Judaism*. Chicago: Loyola University Press, 1989.
Bellah, Robert, et al. *Habits of the Heart*. New York: Harper & Row, 1985.
Benedict. *The Rule of Saint Benedict*. Edited by Timothy Fry. New York: Vintage, 1981.
Benjamin, Walter. *Illuminations*. Edited by Hannah Arendt. New York: Schocken, 1968.
Berdyaev, Nikolai. *Slavery and Freedom*. Translated by R. M. French. New York: Scribner's, 1944.
Bernard of Clairvaux. *The Steps of Humility and Pride*. Kalamazoo, MI: Cistercian, 1989.
Blanchot, Maurice. *The Infinite Conversation*. Translated by Susan Hanson. Minneapolis: University of Minnesota Press, 1993.
———. "Our Clandestine Companion." Translated by D. B. Allison. In *Face to Face With Levinas*, edited by Richard A. Cohen, 41–50. Albany: State University of New York Press, 1986.
———. *The Writing of the Disaster*. Translated by Ann Smock. Lincoln: University of Nebraska Press, 1986.
Bonhoeffer, Dietrich. *Christology*. Translated by J. Bowden. London: Collins, 1966.
Bosker, Ben Zion, and Baruch M. Bosker. "Introduction: The Spirituality of the Talmud." In *The Talmud: Selected Writings*, edited by Ben Zion Bosker and Baruch M. Bosker. New York: Paulist, 1989.
Brodine, Karen. *Illegal Assembly*. Brooklyn, NY: Hanging Loose, 1980.
Buber, Martin. *Between Man and Man*. New York: Collier, 1965.
———. *Eclipse of God: Studies in the Relation between Religion and Philosophy*. Atlantic Highlands, NJ: Humanities, 1988.
———. *I and Thou*. Translated by Ronald Gregor Smith. New York: Collier, 1958.
———. *I and Thou*. Translated by Walter Kaufmann. Edinburgh: T. & T. Clark, 1970.
———. *Pointing the Way: Collected Essays*. Translated and edited by Maurice Friedman. Atlantic Highlands, NJ: Humanities, 1990.
———. *Tales of the Hasidim*. New York: Schocken, 1947/1991.

Bibliography

———. *Two Types of Faith*. Translated by Norman P. Goldhawk. Syracuse: Syracuse University Press, 2003.

Burggraeve, Roger. *The Wisdom of Love in the Service of Love: Emmanuel Levinas on Justice, Peace, and Human Rights*. Translated by Jeffrey Bloechl. Milwaukee: Marquette University Press, 2002.

Burton-Christie, Douglas. *The Word in the Desert: Scripture and the Quest for Holiness in Early Christian Monasticism*. New York: Oxford University Press, 1993.

Caputo, John D. *Against Ethics: Contributions to a Poetics of Obligation with Constant Reference to Deconstruction*. Bloomington: Indiana University Press, 1993.

———. *The Prayers and Tears of Jacques Derrida: Religion without Religion*. Bloomington: Indiana University Press, 1997.

Celan, Paul. *Selected Poems*. Translated by Michael Hamburger. London: Penguin, 1972.

———. *Selected Poems and Prose of Paul Celan*. Translated by John Felstiner. New York: Norton, 2001.

Chardin, Teilhard de. *The Divine Milieu*. New York: Harper & Row, 1960.

Charlesworth, Max, ed. *Jesus' Jewishness: Exploring the Place of Jesus in Early Judaism*. New York: Crossroad, 1991.

Charry, Ellen. *By the Renewing of Your Minds: The Pastoral Function of Christian Doctrine*. Oxford: Oxford University Press, 1997.

Cixous, Hélène. *"Coming to Writing" and Other Essays*. Edited by Deborah Jenson. Translated by Sarah Cornell et al. Cambridge: Harvard University Press, 1991.

———. *Three Steps on the Ladder of Writing*. Translated by Sarah Cornell and Susan Sellers. New York: Columbia University Press, 1993.

Cohen, Leonard. *Book of Longing*. London: Penguin, 2006.

———. "Love Calls You by Your Name." From the CD *Songs of Love and Hate*. Columbia, 1971.

———. *Stranger Music: Selected Poems and Songs*. New York: Vintage, 1993.

Cohen, Richard, ed. *Face to Face with Levinas*. Albany: State University of New York Press, 1986.

Day, Dorothy. *The Duty of Delight: The Diaries of Dorothy Day*. Edited by Robert Ellsberg. Milwaukee: Marquette University Press, 2008.

Derrida, Jacques. *Adieu: To Emmanuel Levinas*. Translated by Pascale-Anne Brault and Michael Naas. Stanford: Stanford University Press, 1999.

———. *Deconstruction in a Nutshell: A Conversation with Jacques Derrida*. Edited with a commentary by John D. Caputo. New York: Fordham University Press, 1997.

———. "Force of the Law: The 'Mystical Foundation of Authority.'" In *Deconstruction and the Possibility of Justice*, edited by Drucilla Cornell, Michael Rosenfeld, and David Gray Carlson, 3–67. London: Routledge, 1992.

———. *The Gift of Death*. Translated by David Wills. Chicago: University of Chicago Press, 1995.

———. *Points . . . Interviews 1974–94*. Edited by Elisabeth Weber. Translated by Peggy Kamuf et al. Stanford: Stanford University Press, 1995.

———. *Writing and Difference*. Translated by Alan Bass. Chicago: University of Chicago Press, 1978.

Descartes, René. *Discourse on Method* and *Meditations on First Philosophy*. Translated by Donald A. Cress. Indianapolis: Hackett, 1993.

Edgerton, W. Dow. *The Passion of Interpretation*. Louisville: Westminster John Knox, 1992.

Ferreira, Jamie M. "Kierkegaard and Levinas on Four Elements of the Biblical Love Commandment." In *Kierkegaard and Levinas: Ethics, Politics and Religion*, edited by

J. Aaron Simmons and David Wood, 82–98. Bloomington: Indiana University Press, 2008.
Fischer, Norman. *Opening to You: Zen-Inspired Translations of the Psalms*. New York: Penguin Compass, 2002.
Fishbane, Michael. *The Garments of Torah: Essays in Biblical Hermeneutics*. Bloomington: Indiana University Press, 1989.
Flusser, David. *The Sage from Galilee*. Grand Rapids: Eerdmans, 2007.
Forché, Carolyn, ed. *Against Forgetting: Twentieth-Century Poetry of Witness*. New York: Norton, 1993.
Freire, Paulo. *Pedagogy of the Oppressed*. Ringwood, Victoria: Penguin, 1972.
Furnish, Victor Paul. *The Love Command in the New Testament*. London: SCM, 1972.
Gadamer, Hans-Georg. *Gadamer on Celan: "Who Am I and Who Are You?" and Other Essays*. Translated by Richard Heinemann and Bruce Krajewski. Albany: State University of New York Press, 1997.
———. *Truth and Method*. Translated by Joel Weinsheimer and Donald Marshall. 2nd ed. New York: Crossroad, 1989.
Gandhi, Mohandas. *Essential Writings*. Selected with an Introduction by John Dear. Maryknoll, NY: Orbis, 2002.
Geffré, Claude, and Gustavo Gutiérrez, eds. *The Mystical and Political Dimension of the Christian Faith*. New York: Herder and Herder, 1974.
Gibbs, Robert. *Correlations in Rosenzweig and Levinas*. Princeton: Princeton University Press, 1992.
Gilles, Michael. "Emmanuel Levinas' Lectures Talmudiques: Talmudic Hermeneutics and Pedagogy." Unpublished chapter.
Goodman, Lenn. *Love Thy Neighbor as Thyself*. Oxford: Oxford University Press, 2008.
Gottlieb, Roger. "Ethics and Trauma: Levinas, Feminism, and Deep Ecology." *Cross Currents* (1994), http://www.crosscurrents.org/feministecology.htm.
Gutiérrez, Gustavo. "Bartolome de Las Casas: Defender of the Indians." *Pacifica* 5 (1992) 262–73.
———. *Essential Writings*. Edited by James B. Nickoloff. Minneapolis: Fortress, 1996.
Hall, David W. *Paul Ricoeur and the Poetic Imperative: The Creative Tension between Love and Justice*. Albany: State University of New York Press, 2007.
Handelman, Susan. *Fragments of Redemption: Jewish Thought and Literary Theory in Benjamin, Scholem, and Levinas*. Bloomington: Indiana University Press, 1991.
———. *The Slayers of Moses: The Emergence of Rabbinic Interpretation in Modern Literary Theory*. Albany: State University of New York Press, 1982.
Heidegger, Martin. *Being and Time*. Translated by Joan Stambaugh. Albany: State University of New York Press, 2010.
———. *On the Way to Language*. Translated by Peter D. Hertz. San Francisco: Harper, 1971.
Heilman, Samuel. *The People of the Book*. Chicago: University of Chicago Press, 1983.
Heschel, Abraham. *Between God and Man: An Interpretation of Judaism, from the Writings of Abraham J. Heschel*. Selected, edited, and introduced by Fritz A. Rothschild. New York: Free Press, 1959.
———. *God in Search of Man: A Philosophy of Judaism*. New York: Farrar, Straus and Cudahy, 1955.
———. *Heavenly Torah: As Refracted through the Generations*. Edited and translated by Gordon Tucker with Leonard Levin. New York: Continuum, 2010.

Bibliography

———. *Man Is Not Alone: A Philosophy of Religion*. New York: Farrar, Straus and Young, 1951.

———. *The Prophets*. 2 vols. New York: Harper Torchbooks, 1962.

———. *Who Is Man?* Stanford: Stanford University Press, 1965.

Hilton, Michael, and Gordian Marshall. *The Gospels and Rabbinic Judaism*. London: SCM, 1988.

Holcomb, Justin, ed. *Christian Theologies of Scripture: A Comparative Introduction*. New York: New York University Press, 2006.

Holtz, Barry W., ed. *Back to the Sources: Reading the Classic Jewish Texts*. New York: Simon and Schuster, 1984.

Irigaray, Luce. *To Be Two*. Translated by Monique M. Rhodes and Marco F. Cocito-Monoc. New York: Routledge, 2001.

Jabès, Edmond. *The Book of Dialogue*. Translated by Rosmarie Waldrop. Middletown, CT: Wesleyan University Press, 1987.

———. *The Book of Margins*. Translated by Rosmarie Waldrop. Chicago: University of Chicago Press, 1993.

———. *The Book of Questions. I, II, III. The Book of Questions, The Book of Yukel, Return to the Book*. Published as vol. 1. Translated by Rosmarie Waldrop. Hanover, NH: University of New England Press/Wesleyan University Press, 1972.

———. *The Book of Questions. IV, V, VI. Yael, Elya, Aely*. Published as vol. 2. Translated by Rosmarie Waldrop. Middletown, Conn.: Wesleyan University Press, 1983.

———. *The Book of Questions. VII. El (or the last book)*. Translated by Rosmarie Waldrop. Middletown, CT: Wesleyan University Press, 1984.

———. *The Book of Resemblances. I*. Translated by Rosmarie Waldrop. Hanover, NH: University Press of New England/Wesleyan University Press, 1990.

———. *The Book of Resemblances. II. Intimations, The Desert*. Translated by Rosmarie Waldrop. Hanover, NH: University Press of New England/Wesleyan University Press, 1991.

———. *The Book of Resemblances. III. The Ineffaceable, The Unperceived*. Translated by Rosmarie Waldrop. Hanover, NH: University Press of New England/Wesleyan University Press, 1991.

———. *From the Desert to the Book: Dialogues with Marcel Cohen*. Translated by Pierre Joris. New York: Station Hill, 1990.

John XXIII, Pope. *Mater et Magistra: Christianity and Social Progress*. http://www.vatican.va/holy_father/john_xxiii/encyclicals/documents/hf_j-xxiii_enc_15051961_mater_en.html.

John Paul II, Pope. *Dives in Misericordia: On the Mercy of God*. Homebush, NSW: St. Paul Publications, 1980.

Kafka, Franz. *Letters to Friends, Family, and Editors*. New York: Schocken, 1978.

Kant, Immanuel. "What Is Enlightenment?" In *Critique of Practical Reason*, translated by Lewis White Beck. Chicago: University of Chicago Press, 1949.

Kaufmann, Walter. "I and You: A Prologue." In Martin Buber, *I and Thou*, translated by Walter Kaufmann. Edinburgh: T. & T. Clark, 1970.

Kierkegaard, Søren. *Fear and Trembling* and *The Sickness Unto Death*. Translated by Walter Lowrie. Princeton: Princeton University Press, 1968.

———. *Provocations: Spiritual Writings of Kierkegaard*. Edited by Charles E. Moore. Farmington, PA: Plough, 1999.

———. *Works of Love*. Translated by Howard and Edna Hong. New York: Harper, 1962.

King, Martin Luther, Jr. *A Testament of Hope: The Essential Writings and Speeches of Martin Luther King.* Edited by James M. Washington. San Francisco: Harper and Row, 1986.
Kundera, Milan. *The Unbearable Lightness of Being.* New York: Harper, 1984.
LaCugna, Catherine Mowry. *God for Us: The Trinity and Christian Life.* San Francisco: HarperSanFrancisco, 1991.
Lee, Bernard J. *The Galilean Jewishness of Jesus: Retrieving the Jewish Origins of Christianity.* New York: Paulist, 1988.
Leibowitz, Nehama. *New Studies in Bereshit (Genesis): In the Context of Ancient and Modern Jewish Bible Commentary.* Jerusalem: Eliner Library, n.d.
———. *New Studies in Vayikra (Leviticus).* Jerusalem: Eliner Library, n.d.
Levine, Amy-Jill, and Marc Zvi Brettler, eds. *The Jewish Annotated New Testament: New Revised Standard Version.* Oxford: Oxford University Press, 2011.
Lewis, C. S. *A Grief Observed.* London: Faber and Faber, 1961.
Lodahl, Michael E. *Shekinah Spirit: Divine Presence in Jewish and Christian Religion.* New York: Paulist, 1992.
Lubac, Henri de. *Medieval Exegesis: The Four Senses of Scripture.* Translated by Mark Sebanc. 3 vols. Grand Rapids: Eerdmans, 1998.
Malka, Salomon. *Emmanuel Levinas: His Life and Legacy.* Pittsburgh: Duquesne University Press, 2006.
Mandela, Nelson. *Long Walk to Freedom.* London: Abacus, 1994.
Matt, Daniel. *The Essential Kabbalah.* San Francisco: HarperSanFrancisco, 1996.
Meir, Ephraim. "Hellenic and Jewish in Levinas's Writings." *Veritas* 51 (2006) 79–88.
Merton, Thomas. *The Seven Storey Mountain.* New York: Harvest, 1976.
Meskin, Jacob. "Textual Reasoning, Modernity, and the Limits of History." *Cross Currents* 49 (1999) 475–90.
Mole, Gary D. *Levinas, Blanchot, Jabès: Figures of Estrangement.* Gainesville: University Press of Florida, 1997.
Morrison, Van. "Carrying a Torch." From the CD *Hymns to the Silence.* New York: Columbia Productions, 1991.
———. "Help Me." From *It's Too Late to Stop Now.* Exile Productions, 1974.
———. "Hungry for Your Love." From *Wavelength.* Warner Bros. Records, 1978.
———. "A Town Called Paradise." From *No Guru, No Method, No Teacher.* Exile Productions, 1986.
Moyn, Samuel. "Emmanuel Levinas' Talmudic Readings: Between Tradition and Invention." *Prooftexts: A Journal of Jewish Literary History* 23 (2003) 42–68.
———. "Judaism against Paganism: Emmanuel Levinas' Response to Heidegger and Nazism in the 1930s." *History and Memory* 10 (1998) 25–58.
Nadel, Ira B. *Various Positions: A Life of Leonard Cohen.* Austin: University of Texas Press, 1996.
Nemo, Philippe. *Job and the Excess of Evil.* Translated by Michael Kigel. With a postface by Emmanuel Levinas. Pittsburgh: Duquesne University Press, 1998.
Neusner, Jacob. *Torah: From Scroll to Symbol in Formative Judaism.* Minneapolis: Fortress, 1985.
Nussbaum, Martha C. *Love's Knowledge: Essays on Philosophy and Literature.* New York: Oxford University Press, 1990.
Ouaknin, Marc-Alain. *The Burnt Book: Reading the Talmud.* Translated by Llewellyn Brown. Princeton: Princeton University Press, 1995.

Bibliography

Palmer, Parker. *Let Your Life Speak: Listening to the Voice of Vocation.* San Francisco: Jossey-Bass, 2000.

Paul VI, Pope. *Octogesima Adveniens: A Call to Action.* http://www.vatican.va/holy_father/paul_vi/apost_letters/documents/hf_p-vi_apl_19710514_octogesima-adveniens_en.html.

Pearl, Chaim. *Theology in Rabbinic Stories.* Peabody, MA: Hendrickson, 1997.

Peperzak, Adriaan. *Beyond: The Philosophy of Emmanuel Levinas.* Evanston: Northwestern University Press, 1997.

———, ed. *Ethics as First Philosophy: The Significance of Emmanuel Levinas for Philosophy, Literature and Religion.* New York: Routledge, 1995.

———. *To the Other: An Introduction to the Philosophy of Emmanuel Levinas.* West Lafayette, IN: Purdue University Press, 1993.

Pirkei Avos, Ethics of the Fathers. Commentary by Rabbi Meir Zlotowitz. New York: Mesorah, 1989.

Rahner, Karl. "The 'Commandment' of Love in Relation to the Other Commandments." In vol. 5 of *Theological Investigations*, 439–59. London: Darton, Longman and Todd, 1966.

Rich, Adrienne. *The Dream of a Common Language.* New York: Norton, 1987.

———. *What Is Found There: Notebooks on Poetry and Politics.* London: Virago, 1993.

Ricoeur, Paul. *The Course of Recognition.* Translated by David Pellauer. Cambridge: Harvard University Press, 2005.

———. *Critique and Conviction: Conversations with Francois Azouvi and Marc de Launay.* Cambridge: Polity, 1998.

———. *Figuring the Sacred: Religion, Narrative and Imagination.* Minneapolis: Fortress, 1995.

———. *Hermeneutics and the Human Sciences: Essays on Language, Action, and Interpretation.* Translated by John B. Thompson. Cambridge: Cambridge University Press, 1981.

———. "In Memoriam Emmanuel Levinas." *Philosophy Today* 40 (1996) 331–33.

———. *Living Up to Death.* Translated by David Pellauer. Chicago: University of Chicago Press, 2009.

———. *Oneself as Another.* Translated by Kathleen Blamey. Chicago: University of Chicago Press, 1992.

———. *The Symbolism of Evil.* Translated by Emerson Buchanan. Boston: Beacon, 1967.

Rilke, Rainer Maria. *Rilke's Book of Hours: Love Poems to God.* Translated by Anita Barrows and Joanna Macy. New York: Riverhead, 1996.

Rosenak, Michael. *Commandment and Concern: Jewish Religious Education in Secular Society.* Philadelphia: Jewish Publication Society, 1987.

———. *Roads to the Palace: Jewish Texts and Teaching.* Providence, RI: Berghahn, 1995.

———. *Tree of Life, Tree of Knowledge: Conversations with the Torah.* Boulder, CO: Westview, 2001.

Rosenzweig, Franz. *Philosophical and Theological Writings.* Translated by Paul W. Franks and Michael L. Morgan. Indianapolis: Hackett, 2000.

———. *The Star of Redemption.* Translated by William W. Hallo. Notre Dame: University of Notre Dame Press, 1970.

Sacks, Jonathan. *The Dignity of Difference: How to Avoid the Clash of Civilizations.* London: Continuum, 2002.

Schillebeeckx, Edward. *Church: The Human Story of God.* New York: Crossroad, 1990.

———. *God Is New Each Moment*. In conversation with Huub Oosterhuis and Piet Hoogeveen. Translated by David Smith. New York: Seabury, 1983.
———. *The Schillebeeckx Reader*. Edited by Robert Schreiter. New York: Crossraod, 1987.
Scholem, Gershom. *Kabbalah*. New York: Dorset, 1974.
———. "Tradition and Commentary as Religious Categories in Judaism." *Judaism* 15 (1966) 23–39.
Schreiter, Robert. *The Ministry of Reconciliation*. Maryknoll, NY: Orbis, 1998.
Shanks, Hershel, ed. *Christianity and Rabbinic Judaism: A Parallel History of Their Origins and Early Development*. Washington, DC: Biblical Archaeology Society, 1992.
Steiner, George. *Real Presences*. Chicago: University of Chicago Press, 1989.
Steinsaltz, Adin. *The Essential Talmud*. Translated by Chaya Galai. New York: Basic Books, 1976.
———. *The Thirteen Petalled Rose*. Translated by Yehuda Hanegbi. Lanham, MD: Rowman & Littlefield, 2004.
Stern, David. "Midrash and Indeterminacy." *Critical Inquiry* 15 (1988) 132–61.
———. *Parables in Midrash: Narrative and Exegesis in Rabbinic Literature*. Cambridge: Harvard University Press, 1991.
Stone, Ira F. *Reading Levinas/Reading Talmud*. Philadelphia: Jewish Publication Society, 1998.
Talmud: The Steinsaltz Edition. Vols. 2 and 3. New York: Random House, 1990.
Tracy, David. *The Analogical Imagination: Christian Theology and the Plurality of Cultures*. New York: Crossroad, 1981.
———. *On Naming the Present: God, Hermeneutics, and Church*. Maryknoll, NY: Orbis, 1994.
———. "Theology and the Many Faces of Postmodernity." *Theology Today* 51 (1994) 104–14.
United States Conference of Catholic Bishops. *Economic Justice for All: Pastoral Letter on Catholic Social Teaching and the U.S. Economy*. 1986. http://www.usccb.org/upload/economic_justice_for_all.pdf.
Veling, Terry. *The Beatitude of Mercy: Love Watches Over Justice*. Mulgrave, Victoria: John Garratt, 2010.
———. "God in Translation." *Pacifica* 24 (2011) 210–28.
———. *Living in the Margins: Intentional Communities and the Art of Interpretation*. 1996. Reprint, Eugene, OR: Wipf & Stock, 2002.
———. "The Personal and Spiritual Life: All Too Human, All Too Divine." *The Way* 52 (2013) 7–21.
———. *Practical Theology: On Earth as It Is in Heaven*. Maryknoll, NY: Orbis, 2005.
Ward, Benedicta, trans. *The Desert Fathers: Sayings of the Early Christian Monks*. New York: Penguin, 2003.
Weil, Simone. *Simone Weil: An Anthology*. Edited by Siân Miles. London: Penguin, 2005.
———. *Waiting on God: Letters and Essays*. London: Fount, 1977.
Westphal, Merold. *Transcendence and Self-Transcendence: On God and the Soul*. Bloomington: Indiana University Press, 2004.
Wiesel, Elie. *Legends of Our Time*. New York: Schocken, 1968.
Williams, Rowan. *On Christian Theology*. Oxford: Blackwell, 2000.
Wojtyla, Karol. *The Acting Person*. Translated by Andrzej Potocki. Dordrecht: D. Riedel, 1979.

Bibliography

Wyschogrod, Edith. *Saints and Postmodernism: Revisioning Moral Philosophy.* Chicago: University of Chicago Press, 1990.

Young, Brad H. *The Parables: Jewish Tradition and Christian Interpretation.* Peabody, MA: Hendrickson, 1998.

Zohar: The Book of Enlightenment. Translated by Daniel Chanan Matt. Mahwah, NJ: Paulist, 1983.

Name Index

Anselm, 128–29
Aquinas, 84, 96–97
Arendt, Hannah, 74–75, 119, 134–35, 149
Armstrong, Karen, 154–55
Augustine, 33, 61–62, 96–97, 129, 135, 149

Bakhtin, M. M., 130–31
Bellah, Robert, 9
Benjamin, Walter, 176
Berdyaev, Nikolai, 148–50
Bernard of Clairvaux, 151
Blanchot, Maurice, 2–4, 60, 163–65
Bonhoeffer, Dietrich, 50
Bosker, Baruch, 93–94, 162
Bosker, Ben Zion, 93–94, 162
Buber, Martin, xii–xiii, 7–8, 24, 49, 56–57, 63, 106, 147, 150, 159
Burggraeve, Roger, 76–77, 81
Burton-Christie, Douglas, 136–37, 155

Caputo, John, 41, 43, 62, 127, 134, 136
Celan, Paul, 14, 20, 22–23, 48, 62, 66, 148
Charlesworth, Max, 147
Charry, Ellen, 96–97
Chardin, Teilhard de, 170–71
Cixous, Hélène, 8, 51
Cohen, Leonard, 52, 61, 159–61, 174–75

Day, Dorothy, 152
Derrida, Jacques, 3, 7–9, 38, 40–41, 50–51, 63, 80–81, 134
Descarte, René, xi–xii, 126–27, 129
Desert Fathers, 136–38, 155
Dostoyevsky, Fyodor, 1, 41

Edgerton, W. Dow, 91–92
Fine, Lawrence, 168
Fischer, Norman, xvi
Fishbane, Michael, 109
Flusser, David, 147
Freire, Paulo, 173
Furnish, Victor Paul, 146, 156–57

Gadamer, Hans-Georg, 48–49, 102, 115–16, 120–21
Gandhi, Mohandas, 173
Gibbs, Robert, 7
Goodman, Lenn, 145, 153
Gottlieb, Roger, 25
Gutiérrez, Gustavo, 37–38, 146

Handelman, Susan, 8, 12, 25, 58
Heidegger, Martin, 1, 21–22, 25, 32, 102,
Heilman, Samuel, 95–96
Heschel, Abraham, xv, 8, 10–11, 23–24, 51, 98–99, 106, 109–12, 130–33, 139–40, 142–43, 146, 151–52, 156, 167–70, 172
Hilton, Michael, 143

Irigaray, Luce, 50–52

185

Name Index

Jabès, Edmond, 40, 57, 85, 94–95, 122–23
John XXIII, Pope, 76
John Paul II, Pope, 3, 81–84, 131
Jonas, Hans, 64

Kafka, Franz, 42
Kant, Immanuel, xii
Kaufmann, Walter, 8
Kierkegaard, Sören, 20, 127–28, 151–56, 158–60
King, Martin Luther, 75, 146
Kundera, Milan, 21

Lee, Bernard J., 93, 131–32
Leibowitz, Nehama, 45, 145, 147–48, 150–51
Lewis, C. S., 161

Mandela, Nelson, 172–73
Malka, Salomon, 1–3, 15, 67, 89–90, 100, 113–14, 119
Merton, Thomas, 140–41
Meskin, Jacob, 8
Moyn, Samuel, 21, 64, 102–3
Morrison, Van, 13, 62, 161, 168

Nadel, Ira B., 175
Nemo, Philippe, 59, 85
Nussbaum, Martha, 78

Palmer, Parker, 152
Paul VI, Pope, 75, 77, 79
Peperzak, Adriaan, 1, 8, 12, 42–43, 71, 76, 159

Rahner, Karl, 158–60
Rich, Adrienne, 26
Ricoeur, Paul, xiv, xvi, 3, 8, 64, 79, 94, 117–18, 152–54, 157–58
Rosenak, Michael, 136
Rosenzweig, Franz, 66, 147, 155–56, 161

Sacks, Jonathan, 113–14
Schillebeeckx, Edward, 145, 170
Scholem, Gershom, 107
Schreiter, Robert, 164
Steiner, George, 61
Steinsaltz, Adin, 15, 93
Stern, David, 107–8

Tracy, David, 31, 37, 112, 119

Weil, Simone, 21, 83, 150, 171
Westphal, Merold, 44–45
Wiesel, Elie, 90
Williams, Rowan, 113
Wyschogrod, Edith, 43

www.ingramcontent.com/pod-product-compliance
Lightning Source LLC
Chambersburg PA
CBHW031427150426
43191CB00006B/425